Sincerely yours,

Stanley J. Stuber

PRIMER ON ROMAN CATHOLICISM FOR PROTESTANTS

Books by Stanley I. Stuber

THE LIVING WATER

HOW WE GOT OUR DENOMINATIONS

TREASURY OF THE CHRISTIAN FAITH

PUBLIC RELATIONS MANUAL FOR CHURCHES

THE CHRISTIAN READER

PRIMER ON ROMAN CATHOLICISM FOR PROTESTANTS

Primer on
ROMAN CATHOLICISM
for PROTESTANTS

*An Appraisal of the Basic Differences Between
the Roman Catholic Church and Protestantism*

by
STANLEY I. STUBER

ASSOCIATION PRESS   **NEW YORK**

55
Printed in the United States of America
American Book–Stratford Press, Inc., New York

Dedicated

to

EMIL BRUNNER

Professor of Christianity at the International Christian University in Japan

and

To all those Protestants who are re-examining the Scriptures for new light on old doctrines and who dare to proclaim boldly the great creative principles of the Protestant Reformation.

Preface

This is a book for Protestants about Roman Catholicism. Its aims are: (1) to explain in as factual, objective, and simple a way as possible the basic beliefs and practices of the Roman Catholic Church; (2) to let the reader view these beliefs and practices as Roman Catholics themselves view them; (3) to present the author's interpretation of the general Protestant point of view in relation to each of these beliefs and practices; (4) to provide basic information that can encourage intelligent co-operation and equally intelligent but unemotional disagreement within a spirit of Christian love and understanding.

As Bishop Fulton J. Sheen and many others have pointed out, Protestants have strange and peculiar notions concerning Roman Catholicism. This is no credit to Protestantism. This book attempts to look at Roman Catholicism from the inside, as far as that is possible for a Protestant to do. Only Roman Catholic source material, including the authentic fifteen-volume *Catholic Encyclopedia,* is used as the basis for the Roman Catholic portions of this book. This material has been used not only in an objective, factual way, but in terms of catching the true spirit of Roman Catholicism. Several Roman Catholic scholars, among whom were two official censors of the Roman Catholic Church, examined drafts of the manuscript line by line and word by word. Many Roman Catholic leaders and theologians provided unlimited help in making this manuscript objective and accurate in its description of Roman Catholicism.

In each chapter, after presenting the Roman Catholic material, a frank appraisal is made of it from the Protestant viewpoint. Without bitterness or prejudice, each chapter notes how Protestants and Roman Catholics differ, and why. Protestant churchmen and theologians helped evaluate two successive drafts of the manuscript to make the Protestant comments about Roman Catholicism concise, positive, and constructive. The author has included suggestions for further reading and scriptural references for Protestants who wish to become more familiar with any specific area.

The issues dealt with here have been the basis of controversy, even of wars. These are not simple issues. No primer can cover all of this vast area of religious belief and practice. Only the major points can be emphasized here.

It is the hope of the author, and the publisher, that this primer may help Protestants know better the beliefs and practices of the Roman Catholic Church. Roman Catholics and Protestants have much in common. There are, however, many aspects of Roman Catholicism with which Protestants cannot agree; there are teachings of Roman Catholics that Protestants must oppose. While recognizing Christian truth wherever it may be found, Protestants and Roman Catholics may learn to disagree on the basis of firm mutual understanding and within the framework of full religious liberty.

To every one of the many Protestant and Roman Catholic readers who gave such willing help, I want to express my very deepest appreciation.

STANLEY I. STUBER

Acknowledgments

Appreciation is expressed for permission to quote from the following publications having the official *Nihil obstat* and *Imprimatur* of the Roman Catholic Church: The Confraternity of Christian Doctrine, Washington, D.C., for permission to quote from Father McGuire's *New Baltimore Catechism and Mass*, No. 2, Official Revised Edition, the Revised Edition of the *Baltimore Catechism*, No. 2, and *The Call of the Popes to the Laity;* Saint Anthony's Guild, Paterson, New Jersey, for permission to quote from the *1952 National Catholic Almanac*, and *The Catechism of Christian Doctrine*, No. 3, Revised Edition; the Paulist Press, New York City, for permission to quote from papal encyclical letters, from *American Separation of Church and State* by Jeffrey Keefe, *Our Parish: House of God and Gate of Heaven* by H. A. Reinhold, *Are Anglican Ministers Catholic Priests?* by F. Woodlock, *The Popes, Infallible Teachers* by J. B. Harney, *Freedom of Worship* by Francis J. Connell, *A Brief History of the Church* by Stephen McKenna, *History of the Popes* by Ludwig Pastor, *The Question Box* by B. L. Conway, *Birth Control* by D. Pruemmer, *The Ceremonies of the Mass* by Carroll C. Smyth; the Our Sunday Visitor Press, Huntington, Indiana, for permission to quote from *Sharing the Faith* by John A. O'Brien, *The Faith of Millions* by John A. O'Brien, *Father Smith Instructs Jackson* by Fathers Noll and Fallon, *Catholic Liturgy and Catholic Life* by Albert Muntsch.

Also M. H. Gill & Son, Ltd., Dublin, Ireland, for permission to quote from *Apologetics and Catholic Doctrine*, Second and Revised Edition; Radio Replies Press, St. Paul, Minnesota, for permission to quote from *Radio Replies*, I, II, III, by Fathers Rumble and Carty; the Liguorian Pamphlet Office, Liguoria, Missouri, for permission to quote from *How To Become A Catholic* by D. J. Corrigan; The Macmillan Company, New York City, for permission to quote from *A Catholic Dictionary*, edited by Donald Attwater, copyrighted 1949; the Benedictine Convent of Perpetual Adoration, Clyde, Missouri, for permission to quote from *Confession, Its Fruitful Practice;* and P. J. Kenedy & Sons, New York City, for permission to quote from Cardinal Gibbons' *Faith of Our Fathers;* and to William J. Hirten Co., New York City, for permission to quote from *Within the Sanctuary, The Mass, With Manual of Prayers.*

Appreciation is also expressed to Harper & Brothers for permission to quote from *The Kingdom of God in America* by H. Richard Niebuhr; to G. P. Putnam's Sons for permission to quote from *Our Fathers Faith and Ours* by David Schaff; to The Macmillan Company for permission to quote from *The Church Looks Forward* by William Temple; and to Abingdon-Cokesbury Press for permission to quote from *A Protestant Manifesto* by Winfred E. Garrison.

                                                                                              S.I.S.

Contents

PART I
Historical Background

1

When All Christians Were One

If we are to understand Roman Catholicism we must go back to the first century and look at Christian origins. In this primer we shall find that Catholic authorities base the claims of their Church principally upon this period of history. Everything else, they claim, is interpretation and clarification of what actually was said and done by Christ and the apostles. The difficulty between Roman Catholics and Protestants arises over the radically different views concerning the same events of the early church as recorded in the New Testament, and over Christ's intentions in regard to the establishment of a divine institution to be known as the Christian Church.

Christ prayed that his disciples might be one. In the Great Commission he gave them a world-wide field of service. His principles were of a universal nature. But as we read the various books of the New Testament it is evident that the disciples had different points of view, programs, and personalities. And they had many varieties of local practice.[1] Paul spent much of his time trying to bring some measure of harmony among the early Christians. Yet there was one great experience which they did have in common, and that was the presence of their Lord. While there were various interpretations of him, he was the center of their faith and the basis of their hope.

Roman Catholics look upon Christ as the founder of the Church, giving to it, from the beginning, its Catholic characteristics. Just why they believe this, and how this belief affects the whole conception of their faith and practice, we shall see in this chapter.

---

[1] See *The Varieties of New Testament Religion* by Ernest F. Scott, Charles Scribner's Sons.

THE ROMAN CATHOLIC POSITION

The Birth of the Church

The Roman Catholic Church teaches that Christ himself was the founder of the Church. He completed the task just prior to his ascension when he commissioned the apostles to make disciples of all nations. Before this he had instituted the sacraments, chosen the twelve apostles, instructed them by word and deed, and conferred upon them the power of teaching, ruling, and sanctifying.

According to Roman Catholics, Christ founded the Church in the form of a visible, hierarchical society, being made up of subjects and superiors who rightfully rule the subjects. Christ made Peter the first head of the Church, the first Roman Pontiff. The Church is a monarchical society in which the pope rules with full power, having jurisdiction over the entire Church.

After Pentecost, when the Holy Spirit was first visibly manifested within the Church, the apostles at the command of Christ began to carry out their mission, which through them and their successors continues and will continue until the end of time. (*A Catechism of Christian Doctrine,*[2] No. 3, Official Revised Edition, pp. 103-104)

The Nature of the Church

"The Church is the congregation of all baptized persons united in the same true faith, the same sacrifice, and the same sacraments, under the authority of the Sovereign Pontiff and the bishops in communion with him." (*A Catechism of Christian Doctrine,* p. 102)

Robert Bellarmine, the Catholic authority, puts it this way: "The Church is a society of men who are united together by the profession of the same Christian faith, and by participation of the same Sacraments, and who are governed by their lawful pastors under the Roman Pontiff, the only vicar of Christ on earth."

---

[2] *A Catechism of Christian Doctrine,* No. 3, Official Revised Edition, is Catechism No. 2, Revised Edition of the *Baltimore Catechism,* with supplementary statements and quotations from Holy Scripture. This same text is used throughout this primer by permission of the Confraternity of Christian Doctrine. The text of the *Baltimore Catechism,* also used by permission of the Confraternity of Christian Doctrine, is the Revised Edition No. 2. Both are published by the St. Anthony Guild Press, Paterson, N. J.

The Roman Catholic Church teaches that baptism, according to the ruling of Christ, is the gateway to the Church. A person becomes a member of the Church upon receiving this sacrament. In order to remain a real member of the Church after baptism a person must continue to profess the one true faith and must not withdraw from the unity of the body of the Church by schism or heresy, or be excommunicated (in the most severe procedure) by legitimate authority because of serious sins.

The Scriptures refer to the Church as the Body of Christ, as a sheepfold, as the Kingdom of God, and as the Kingdom of Heaven (Matt. 13:24; Luke 11:20; John 10:14-16; I Cor. 12:12, 27; and Eph. 4:4-6).

The Special Powers Given to St. Peter

Christ gave special power to Peter, Roman Catholics believe, by making him the head of the apostles and the chief teacher and ruler of the entire Church. The power of the keys (Matt. 16:17-19) was promised to Peter and was actually conferred upon him (John 21:15-17). He was recognized by the early Christians, from the very beginning, as the head of the Church. (*A Catechism of Christian Doctrine*, p. 111)

The Apostolic Succession

The Roman Catholic Church believes that Christ did not intend that the special power of chief teacher and ruler of the entire Church should be exercised by Peter alone. This power was to be passed on from one Bishop of Rome to another pope, who serves on earth as the Vicar of Christ. The popes, along with the other bishops, are the successors of the apostles and have received their episcopal power by valid consecration through an unbroken line of successors of the apostles. Priests, especially parish priests, assist the bishops in the care of souls. (*A Catechism of Christian Doctrine*, pp. 112-113)

The Tests of the One True Church

It is the belief of Roman Catholics that the one true Church has four chief marks or signs: it is one, holy, catholic or universal, and apostolic. All of these tests are met only by the Roman Catholic Church.

The Roman Catholic Church is one because all of its members, in response to the desire of Christ, profess the same faith, have the same sacrifices and sacraments, and are united under one visible head, the pope.

It is holy "because it was founded by Jesus Christ, who is all-holy, and because it teaches, according to the will of Christ, holy doctrines, and provides the means of leading a holy life." (*A Catechism of Christian Doctrine,* p. 119)

It is universal because, "destined to last for all time," it fulfills the commandment of Christ to go forth and make disciples of all nations, and it teaches today everywhere the same doctrine which it first received from Christ.

It is apostolic because it is the Church which Christ founded upon the apostles, particularly upon Peter whom he called the rock on which the Church would be built (Matt. 16:18; Eph. 2:19-20). This supreme power of Peter has been passed down, through the centuries, in unbroken line of his successors in the see of Rome. (*A Catechism of Christian Doctrine,* pp. 116-122)

No Other True Church

"We know that no other church but the Catholic Church is the true Church of Christ because no other church has these four marks." (*A Catechism of Christian Doctrine,* p. 123)

Roman Catholics declare that other churches recognize no authority in religious matters vested in an individual who is the vicar of Christ. Other churches have all had human founders. Other churches are not truly universal, nor do they trace their origin to the apostles. They have rejected the authority of the pope, certain doctrines of faith, and have broken away from Catholic unity.

The Chief Attributes of the Roman Catholic Church

Roman Catholic teaching is that the chief attributes of the one true Church are authority, infallibility, and indefectibility. (1) The authority comes directly from Christ through Peter, and the other apostles, when he bestowed the power of binding and loosing, of teaching and baptizing. (2) Infallibility comes through the special assistance of the Holy Ghost, and the Church therefore cannot err when it teaches or believes a doctrine of faith or morals. The Church teaches infallibly when, through the pope alone, or by the pope with a General Council, or through the bishops in their respective sees together with the pope, it defines a doctrine of faith or morals to be held by all the faithful.[3] (3) By indefectibility is meant the permanent and substantially unchangeable nature of the Roman Catholic Church. This is in conformity with the will of Christ who promised to be with his Church until the end of time (I Cor. 11:26).

Salvation Only Through the Roman Catholic Church

"No one can be saved without sanctifying grace, and the Catholic Church alone is the divinely established means by which grace is brought to the world and the full fruits of Our Lord's Redemption are applied to men." (*A Catechism of Christian Doctrine*, p. 129)

The teaching that "outside the Church there is no salvation" does not mean that everyone who is not a Roman Catholic will necessarily go to hell. It does mean, however, that no person can be saved unless he belongs in some manner to the Roman Catholic Church—either actually or *in desire*. The desire may be unconscious. Those who, for one reason or another, remain outside of the Church through no grave fault of their own and do not know it is the true Church, can be saved by making use of the graces given them by God. According to Roman Catholic authorities the true doctrine is that a person may be fully convinced of another creed in all sincerity, and may be striving to serve God according to his conscience and to love God with all his heart. Such a person is not *outside* the Roman Catholic Church in the sense of the above axiom, for although not an actual member, he has an *implicit* desire of the one true Church.

The Mystical Body of Christ

The Roman Catholic Church is declared to be the Mystical Body of Christ because "its members are united by supernatural bonds with one another and with Christ, their Head, thus resembling the members and head of the living human body." (*A Catechism of Christian Doctrine*, p. 129) [4]

---

[3] "As the divinely appointed teacher of revealed truth, the Church is infallible. This gift of inerrancy is guaranteed to it by the words of Christ, in which He promised that His spirit would abide with it for ever to guide it unto all truth (John 14:16; 16:13). It is implied also in other passages of Scripture, and asserted by the unanimous testimony of the Fathers."— *The Catholic Encyclopedia*.

[4] Another definition of the Mystical Body is found in the encyclical *Mystici Corporis* of Pope Pius XII.

Early Heresies

While some of the early Christians were influenced by Gnosticism, the great heresies within the Church occurred in the fourth century. Arius taught that Christ was not truly God. Eutyches and Sergius went to the other extreme and declared that Christ was not truly man. Nestorius maintained that Mary was the mother of a purely human person, who was only a man, not the Son of God. Pelagius claimed that a person by his own efforts could reach the Kingdom of Heaven, thus doing away with the supernatural element in Christianity.

According to Roman Catholics, this period of the great heresies was a very critical one for the Church because two of the heretics, Nestorius and Sergius, were patriarchs of Constantinople. They enjoyed tremendous prestige and authority among both the clergy and laity. The others succeeded in gaining support of some members of the hierarchy, and many bishops became recognized as champions of the heretical doctrines. To make matters even worse, the heretics had acquired a reputation for holiness. For this reason many people found it difficult to condemn them because of their doctrines. Another reason for confusion was that the heretics were skillful in concealing their errors in language which sounded quite orthodox. (*A Brief History of the Church*, by Stephen McKenna, pp. 10, 11) Matters grew so difficult that the Church, to protect its unity, was forced to take drastic action.

The Council of Nicea

Arius would not submit to the Church, but went on teaching his errors, winning many followers and causing immense disturbances within both the Church and the State. Finally matters reached the breaking point and Emperor Constantine demanded that a General Council be called to settle the issue. The bishops of the Church met at Nicea in A.D. 325.

"They condemned the teaching of Arius because he denied the Deity of Christ, and he was excommunicated because he would not submit to the authority of the Church. His heresy led multitudes astray, and for over four centuries Arian heretics were proportionately as numerous as the various forms of Protestantism during the last four centuries. Arius himself died in 335 A.D., and his movement died out also in the seventh century." (*Radio Replies*, by Fathers Rumble and Carty, Vol. II, p. 304)

The Nicea Council "condemned heresy of Arius; defined clearly that the Son of God was consubstantial (homoousios) with the Father; formulated the Nicene Creed." (*National Catholic Almanac,*[5] p. 93) It should be pointed out that *homoousios* is the Greek word meaning "of the same nature."

The Schism of the Eastern Church

The schism of the Eastern Church from Rome did not occur suddenly but developed over hundreds of years. There were differences of customs and manner between the East and the West. Some of the popes permitted the East, so long as it submitted to the supremacy of Rome, to follow its own rituals. Gradually, because of growing tensions, many of them more political than religious, the final break became inevitable.

During the years there had developed a strong anti-Rome party led by Photius, the Patriarch of Constantinople. In A.D. 867 he "purported to excommunicate the pope because (1) the Latins fast on Saturdays, (2) do not begin Lent until Ash Wednesday instead of three days earlier, as in the East, (3) do not allow priests to be married, (4) do not allow priests to administer confirmation, and have added the *filioque* to the creed." (*The Testimony of History for the Roman Catholic Church,* p. 12)

Although Photius was excommunicated by the pope, and banished by Emperor Leo VI, his influence grew. It came to a head in the person of Michael Caerularius, Patriarch of Constantinople. He led the strong anti-Latins and revived the old accusations. He finally declined to hold communion with legates sent to Constantinople and was excommunicated. The break with Rome came in A.D. 1054 and has lasted ever since. From that time to this no Patriarch of Constantinople has sought confirmation of his appointment from Rome, nor has submitted to the jurisdiction of the pope.[6]

---

[5] All quotations throughout this primer, taken from the *National Catholic Almanac,* are from the 1952 edition.

[6] The Eastern Orthodox Church, while not of the Protestant tradition, has membership in the World Council of Churches. Like Protestant churches, it considers itself to be truly "Catholic."

The Eastern Orthodox Church (the second largest Christian body in the world), according to the *Catholic Dictionary* (p. 360), has been regarded ever since the break in 1054 as "being only in schism." Eastern Orthodox theologians, however, point to certain dogmatic differences such as: (1) the Roman Catholic Church must have no visible head, but must speak through

"The Greek Orthodox Churches are separated from the Catholic Church by schism, or division from its authority; and also by heresy, insofar as they refuse to admit certain Catholic dogmatic teachings." (*Radio Replies*, by Fathers Rumble and Carty, Vol. II, p. 307)

THE PROTESTANT POINT OF VIEW
On the Return to the Early Church

Protestantism denies that the Roman Catholic Church is the only true Church because it has its own spiritual foundations resting firmly upon New Testament origins and is therefore a real part of the "Holy Catholic Church" as stated in the Apostles' Creed.

Protestants agree that Christ founded the Church, but they conceive it to be more a spiritual fellowship than a rigid hierarchy. They think of Peter as one of the apostles, but with no special authority or powers. Some Protestant churches accept the theory of the apostolic succession, although many do not. While Protestants understand the contention of the Roman Catholic Church that it is the only true Church, they cannot discover in the New Testament any statement which would indicate that the Church must be organized as one visible body under the sole domination of a pope. They can, however, find much evidence supporting the belief that the true Church is of the Spirit; is of those who love Christ and obey His commandments. Protestants

the bishops; (2) only the first seven councils are recognized as ecumenical; (3) rejection of the *filioque* clause; (4) the Virgin Mary was purified from original sin at the Annunciation; (5) reject indulgences, claiming that sacramental absolution remits all temporal punishment; (6) permit divorce; (7) have a married clergy.

Father Conway in his *Question Box* (pp. 108-109) adds that the Eastern Orthodox Church believes itself to be the only true Church; rejects both the primacy and infallibility of the pope; accepts an objective real presence in the Eucharist, believing that the change takes place not when the words of consecration are pronounced, but at the invocation of the Holy Ghost (Epiklesis); denies purgatory in any sense as a cleansing fire, while praying for the dead; denies the Immaculate Conception; has baptism by immersion and administers Confirmation directly after baptism; gives Communion under both bread and wine four times a year (Christmas, Easter, Whitsunday, and the Feast of the Assumption); accepts all the books of the Old and New Testament; believes in the Mass and the priesthood; has seven sacraments; honors and prays to the saints and to the Virgin Mary.

therefore do not exclude Roman Catholics, but accept them as part of the fellowship of Christ in the Church Universal.

Protestants differ widely in regard to rites and practices, but they are united in the belief that salvation comes not through a Church organization but through the grace of God manifested in Jesus Christ. As long as the Roman Catholic Church insists that salvation must be found in the "one true Church," [7] so long will the principles of the Protestant Reformation be proclaimed in protest. This protest is positive and creative; it is not merely negative. Protestants are *testifying for* great spiritual principles as their name (*pro testare*) indicates they should. Protestant beliefs are realistic and, being based upon deep, personal religious experience, lead to God directly through Jesus Christ.

The Kingdom of God, which Jesus emphasized so much, is the concern of Protestants; along with the visible Church here upon this earth. Those who belong to the Church are not necessarily born into the Kingdom. Members of the Kingdom possess a particular inner spiritual quality; they have within their hearts the ever-living, creative spirit of Christ. The Kingdom has no denominational or sectarian barriers. Roman Catholics, as well as Protestants, are members of it. In the Kingdom of God all earnest Christians, Eastern Orthodox, Roman Catholics, and Protestants alike, walk upon common ground. The visible Churches, for the moment, separate us; but the Kingdom brings us together in a great redemptive program.

Return to Original Christianity

Protestants glory in the fact that the Protestant Reformation broke the rigid pattern of the Roman hierarchy and re-established in their minds, hearts, and practice the teachings and the spirit of the New Testament and the early church. Distinct features of the Reformation, such as the priesthood of all believers, the worth of the individual, soul freedom, justification by faith, and the all-sufficiency of the Scriptures for faith and life, had their rebirth in the rediscovery of the early Christian church.

This return to the precepts of original Christianity is reflected in the formal creedal statements of Protestantism. The *Westminster Confession* declares that "the whole counsel of God, covering all things necessary for His own glory, man's salvation, faith and life, is either expressly set down in Scripture or by good and

---

[7] See the interpretation of this as found on pages 5-6.

necessary consequence may be deduced from Scripture, unto which nothing at any time is to be added, whether by new revelations of the Spirit or traditions of men."

The *Augsberg Confession* (1530) gives the official Protestant view of the church: "The church is the congregation of the saints in which the Gospel is rightly taught and the sacraments rightly administered." Supporting this is the definition contained in the *Thirty-nine Articles* of the Church of England (1571): "The visible Church of Christ is a congregation of faithful men in which the pure Word of God is preached and the sacraments be duly administered according to Christ's order in all those things which of necessity are requisite to the same."

"Where true faith is, there is the new birth and where the new birth is there is the church," declared Anabaptist Adam Pastor.

In an encyclical letter issued from the Lambeth Conference in 1948, 329 archbishops and bishops of the "Anglican Communion" (part of the "Holy Catholic Church"), under the presidency of the Archbishop of Canterbury, declared, "The Church is not something made by men. It is the instrument of the living God for the setting-forward of His reign on earth. God in Christ has won the victory. The Church lives in the power of the Resurrection. The gates of Hell cannot prevail against it."

A committee report of the same conference stresses the fact that "the Churches of the Anglican Communion are Catholic in the sense of the English Reformation. They are Catholic but reformed; they are reformed but Catholic. . . . The English Reformers were not trying to make a new Church. It continued to be the Church of England, the *Ecclesia Anglicana,* as Magna Carta described it in 1215. For this reason the Anglican Communion is not a sect. It is a true part of the Church Catholic."

The Bishop of Monmouth, Dr. Edwin Morris, declared in 1952 that the Church of England is not Protestant, nor has it *ever* been Roman Catholic. "Our medieval cathedrals and churches did not formerly 'belong to the Roman Catholics.' They have always belonged to the Church of England." Some Protestants question this, however.

Scriptural Basis for Protestant Beliefs

Protestant churches carry their origins back directly to the New Testament. The Anglican Communion, for example, does not think of the Protestant Reformation as its true origin. Southern Baptists do not think of themselves as Protestants, but as direct descendants of first century Christians. While historically many churches had their physical birth in the period of the Protestant Reformation, spiritually they are of the New Testament and claim Christ as their Founder and Head. They think of the Church as being founded by Christ at Pentecost.

"Then they that gladly received his word were baptized; and the same day there were added unto them about three thousand souls. And they continued steadfastly in the apostles' doctrines and fellowship, and in breaking of bread, and in prayer. . . . And all that believed were together, and had all things common; and sold their possessions and goods, and parted them to all men, as every man had need. And they, continuing daily with one accord in the temple, and breaking bread from house to house, did eat their meat with gladness and singleness of heart, praising God, and having favour with all the people. And the Lord added to the church daily such as should be saved" (Acts 2:41-42, 44-47).

Other Scripture passages which support the Protestant position are: Matthew 28:18-20; John 14:26; 16:7, 13; Acts 6:5-6; 14:23; 20:17; Romans 12:4-5; Ephesians 4:11-12; I Timothy 4:12-14; James 5:14; I Peter 5:1. The letters of Paul to the churches, and the Book of Revelation, give Protestants a firm basis of conviction in regard to the divine origin of their churches. I Corinthians 12:28 and Ephesians 4:11 list the specific leadership of the early church.

PROTESTANT REFERENCE BOOKS: The reader who desires an authentic refutation of most of the Roman Catholic positions covered in this primer should consult David S. Schaff's *Our Fathers Faith and Ours: A Comparison between Protestantism and Romanism* (G. P. Putnam's Sons, 1928). Books dealing with the issues raised in this chapter from a distinctly Protestant viewpoint are: *What Did Jesus Think?* by Stanley Brown-Serman and Harold Adye Pichard, Chap. IV; *A Source Book for the Study of the Teaching of Jesus* by Ernest DeWitt Burton; *The Christian Faith* by Nels F. S. Ferré; *A Protestant Manifesto* by Winfred E. Garrison; *The Church and the Christian* by Shailer Mathews; *What Is Christianity?* by Charles Clayton Morrison; *Primer for Protestants* by James Hastings Nichols, Chap. VII; *The Kingdom of God and History*, an Oxford Conference Book; *According to Paul* by Harris Franklin Rall; *The Varieties of New Testament Religion* by Ernest T. Scott.

2

How the Roman Catholic Church
Interprets the Protestant Reformation

Few Protestants realize that the Roman Catholic Church, while losing millions of members because of the Protestant Reformation, had its own Counter-Reformation which in a real sense made it stronger than ever.[1] While most of our attention has been upon Luther and the other reformers, we have missed almost altogether the fact that the Roman Catholic Church, admitting that many of its members had sinned and that some of the hierarchy had done wrong, went forward to the Council of Trent determined to right the wrongs and to reaffirm the true values of the true Church.

The accomplishments of the Council of Trent deserve careful consideration. We may not agree with them. But we will have to admit that, from the Catholic point of view, it was the great rallying force of the Catholic Church.

In our study of Roman Catholicism we must always keep in mind that while it is claimed that the Church, in its official teaching and guidance, can do no wrong, individual members, priests, bishops, and even popes, can commit grievous sins. They are human and can err. The contention is that the reformers had a case against the *members* of the Roman Catholic Church, but not against the one true Church. Reforms were made to correct human mistakes. The Church, even though seriously wounded by Martin Luther, issued pronouncements at Trent which clarified issues and helped its members to bypass the Protestant Reformation successfully.

---

[1] "The name suggests that the Catholic movement came after the Protestant; whereas in truth the reform originally began in the Catholic Church, and Luther was a Catholic Reformer before he became a Protestant. By becoming a Protestant Reformer, he did indeed hinder the progress of the Catholic reformation, but he did not stop it."—*The Catholic Encyclopedia.*

14

THE ROMAN CATHOLIC POSITION

Causes Which Led to the Protestant Reformation

Roman Catholics readily admit that there were many wrongs which led to the Protestant Reformation. These were basic causes, like the growth of nationalism and secularism. Political causes had weakened the authority of the pope. The German princes, for example, had great personal ambitions for their States and were ready to free themselves from all relationships with Rome. Some who were covetous and avaricious saw the possibility of plunder in the confiscation of Church property.

The spirit of the Renaissance, through its revival of the pagan Greek and Latin classics, paved the way also for a rebellion against ecclesiastical control.

"Catholics readily grant that a reformation in the lives of many unworthy Catholic clerics and laymen was indeed called for in the sixteenth century, and historians like Pastor have admitted the worldliness, immorality, nepotism, and avarice that marked many of the clergy." [2]

"The weakening of moral discipline among the clergy and people was the chief factor in bringing about the Protestant revolt." (*The Question Box,* by Bertrand L. Conway, pp. 91-92)

"There was nothing whatever wrong with the Catholic religion itself. But there were a good many things wrong with great numbers of Catholics, or the Reformation would have been impossible." (*Radio Replies,* by Fathers Rumble and Carty, Vol. II, p. 68)

Inner Purification All That Was Necessary

Roman Catholics believe that the necessary reforms should have been carried out altogether within the Church, as advocated by Erasmus. In fact, such a development had begun to take place when Luther rebelled against the pope and started a reformation of his own. This, from the Roman Catholic point of view, was heresy.

"The Church of course understood that the worldliness and corruption must be purged from her ranks. Councils for that purpose had already been called and many excellent reforms had been initiated. If this plan could have proceeded without inter-

---

[2] See *History of the Popes,* Vol. VII, by Pastor, pp. 291-328.

ruption, the cleansing of society would have taken place peacefully within the framework of Catholic Christendom. But in 1517
a German monk named Martin Luther revolted and succeeded
in getting a majority of the German rulers to follow him. Though
this development is called in secular histories 'the Reformation,'
we should use the word cautiously. Some of the leaders of the
new movement, it is true, began with a praiseworthy desire to
reform what was morally wrong in the lives of Christians; but
having thrown off the restraint of Divine authority, represented
by the Church, their unaided human judgment quickly led them
to attack Christian teaching and even Christian morality. Luther,
for example, denied the freedom of the will, asserted that men
are saved by 'faith alone and not by good works,' attacked the
Mass and the sacraments, and taught 'that priests and nuns
should marry.' " (*Church History Through Biography*, published
by the Confraternity of Christian Doctrine, pp. 134-135)

Selling of Indulgences

From the Roman Catholic point of view, the spark which set
off the Protestant Reformation was the accusation that John
Tetzel, a Dominican monk who had been commissioned by the
pope to preach in Germany a special indulgence, was guilty of
selling indulgences. This was contrary to the teaching of the
Church and Tetzel's conduct was disavowed and condemned by
a representative of the Holy See. Nevertheless, Martin Luther
made a great issue of it.

The fact of the matter is that Pope Leo X proclaimed the indulgence "which afforded Luther a pretext for his apostasy." The
pope wanted to bring to completion the Church of St. Peter in
Rome. With this purpose in mind he issued a Bull granting an
indulgence to all who would contribute voluntary offerings toward this cause. But each gift had to be accompanied by sincere
repentance and confession of sins. Moreover, those who contributed nothing, but otherwise met the requirements of the indulgence, were to share equally in the spiritual treasury of the
Church. On the other hand, no matter how large the gift might
be, unless it had back of it a true contribution of the heart, it
would be of no avail.

Roman Catholics maintain that there was, therefore, to be no
traffic or sale of indulgences. Such was never authorized, and
never would be countenanced by the pope. In order to keep indulgences free from the desire of individual gain it was charged

that, under the severest penalties, those who preached the indulgence could not receive the money.

The Council of Trent, soon after the Reformation, took effective measures to put a stop to all irregularities regarding indulgences by issuing the following decree: "Wishing to correct and amend the abuses which have crept into them, and on occasion of which this signal name of Indulgences is blasphemed by heretics, the Holy Synod enjoins in general, by the present decree, that all wicked traffic for obtaining them, which has been the fruitful source of many abuses among the Christian people, should be wholly abolished."

James Cardinal Gibbons in his *The Faith of Our Fathers* (p. 312), in commenting on the indulgence to which Luther took exception, declares, "Nor did the Pope exceed his legitimate powers in promising to the pious donors spiritual favors in exchange for their donations. For if our sins can be redeemed by alms to the poor, as the Scripture tells us, why not as well by offerings in the cause of religion?"

Catholic Opinion of Martin Luther

To Roman Catholics, Martin Luther is a heretic, a rebel against the true Church. The denominations which grew out of his rebellion are not true churches at all and will have no divine authority until they are reunited with Rome.

Typical of the Roman Catholic attitude toward Luther is that expressed by the Reverend John A. O'Brien, Ph.D., professor at the University of Notre Dame, when he writes in his book *The Faith of Millions* (The Credentials of the Catholic Religion):

"When Martin Luther, an Augustinian monk, on October 31, 1517, nailed his ninety-five theses to the doors of the church at Wittenberg, and later proceeded to establish a religion of his own, he set loose in the religious world a principle which was destined to produce consequences far beyond the ken of himself or his fellow reformers. It was the principle of the supremacy of private judgment in the interpretation of the Scriptures and as a guide in the religious life.

. . . "Far from being indifferentists in religion, these reformers were fanatics, each believing his own particular creed was correct, and willing to persecute unto death all who contumaciously held a contrary interpretation. Far too from being the founders of religious tolerance, as a modern myth is fond of picturing them, they set an example of intolerance and persecution which in cruelty and fanaticism has seldom, if ever, been equalled in the long annals of Christendom.

"Insisting with despotic finality that his judgment be accepted as supreme in all matters of religion, Martin Luther pronounced every one who differed with him in doctrine a heretic, and condemned him in coarse and vulgar language.

. . . "When the peasants, led astray by Luther's example of the private interpretation of Scripture to suit one's fancy, sought to carry out their own ideas of the meaning of the Bible, thus provoking the Peasant's War, Luther turned on them with savage ruthlessness, urged the nobles to track them down like dogs and to kill these 'children of the devil.' His advice was followed literally.

. . . "Instead of becoming gentler and more tolerant with age, Luther grew more rancorous and vituperative." (pp. 28-29)

Success of the Council of Trent

The Council of Trent was called to settle the controversies growing out of the Protestant "revolt." It met in December, 1545, after years of delay, and lasted for eighteen years, that is, to December, 1563. It is said to be, from the Roman Catholic position, not only one of the most remarkable of all the ecumenical councils, but was one of the most successful. During the eighteen years in which it met the council did more than define the doctrines which had been brought into question by Protestants. It also gave explicit directions for reform where reform was needed, and supplied an example of the inner vitality and unity of the Church. From Trent went a force "of order, of holiness, of firmness of purpose, of unity, of Catholicity. It was ultimately to cleanse and remake Catholic society, and regain many of the souls lost in the Protestant revolt." (*Church History Through Biography*, p. 144)

Members of the council discussed the dogmatic questions with great frankness and thoroughness. They devoted, for example, six full months to the study of Justification, the central doctrine of Protestantism. After reaching a decision they rejected the "errors" of their opponents in no uncertain terms. The definitions which they formulated are considered by Roman Catholics as "models of theological precision." They have, of course, been binding upon Roman Catholics ever since.

According to the *Catholic Dictionary*, edited by Donald Attwater (p. 500), some of the principal decisions reached at the Council of Trent are as follows:

The confirmation of the Nicene Creed.

The authenticity of the Latin Vulgate and the canonicity of all books contained therein and of them only.

The definition of the doctrine of original sin.

The precision of the doctrine of Justification, condemning justification by faith alone and imputation of grace.

The condemnation of errors about the sacraments.

The definition of the Real Presence and of Transubstantiation as its mode.

The precision of the doctrine of the sacraments of Penance and Extreme Unction.

The declaration that holy communion in both kinds was not necessary for lay-people and clerics not celebrating, Christ being received whole and entire under either species.

The precision of the doctrine concerning the sacrifice of the Mass and the sacraments of Holy Orders and Matrimony.

The affirmation of the doctrines of Purgatory, of the invocation of saints and the veneration of them, their relics and images, and of Indulgences.

Stephen McKenna summarizes the work of the Council of Trent in his *A Brief History of the Church* in this way: "The Council of Trent failed in one of its main objectives: to win back the Protestants to the Church which they had abandoned. Its decrees on reform were not accepted immediately in all Catholic countries. Yet, its importance can hardly be overestimated. It furnished an impetus to theological, scriptural, and historical studies among Catholics that have continued down to the present time. It proved that the Church possessed a spiritual vitality that enabled her to triumph over her enemies both within and without. It marked the first definite check to Protestantism and the real beginning of what is called the 'Counter-Reformation.'" (pp. 24-25)

THE PROTESTANT POINT OF VIEW
On the Meaning of the Reformation

> Protestantism continues to believe in the basic principles of the Protestant Reformation because the Reformation, more than anything else, opened and revitalized New Testament concepts of religion.

Protestants are concerned with the Counter-Reformation only in relation to the effect which the Reformation had on the Roman Catholic Church. It is clearly evident that the Reformers had a real case. So strong was the case that it forced the Roman Catholic Church to correct some of the abuses, such as the "selling" of indulgences, and to restate its theological position. There is no doubt that the Roman Catholic Church came away from the Council of Trent in a much stronger position morally and spiritually. But, from the Protestant point of view, the Council, on the dogmatic side, did Christianity a grave disservice. For it declared as *dogmas* certain beliefs, such as the "real presence," holy orders, penance, purgatory, and indulgences, which are considered by Protestants as being contrary to the teachings of Christ. Instead of bringing Christians closer together, the Council of Trent made it impossible for Protestants and Roman Catholics to agree upon the essentials of the Christian gospel.

Protestantism also has theological statements and creeds which tend to divide. Many feel that there is great need today for Protestants to re-examine the doctrines, the forms of church government, and the practices which came out of the Reformation. Many conferences have been held at which "we looked at our differences." The need now is to move past differences to a new, creative aspect of Protestantism. The hope of the Protestant churches is not in the process of redefining dogmas which separate, but in building around the creative elements of the Reformation which will send all earnest Christians forth to fulfill the basic principles of the Kingdom of God.

Positive Quality of the Reformation

Those who separated themselves from the Roman Catholic Church in the sixteenth century were known as "heretics," "arch-Lutherans," "Evangelicals," and as members of Reformed churches. In 1520, Luther used the word "Protestation" as the title of a document in which he called upon the emperor for protection against false charges being made against him. The actual term "Protestant" was first used in 1529 and relates to the protest offered by the evangelical minority of the Diet of Spires to the action of the Roman Catholic majority.

But from the very beginning Protestantism was more than a protest. It was never a protest against the Church itself; it was a protest against certain abuses within the Christian body. It became a positive, creative force which has given new meaning and direction to the Christian religion. Protestantism looks to Christ as its head; to the Bible as its authority; to the Holy Spirit

as its inspiration; to the active membership of its fellowship as
its strength; and to personal experience in Christ as the way to
salvation. Martin Luther set the scene for the Reformation when
he declared, "If a thousand Augustines and a thousand churches
were against me, I am sure that the true church holds with me
to the Word of God." (In his reply to John Eck, 1519)

In regard to the head of the church, the *Westminster Confession,* in its original form, had this to say: "There is no other
head of the church but the Lord Jesus Christ, nor can the pope
of Rome in any sense be the head thereof." Historic words of
the Reformation were uttered by Luther as he stood before Emperor Charles V at the Diet of Worms in April of 1521: "Unless
I am persuaded by testimonies from Scriptures or clear arguments—for by themselves, I believe neither pope nor council—I
stand convinced by the Holy Scriptures adduced by myself and
my conscience is bound up in God's Word. Retract, I do not and
will not, for to do anything against conscience is unsafe and dangerous. Here I stand. I can do no other. God help me. Amen."

Following this, Protestantism took shape rapidly. The New
Testament was translated into German; the miraculous element
was removed from the Mass; the cup was restored to the laity;
the "worship" of images and saints was abolished; preaching became the central part of public worship; congregational singing
was introduced; catechisms were prepared; enforced celibacy of
Christian pastors was abolished; and in 1530 the Augsburg Confession formulated in writing the basic principles of the Reformation.

It should be emphasized that Protestants have never separated themselves from the Holy Catholic Church. This is evident
every time the Apostles' Creed is repeated in Protestant churches.
Protestants do not intend to forfeit the word "Catholic" when it
means universal, world-wide, or a global fellowship. This awareness of the catholicity of Protestantism is well expressed by
Dr. Douglas Horton, minister of the Congregational Christian
Churches in the United States: "In St. Mary's in Oxford, and
later in St. Giles' in Edinburgh, there came to us such a sense
of spiritual oneness about the altar of God as to make all those
who partook of the experience mystically aware of the presence
of the church. That church, one, holy, catholic, appeared in her
beauty to eyes no longer holden, and all responded to the impulse of the same Spirit."

Protestantism's catholicity is found in one Christ, in one Bible, in one Holy Spirit, in one Kingdom.

Scriptural Foundations

The Protestant Reformation had its birth and inspiration in Holy Scripture. Martin Luther was challenged by the reading of the Bible. The central verse of the Reformation was: "The just shall live by faith" (Rom. 1:17b). This is the scriptural basis for the great Reformation principle, "justification by faith." Moreover, the Bible itself became the sole necessity for faith, life, and salvation for Protestantism. This is why Chillingworth declared: "The Bible and the Bible alone is the religion of Protestants."

Scripture passages which form a solid foundation for the Protestant Reformation are: "For by grace are ye saved through faith; and that not of yourselves; it is the gift of God: not of works" (Eph. 2:8, 9). "Stand fast therefore in the liberty wherewith Christ hath made us free, and be not entangled again with the yoke of bondage" (Gal. 5:1). John 8:32 declares the spiritual attitude of the Protestant: "And ye shall know the truth, and the truth shall make you free."

Paul, the apostle to the Gentiles, in writing to the young preacher Timothy, established in Scripture some of the basic principles which were to be developed in the sixteenth century by the Protestant reformers:

"God hath not given us the spirit of fear; but of power, and of love, and of a sound mind. Be not thou therefore ashamed of the testimony of our Lord, nor of me his prisoner: but be thou partaker of the afflictions of the gospel according to the power of God; who hath saved us, and called us with an holy calling, not according to our works, but according to his own purpose and grace, which was given us in Christ Jesus before the world began, but is now made manifest by the appearing of our Saviour Jesus Christ who hast abolished death, and hath brought life and immortality to light through the gospel: whereunto I am appointed a preacher, and an apostle, and a teacher of the Gentiles" (II Tim. 1:7-11).

PROTESTANT REFERENCE BOOKS: Most helpful to the first three chapters of this primer is the complete set of historical studies by Kenneth Scott Latourette, *A History of the Expansion of Christianity.*

Other supplemental reading recommended is as follows: *Here I Stand* (A Life of Martin Luther) by Roland Bainton; *A History of the Reformation* by Thomas M. Lindsay; *Luther and the German*

Reformation by Thomas M. Lindsay; *History of Christian Doctrine* by George Park Fisher; *Great Voices of the Reformation,* edited by Harry Emerson Fosdick; *The Church and Its Function in Society,* edited by W. A. Visser 't Hooft and J. H. Oldham (an Oxford Conference book); *The Reformation* by Williston Walker; *Christian Thought to the Reformation* by Herbert B. Workman.

3

The Roman
Catholic Church in America

In dealing with this vital subject, we must always keep in mind that there is no such thing as an *American* Catholic Church. The Church is universal. It is never divided on a national basis. Because the Head of the Roman Catholic Church abides at Rome, all Catholics everywhere accept Rome as the Holy City and as the seat of the Church Universal. The pope, at Rome, is the supreme spiritual ruler of world Catholicism.

Many conjectures have arisen in the United States because of this allegiance to Rome. There is the matter of citizenship, and whether a Catholic President would be under the direct domination of the pope. There are the vital issues concerning the public schools and taxation. Many other problems and misunderstandings grow out of this issue of the control of the Papacy, including whether or not an Ambassador should be sent to the Vatican.

Since the Roman Catholic Church in the United States is so important a part of the Roman Catholic Church, this chapter will present, in summary form, the U.S. hierarchy, its work and organization, and statistics on the church membership and growth of the Roman Catholic Church in the United States.

THE ROMAN CATHOLIC POSITION

Catholic Aid in the Founding of the U.S.A.

According to the *National Catholic Almanac,* "The Catholic contribution to the founding of the United States was two-fold: (1) The fundamental documents of American liberty derived from traditional Catholic thought and philosophy. The culture of our fathers was predominantly that of Western Europe, which

24

for more than a thousand years had been Catholic. It had produced the doctrine of the fundamental equality of all souls; and this, in turn, produced the democratic ideal that all citizens have equal rights. (2) The Revolutionary War was successfully concluded through the assistance of a number of Catholic soldiers and statesmen." (p. 199)

Catholic Philosophy in the Declaration of Independence

Some Roman Catholics point with pride to two outstanding churchmen whose social ideals and concepts of human rights, they maintain, contributed much to the Declaration of Independence: St. Thomas Aquinas (1225–74) and Robert Bellarmine (1542–1621). The former is representative of the learning and thought of the Middle Ages; the latter, that of the sixteenth century. A comparison of various sections of the Declaration of Independence, according to Catholics, harmonizes with the writings of these two theologians in thought and political principle. It is said that Thomas Aquinas discovered America politically two hundred years before Columbus discovered it geographically. (*National Catholic Almanac*, pp. 199-201)

John Carroll and George Washington

Pope Pius XII in an encyclical letter to the Church in the United States, issued in 1939 on the occasion of the one hundred and fiftieth anniversary of the establishment of the American hierarchy, had this to say about Catholic influence in the Revolutionary War:

"When Pope Pius VI gave you your first Bishop in the person of the American John Carroll and set him over the See of Baltimore, small and of slight importance was the Catholic population of your land. At that time, too, the condition of the United States was so perilous that its structure and its very political unity were threatened by grave crisis. Because of the long and exhausting war the public treasury was burdened with debt, industry languished and the citizenry, wearied by misfortunes, was split into contending parties. This ruinous and critical state of affairs was put aright by the celebrated George Washington, famed for his courage and keen intelligence. He was a close friend of the Bishop of Baltimore. Thus the Father of His Country and the pioneer pastor of the Church in that land so dear to Us, bound together by the ties of friendship and clasping, so to speak, each other's hand, form a picture for their descendants, a lesson to all future generations, and a proof that reverence for the Faith of Christ is a holy and established principle of the American people, seeing that it is the foundation of morality and decency, consequently the source of prosperity and progress."

The pope then reviews the Church in the United States today, including missionary associations, solicitude for the Negroes, Catholic charities, the National Catholic Welfare Conference, and closes with the consideration of such American problems as irreligion and education, marriage and divorce, and social justice.

It should be added that while numbering only 25,000, Catholics—at the time of the Revolutionary War—bore a disproportionately great share in the struggle for Independence. They gave outstanding leadership in men like Charles Carroll, member of the Continental Congress and signer of the Declaration of Independence, and large sums of money. Almost 50 per cent of Washington's armies, according to the *National Catholic Almanac,* were either of Irish birth or of Irish descent.

The Civil War

Roman Catholics fought in both Union and Confederate armies. With the Union were some fifty Catholic generals, and with the Confederate forces were more than twenty Catholic generals. On both sides were many Catholic officers of lower rank and thousands of Catholic enlisted men.

World Wars I and II

United States Catholics gave between 800,000 and 1,000,000 to the colors: Catholics suffered 22,552 deaths. For several Roman Catholic "firsts" of World War I, the reader is referred to page 203 of the *National Catholic Almanac.*

According to a survey completed January, 1948, approximately 24 per cent of all the members of the armed services of World War II were Roman Catholics.

Catholics Represented in National Statuary Hall

In the National Statuary Hall are the following Catholics: Charles Carroll (1737–1832), statesman; Rev. Jacques Marquette, S.J. (1637–75), Jesuit missionary; Rev. Junipero Serra (1713–84), Franciscan missionary; and James Shields (1806–79), statesman and soldier.

Present Strength of Catholic Church in U.S.A.

The Roman Catholic Church is the largest religious body in the United States, although grouped together the Protestant denominations have nearly twice the enrollment of the Roman Catholics.

This Roman Catholic population (including Hawaii and Alaska) has:

Archbishops (including 4 Cardinals and 6 Titular Archbishops)	29
Bishops	154
Priests	43,889
Brothers	7,620
Sisters	152,178
Churches with Priests	
Resident	14,709
Non-Resident	824
Missions	4,791
Converts (1951)	121,950
Seminaries	392
Seminarians	28,798
Colleges and Universities	236
High Schools	2,429
Pupils attending Universities, Colleges, Academies, and High Schools	2,575,329
Orphan Asylums	358
Orphans	41,299
Homes for the Aged	262
Hospitals	871

In *1906* the Roman Catholic Church in the U.S.A. had 12,472 churches and 14,210,755 members; in *1916* it had 17,375 churches and 15,721,815 members; in *1926* it had 18,940 churches and 18,605,003 members; in *1936* it had 18,409 churches and 19,914,-937 members. Now it has 29,241,580 members.[1]

The Reverend John A. O'Brien of the University of Notre Dame, speaking of the growth in converts, has this to say in his

---

[1] Based on 1951 figures. According to the *Yearbook of the American Churches,* the Protestant membership for the same year was 52,162,432. Roman Catholic membership contains all baptized persons, including infants and children; Protestant membership represents, from 90-95%, those who are over 13 years of age. Roman Catholics were 16% of the U.S. population in 1926; 18% in 1950; and 19% in 1951. Protestants were 27% of the U.S. population in 1926; 33% in 1950; and 34% in 1951.

book *Sharing the Faith,* "In 1933, a total of 29,872 priests netted 40,226 converts—an average of 1.7; in 1943, a total of 36,970 received 86,905—an average of 2.3 per priest. In a decade the average had increased but .6 of 1 per cent—an acceleration that is surely nothing to get excited about. In 1947, the total of 115,214 converts received by 41,747 priests represents an average of 2.7 per priest. At this snail-like pace, we shall never achieve the goal appointed for us by Christ—the winning of the 80,000,000 churchless people of our country. To accomplish that, we must raise the annual total of converts well beyond the million mark." (p. 9)

American Cardinals and the Apostolic Delegate

The present Apostolic Delegate (nondiplomatic legate) to the United States is His Excellency Most Reverend Amleto Giovanni Cicognani, whose residence is at 3339 Massachusetts Avenue, Washington, D.C. An Apostolic Delegate enjoys precedence over all except the Cardinals, and is sent to foreign countries to watch over the conditions of the Church.

There are four Cardinals in the U.S.A.: Samuel Stritch, Archbishop of Chicago; Edward Mooney, Archbishop of Detroit; Francis Spellman, Archbishop of New York; and Francis McIntyre, Archbishop of Los Angeles.

Public Education and the Roman Catholic Church

The official position of the Roman Catholic Church regarding education is found in the following excerpts from Section XXII of the *Code of Canon Law:*

"Parents are bound by a most grave obligation to provide to the best of their ability for the religious and moral as well as for the physical and civil education of their children, and for their temporal well-being." (*Canon 1113*)

"From childhood all the faithful must be so educated that not only are they taught nothing contrary to faith and morals, but that religious and moral training takes the chief place." (*Canon 1372*)

"In every elementary school religious instruction, adapted to the age of the children, must be given." (*Canon 1373*)

"Catholic children must not attend non-Catholic, neutral or mixed schools. . . . It is for the bishop of the place alone to decide, according to the instructions of the Apostolic See, in what circumstances and with what precautions attendance at such schools may be tolerated without danger of perversion to the pupils." (*Canon 1374*)

"The Church has the right to establish schools of every grade, not only elementary schools, but also high schools and colleges." (*Canon 1375*)

As applied to education in the United States, this official position of the Church was amplified by this law promulgated by the third plenary Council of Baltimore in 1884: "Near every church where there is no parochial school one shall be established within two years after the promulgation of this Council, and shall be perpetually maintained, unless the bishop for serious reasons sees fit to allow delay."

"All parents shall be bound to send their children to a parochial school, unless it is evident that such children obtain a sufficient Christian education at home, or unless they attend some other Catholic school, or unless, for sufficient causes approved by the Bishop, with proper cautions and remedies duly applied, they attend another school."

In 1919, in a pastoral letter, the Hierarchy of the United States declared: "The Church in our country is obliged, for the sake of principle, to maintain a system of education distinct and separate from other systems. It is supported by the voluntary contributions of Catholics who, at the same time, contribute as required by law to the maintenance of public schools.

". . . Our system is based on certain convictions that grow stronger as we observe the testing of all education, not simply by calm theoretic discussion, but by the crucial experience of recent events.

". . . With great wisdom our American Constitution provides that every citizen shall be free to follow the dictates of his conscience in the matter of religious belief and observance.

". . . Our Catholic schools are not established and maintained with any idea of holding our children apart from the general body and spirit of American citizenship. They are simply the concrete form in which we exercise our rights as free citizens, in conformity with the dictates of conscience. Their very existence is a great moral fact in American life. For while they aim, openly and avowedly, to preserve our Catholic Faith, they offer to all people an example of the use of freedom for the advancement of morality and religion." [2]

---

[2] The Catholic view of education and the public school will be considered further in Chapter 19.

Respecting Forms of Government

The Roman Catholic Church believes in authority, both for itself and for the State. Power in each case comes not from the people, but from God. This does not mean that the people cannot "designate" the ruler, yet by so doing they are not conferring the "right to rule." This right is of a divine origin.

Speaking of the forms of government, Pope Leo XIII, in his encyclical letter (June, 1881), "On Civil Government," declares, "There is no question here respecting forms of government, for there is no reason why the Church should not approve of the chief power being held by one man or by more, provided only it be just, and that it tend to the common advantage. Wherefore, *so long as justice be respected, the people are not hindered from choosing for themselves that form of government which suits best either their own disposition, or the institutions and customs of their ancestors.*"

Religious Freedom

Roman Catholics contend that no one has a genuine right, as far as God's law is concerned, to profess any faith except the Catholic religion. Pope Pius IX, in his Syllabus of 1864, condemned the proposition that every man is free to embrace and profess that religion which he believes to be true. All other faiths, except the Catholic, are in error and must be treated with "doctrinal intolerance."

This does not mean, however, that the other religions do not, or should not have, certain *civil* rights.[3] Thus in Catholic countries specific privileges are granted non-Catholics. But there are also certain restrictions as explained by Francis J. Connell, C.SS.R., S.T.D., in *Freedom of Worship:* "If the country is distinctively Catholic, the civil rulers can consider themselves justified in restricting or preventing denominational activities hostile to the Catholic religion. This does not mean that they may punish or persecute those who do not accept the Catholic faith. But they are justified in repressing written or spoken attacks on Catholicism, the use of the press or the mails to weaken the allegiance of Catholics toward their Church, and similar anti-Catholic efforts." (p. 10)

---

[3] A further treatment of this subject is found in Chapter 20 of this primer, "Roman Catholics and Democracy."

Circumstances, however, may justify even in a predominantly Catholic country, the same measure of freedom to non-Catholics as is enjoyed by Catholics. Father Connell declares, "Such a course is justifiable when it is foreseen that a policy of complete toleration will procure greater good than will repressive measures against anti-Catholic activities." (p. 11) For it is one of the basic principles of the Church, as enunciated by Pope Leo XIII, that "no one shall be forced to embrace the Catholic faith against his will."

In the United States, where the Roman Catholic Church is in the minority, it advocates freedom for all religions, not that it recognizes that they are equal, but that there should be the same civil rights for all. The matter of first allegiance of Catholics, whether to the U.S. government or to the pope in Rome, will be discussed in a later chapter.[4]

Duties of the Citizen

According to the *Catechism of Christian Doctrine:* "A citizen must love his country, be sincerely interested in its welfare, and respect and obey its lawful authority.

"A citizen shows a sincere interest in his country's welfare by voting honestly and without selfish motives, by paying just taxes, and by defending his country's rights when necessary."

"Citizens may accept any form of government that does not claim for itself rights that belong to God alone or those that are proper to the individual, to the family, or to the Church. The state exists for the common good of men, and not men for the state. A government may not infringe on the right of an individual or of a family to worship God and to live according to His laws; nor may it forbid parents to instruct their children in the truths of God and to train them in virtuous living. A government may not prohibit the Church from preaching the Gospel, ad-

---

[4] According to the *Catholic Dictionary* (p. 141): "There is nothing sacred about democracy as such: there can be bad and oppressive democracies as well as good ones; if the voice of the people is sometimes the voice of God, it can at other times be the voice of the Devil. The Catholic Church does not undertake to decide which is the best among diverse forms of government; she condemns any which is unjust, irreligious or immoral in its action. Individual Catholics who claim that a good democracy is the form of government most in consonance with Christianity do so because they believe it is the most likely (or least unlikely) to respect human rights."

ministering the sacraments, and legislating in all those matters that pertain to the worship of God and the salvation of souls.

"If a government commands citizens to violate the law of God they must refuse to obey." (pp. 199-201)

THE PROTESTANT POINT OF VIEW
On the Establishment of Free America

Protestantism made a greater contribution to the new democratic state in America because, unlike the Roman Catholic Church, it was truly democratic in its fundamental beliefs concerning man, society, and the state.

Although Roman Catholicism was in America even before the founding of the Republic, it has only been quite recently that it has become a strong, independent power. Protestants, on the whole, do not object to this development as a Christian force. They are glad to grant Roman Catholics all the rights which they themselves enjoy as Christians and as citizens. They will work just as hard for the freedom of the Roman Catholic faith as for their own. But not a few of them are fearful of what might happen if the Roman Catholic Church ever should gain majority control. Even now there are real causes for alarm in regard to Roman Catholic demands for public funds.

This cause for alarm is said, by Roman Catholics, to be without foundation. Yet as their own basic beliefs will reveal, the whole conception of the Roman Catholic Church with regard to its relationship to the State is enough to compel Protestant leaders to rush to their own defenses. If Roman Catholics had their way in this country, many things which Protestants hold dear would be sacrificed or greatly modified. Protestants do not want to be *tolerated*. They want to be free, both in the sight of God and man.

Protestants in America are irritated constantly by the Roman Catholic Church. This is due not only to demands for tax money to support Roman Catholic schools, but to an ever-increasing *Roman Catholic* emphasis. Now we have *Catholic* Boy Scouts, *Catholic* Nurses, the *Catholic* Mother of the Year, *Catholic* dramatic guilds, *Catholic* this and that. All this does not make for good Americanism, to say nothing of good Christianity. Protestants ask of the Roman Catholic Church in America that it use the liberty granted to it by the nation not to divide citizens one from another, but to unite them around Christian principles.

Protestantism in America

As the Pilgrims were about to embark for America, the Reverend John Robinson said to them, "The Lutherans cannot be drawn to go beyond what Luther says, for whatever part of God's will he had further imparted to Calvin, they will rather die than embrace it. And so also the Calvinists: they stuck where he left them, a misery much to be lamented. For, though they were precious shining lights in their times, yet God hath not revealed His whole will to them and, were they now living, they would be ready and willing to embrace further light as they had received."

This spirit of following the new light of truth led the Protestants in America not only to formulate such principles as religious freedom, and the separation of Church and State, but set the stage for true democracy and the writing of the Bill of Rights into the U.S. Constitution. Although full religious freedom was not at first practiced by all Protestants in America, it did find its first home on American soil in the territory of Rhode Island. This was due largely to its chief advocate, Roger Williams.

H. Richard Niebuhr, in his *The Kingdom of God in America,* declares that "any attempt to trace the pattern of the Christian movement in America must begin with the Protestant Reformation. Doubtless Roman Catholicism has made important contributions to American life, and there is also a modicum of truth in the contention that the sources of New World religion must be sought in the sectarian tradition stemming from Wyclif rather than in the Protestant movement led by Luther and Calvin; yet both history and the religious census support the statement that Protestantism is America's 'only national religion and to ignore that fact is to view the country from a false angle.'" (p. 17)

The Protestant position on the liberty of conscience and the priesthood of all believers has been written into the basic opinions and laws of our nation. Not only is this true of the First Amendment to the U.S. Constitution, but also Madison's "Remonstrance" and particularly in the Virginia Bill for Religious Liberty, the *Preamble* of which states that "Almighty God created the mind free." Protestants, establishing in America a free church within a free state, supported and still support the principles of the statute of the Virginia Bill which proclaims that "no man shall be compelled to frequent or support any religious worship, place, or ministry whatsoever, nor shall be enforced, restrained, molested, or burthened, in his body or goods, nor shall otherwise suffer on account of his religious opinions or belief."

Protestants in America established the principle that Christianity must be free from the state and exist independently on the basis of its own inherent merits.

Learned from the Scriptures

Protestants came to America to escape tyranny and to practice the freedom and liberty which they had learned from the Scriptures. They were free men in Christ and they determined to remain such. In the Bible they had found, as in Matthew 23:4 and John 8:32, that they need not carry the heavy and grievous burdens placed upon them by professional religious leaders, but were to be seekers after the truth and thereby find freedom. In Act 15:24, 28, 30-31, they discovered that the Antioch Christians had a perfect right to break away from ancient rites and ceremonies and practice a new religion guided by the Holy Spirit.

Here is the basis of democracy which Protestants established in America: people come before institutions. "The Sabbath was made for man, not man for the Sabbath" (Mark 2:27). As Paul put it in Romans 1:1, he who was called in the Lord as a slave is a freeman of the Lord. Likewise he who was free when called is a slave of Christ.

Writing to the Galatians (5:13) Paul said, "Ye have been called unto liberty; only use not liberty for an occasion to the flesh, but by love serve one another." And in his letter to the church at Corinth (II Cor. 3:17) Paul wrote, "Where the Spirit of the Lord is, there is liberty." In Philippians 2:12 he urges the early Christians "to work out your own salvation with fear and trembling."

Not dogmatism, but greatness of spirit, is the New Testament basis for Christian thinking. This is manifest in the teaching found in Philippians 4:8, "Finally, brethren, whatsoever things are true, whatsoever things are honest, whatsoever things are just, whatsoever things are pure, whatsoever things are lovely, whatsoever things are of good report; if there be any virtue, and if there be any praise, think on these things."

PROTESTANT REFERENCE BOOKS: *Greater Freedom and Catholic Power* by Wade Crawford Barclay; *Protestantism in the United States* by

A. B. Bass; *American Freedom and Catholic Power* by Paul Blanshard; *The Christian Heritage in America* by George Hedley; *Will America Become Catholic?* by John H. Moore; *Can Protestantism Win America?* by Charles Clayton Morrison; *The Kingdom of God in America* by H. Richard Niebuhr; *Toward World-Wide Christianity*, edited by O. Frederick Nolde, Chap. 1, The Interseminary Series; *Religion in America* by Willard L. Sperry; *Religion in the Development of American Culture, 1765–1840,* by William Warren Sweet.

PART II
The Roman Catholic Church and How It Functions

4

Absolute Authority and Power of the Pope

The pope is misunderstood by many Protestants. They fail to see his limitations. They think of him as all-powerful, having absolute authority over approximately 400,000,000 Catholics around the world. They do not realize that the pope, from the Roman Catholic point of view, is merely a man, a man who can sin and therefore is in danger of hell; a man who can make mistakes and is therefore quite fallible; and a man who owes his authority not to his own personal qualifications, but to the position of the office which he holds.

We shall take a look at the pope from the Roman Catholic point of view, not because we accept what is presented, but so that we may know exactly what Roman Catholics believe about the "Vicar of Christ." Beginning with Peter and the Scriptures we will follow the teaching concerning the pope down through the Vatican Council to the present day. Although there are many different issues growing out of the primacy of the pope—some of which we will not have space to mention—we will give the basic positions of the Roman Catholic Church on this great issue which divides the Christian world.

THE ROMAN CATHOLIC POSITION

What Christ Gave to the Apostles

It is the position of the Roman Catholic Church that Christ, as the Founder of the Church, gave to the apostles (the first bishops of the Church) "the power to teach, to rule, and to sanctify." This is evident from the Gospel record. "Christ gave the apostles the power to bind and loose, to baptize, to forgive sin, and to offer the sacrifice of the Mass." (*A Catechism of Christian Doctrine*, p. 109) "The power to teach and to rule is

39

the power of jurisdiction; the power to sanctify is the power of orders. The power to sanctify sometimes requires jurisdiction, as in the sacrament of Penance." (*Ibid.*)

Scripture references for this position are: Matthew 18:18, 28:18; Mark 16:15, 18-20; Luke 10:16, 22:19; John 6:54, 20:21-23; and Acts 1:8.

Not by the Apostles Alone

According to Roman Catholic doctrine, Christ intended that the powers which he gave to the apostles should be passed on to their successors. "Christ founded the Church to last until the end of time. The apostles lived for a short time only. Christ must, then, have intended that the apostles provide duly authorized successors to carry on the work of teaching, sanctifying, and ruling. The Acts of the Apostles and the Epistles of Saint Paul contain references to the work done by the successors of the apostles." (*A Catechism of Christian Doctrine*, p. 110)

Evidence from Scriptures is listed as follows: Acts 1:24-26; I Timothy 3:1; and Titus 1:5.

Chief of the Apostles

Roman Catholics believe absolutely in the appointment by Christ of Peter as the first among the apostles. Moreover, they believe that Christ gave to Peter, and to Peter alone, special powers. Peter, to them, was the first pope.

The official teaching of the Roman Catholic Church is that "Christ gave special power in His Church to Saint Peter by making him the head of the apostles and the chief teacher and ruler of the entire Church. The power of the keys was promised to Saint Peter and was actually conferred upon him. Saint Peter was recognized by the early Christians from the beginning as the head of the Church." (*A Catechism of Christian Doctrine*, p. 111)

This is the Scripture basis for the Roman Catholic claim that Peter was the first pope:

Then Jesus answered and said, "Blessed art thou, Simon Bar-Jona, for flesh and blood has not revealed this to thee, but my Father in heaven. And I say to thee, thou art Peter, and upon this rock I will build my Church, and the gates of hell shall not prevail against it. And I will give thee the keys of the kingdom of heaven; and whatever thou shalt bind on earth shall be bound in heaven, and whatever thou shalt loose on earth shall be loosed in heaven" (Matt. 16:17-19).[1]

---

[1] From the Revised Challoner-Rheims Version.

Apostolic Succession

The doctrine of apostolic succession, unlike in some branches of the Protestant Church, is well established in the Roman Catholic Church. There is no question about it. For it teaches "Christ did not intend that the special power of chief teacher and ruler of the entire Church should be exercised by Saint Peter alone, but intended that this power should be passed down to his successor, the pope, the Bishop of Rome, who is the Vicar of Christ on earth and the visible head of the Church."

"The bishops of the Church are the successors of the apostles because they have received their power of orders by valid consecration through an unbroken line of successors of the apostles, and have received their power of jurisdiction through their union with the Pope, the successor of Saint Peter." (*A Catechism of Christian Doctrine,* pp. 112-113)

Commenting on the primacy of Peter and the apostolic succession, the *Catholic Almanac* says: "Christ completed the founding of His Church shortly before His Ascension, conferring on Peter the promised primacy. . . . Thus Peter was given charge of the whole Church without exception—hierarchy, clergy and laity. . . . 'Upon this rock I will build My Church, and the gates of hell shall not prevail against it' clearly manifests that Christ's Church is destined to exist until the end of time. By divine law the primacy of Peter, indissolubly united with the Roman See, necessarily passes, therefore, to each of his successors in perpetuity."

Catholics firmly believe that when Christ made Peter the foundation of his imperishable Church he founded the papacy.

The Infallibility of the Pope

Roman Catholics claim that it is unthinkable that an institution established by Christ the Son of God for the salvation of souls could possibly lead men into error and therefore turn them away from Himself. Therefore if the Church could and did err in matters of faith or morals it would not be a true teacher, for a doctrine of faith and morals [2] is a truth revealed by God alone. Moreover, the Church cannot change its defined teachings on faith and morals, although it may interpret and and restate them.

This was the case, Catholics believe, in regard to the infallibility of the pope. He has always been infallible, under certain

---

[2] Not all morals are "revealed."

conditions, from the very beginning. The Vatican Council in
1870, when it made the following pronouncement, was not conferring upon the pope any new powers or giving him something
which he did not already possess. The Vatican Council declared
"it to be a dogma of divine revelation that when the Roman
Pontiff speaks *ex cathedra*—that is, when he, using his office as
shepherd and teacher of all Christians, in virtue of his apostolic
authority, defines a doctrine of faith or morals to be held by the
whole Church—he, by the divine assistance promised him in
blessed Peter, possesses that infallibility with which the divine
Redeemer was pleased to invest his Church in the definition of
doctrine on faith and morals, and that, therefore, such definitions
of the Roman Pontiff are irreformable in their own nature and
not because of the consent of the Church." (*A Catholic Dictionary*, p. 253)

The Catholic position is stated in *The Popes, Infallible
Teachers* by John B. Harney, C.S.P., published by the Paulist
Press (pp. 7-8):

"Our belief is that the Pope, without a single exception, from Peter
to Pius XII, has been blessed and protected by Almighty God with
the gift of infallibility in the exercise of his Supreme Teaching Authority. To know when this authority is involved, we must pay close
attention to the following conditions:

1. It must be perfectly clear and certain that the Pope is defining,
   i.e., is handing down a final, authoritative, and irrevocable
   decision.
2. Concerning a matter of either faith or morals;
3. And that he means to make his decision binding on all
   Christians."

When the Pope Is Fallible

The pope is not infallible in everything he says or does. He can
make mistakes like any other mortal man. Catholics, for example,
believe that in certain realms like science the pope may commit
blunders. Stated from a Catholic point of view (Harney's *The
Popes, Infallible Teachers*, pp. 8-9):

"We do not believe that the Pope is infallible, or has any special
Divine assistance in dealing with other branches of human knowledge, such as astronomy, geology, and the physical sciences.

"We do not believe that the Pope is infallible in discussing other
questions which may have a slight bearing on religious truths, or even

a direct and intimate relation with them, except under the conditions and circumstances which have been already specified.

"We do not believe that the Pope can make known new truths or proclaim new revelations.

"We do not believe that the infallibility of the Pope is due in any way, shape, or degree to himself or to any other man. It is not the product of his abilities, his studious researches, or of his keen vision. Neither is it dependent on his character. A scholarly Pope is no more infallible than one whose talents are mediocre. A saintly Pope is no more infallible than one whose behavior is stained with deadly sin."

Popes Can Sin

In spite of papal infallibility popes may, since it is entirely possible, go to hell. They are mortal, sinful men, and have to earn their way to eternal salvation like any other Catholic. In fact, Catholics themselves admit that there have been popes who have committed terrible sins.

In Father Conway's *The Question Box*, which serves as one of the most popular Roman Catholic teaching guides, there is this interesting comment: "Infallibility does not mean that the Pope is incapable of committing sin. He may commit sin like any other Catholic, and he is bound like any other Catholic to use the same divine means of pardon, the Sacrament of Penance. Infallibility is not a personal, but a divine, official prerogative, given by Christ to Peter and his successors to keep them from error in defining the content of the Gospel." (p. 170)

According to the Catholic point of view, *infallibility,* that is, freedom from error in declaring to the world the real meaning of the doctrines of faith and morals, and *impeccability,* that is, freedom from sin, are two quite different things. A pope may be a sinner, yet speak with infallibility for God.

"While we naturally expect the Popes to be of the highest moral character—and most of them have been—the official prerogative of infallibility has nothing whatever to do with the Pope's personal goodness or wickedness.

"But 'just as the intrinsic worth of a jewel is not lessened by an inferior setting, so the sins of a priest cannot essentially affect his power of offering Sacrifice, administering the Sacraments, or transmitting doctrine. . . . Even the supreme high priest can in no way diminish the value of that heavenly treasure which he controls and dispenses, but only as a steward. The gold remains gold in impure as in pure hands.' " (Conway's *Question Box,* quoting Catholic scholar Ludwig Pastor in *History of the Popes*)

Pastor, in the history just quoted, speaking of Pope Alexander VI (1492–1503), admits that he lived the immoral life of a secular prince of his day, both as cardinal and as pope (V, 363; VI, 140); that he obtained the papacy by the rankest simony (V, 385); and that he brought his high office into disrepute by his unconcealed nepotism and lack of moral sense (VI, 139).

Roman Catholics therefore admit that the conduct of some popes, in their personal lives, cannot be justified. This, however, they say, does not affect their official position, nor their power of infallibility.

Three Popes at One Time

During the fourteenth century the Roman Catholic Church had a real problem. There were three ecclesiastical leaders all, at the same time, claiming to be the real, true pope. Naturally, from the Catholic point of view, only one could be pope. The others were only pretenders.

This is how Fathers Rumble and Carty explain the situation in *Radio Replies:* "In 1378 Urban VI was lawfully elected Pope at Rome. Some French Cardinals, wrongly thinking or maintaining that he had not been rightly elected, elected another who called himself Clement VII. . . . To settle the difficulty, another group of Cardinals later on went beyond their rights, declared the rival Popes deposed, and elected a second anti-Pope, Alexander V. This gave rise to three lines of claimants and thus complicated the position. A general Council was called. The legitimate successor in the Urban line, Gregory XII, resigned. The successors of the anti-Popes were declared to be unduly elected, and the difficulty was overcome by the election of Pope Martin V, in 1417. The true succession was never lost; nor was the essential unity. All the time there was but one true Pope, and the mistake on the part of the faithful as to which was the true Pope was not an error in faith." (Vol. I, p. 99)

How a Pope Is Chosen

Next in dignity to the pope are the cardinals, "Princes of the Church." To the College of Cardinals falls the responsibility of electing the new pope when the Holy See is vacant. When complete, the Sacred College numbers seventy members. When the death of the pope is officially proclaimed, word is sent out to all the cardinals around the world to meet at Rome in solemn conclave. This must be held not earlier than fifteen and not later than eighteen days after the death of the pope. They remain in seclusion, within a part of the Vatican Palace specially prepared for them, until the election takes place.

If all the cardinals are present by the fifteenth day, or if not, not later than the eighteenth day, after Holy Mass they go to the Sistine Chapel where the voting takes place. A secret ballot is used for candidates considered fully qualified. Ballots are used which have been specially printed for the purpose. A two-thirds, plus one, majority is required for election. Two ballots are taken each morning and evening until a decision is reached. When no selection is made, the ballots are burned, with damp straw, producing a heavy black smoke. This indicates that no selection has been made. When, however, a two-thirds, plus one, vote is arrived at, the ballots are burned without the damp straw. The light smoke which ascends from the chimney is the signal that a new pope has been elected.

"Acceptance of the office on the part of the one elected must be manifested before he is validly the new Pontiff. If the one elected is not already a bishop, he must be consecrated.

"The Pope is elected for life, although, if he wishes, he may resign. Should he do so, a new Pope is elected. Any male Catholic, regardless of race or color, may be elected Pope, even one who is not a priest. Should a layman be chosen, he would have to be ordained and consecrated." (*National Catholic Almanac,* p. 91)

Uncertainty About the Popes

Roman Catholics themselves are not certain as to the dates and listing of the popes. This is revealed in Appendix III in *A Catholic Dictionary,* edited by Donald Attwater and with the Imprimatur of E. Morrogh Bernard, Vic. gen. (p. 548). Before listing the Bishops of Rome, Supreme Pontiffs of the Universal Church, this note appears: "There are some discrepancies in the lists of popes, owing to conflicting records and the uncertain status of certain pontiffs; the following is an attempt to record historical probabilities. Family names, when known, are given in brackets, and the date of accession follows. The dates up to the third century are extremely uncertain."

As commonly enumerated there have been 262 popes since Peter, although the count is not certain. Of these 105 were Romans, 77 other Italians, 15 French, 14 Greeks, 7 Syrians, 4 Tuscans, 4 Germans, 3 Spaniards, 2 Africans, 2 Dalmatians, 2 Lom-

bards, 2 Sardinians, and one each Alsatian, Burgundian, Cala-
brian Greek, Dutch, English (Adrian VI, 1154–59), Lorrainer,
Ostrogoth, Samnite, Sicilian, Sicilian Greek, Umbrian, and Gali-
lean Jew. Of these, 41 belonged to religious orders; and 76 are
venerated as saints.

A pope may resign or abdicate of his own free will, without
the consent of the cardinals; a pope can only be deposed because
of heresy, expressed or implied, and then only by a general
council.[3] No pope has ever been deposed, although anti-popes
have been.

American Catholics and the Pope

Besides being the spiritual and moral ruler of approximately
400,000,000 Catholics all over the world, the pope is also temporal ruler of the Vatican City State. This came into being by
means of the Lateran Treaty with the Italian government in
1929. It is independent and sovereign. The pope possesses full
legislative, executive, and judiciary powers of Vatican City. It
comprises 108.7 acres.

American Catholics, while under obligation to obey the pope in
faith and morals, are under no obligation to obey him as head of
Vatican City. Catholics make a sharp distinction between the
pope's temporal powers and his universal authority as spiritual
head of the Catholic Church. Catholics obey the laws of their
own nations in temporal affairs;[4] they have only one political
allegiance and this is to their native land.

Fathers Rumble and Carty[5] maintain that (taking a hypo-
thetical case) if the pope, as ruler of the Vatican City State,
should ever have a navy and decide to invade either America
or Australia, they would be obliged to fight against the pope.

Roman Catholics in the United States are conscience bound to
obey the Constitution and the laws of the land. At the same time
they are bound, in moral and spiritual affairs, to obey the pope
in Rome.

---

[3] "In point of fact, heresy is the only legitimate ground. For a heretical
pope has ceased to be a member of the Church, and cannot, therefore, be
its head. A sinful pope, on the other hand, remains a member of the
(visible) Church and is to be treated as a sinful, unjust ruler for whom
we must pray, but from whom we may not withdraw our obedience."—
The Catholic Encyclopedia.

[4] Roman Catholics obey the laws of the nation provided they do not
violate the laws of God.

[5] In *Radio Replies.*

THE PROTESTANT POINT OF VIEW
On the Christian Basis of Authority

Protestantism will not accept the authority of the pope because it firmly believes that Christ alone is Head of the Church and has no other agent outside the Holy Spirit.

Protestants are united in declaring that the pope is not the head of the Church and that he is not Christ's especially chosen vicar. Moreover, they maintain that he has no power and no authority not already granted to other Christian leaders. If there is any one thing upon which Protestants will agree, it is that Christians owe no special allegiance to the pope in Rome. Since the entire Roman hierarchy is built upon the opposite position, it is impossible, at this time, for Protestants and Roman Catholics to come to any agreement in regard to the chief authority of the visible Church.

Protestants are insistent that Christ is head of the Church, and that there need be no other. They vary in church government and polity, but they are united in believing that each soul has direct access to God through Christ. They cannot find anything in the New Testament which says that the successors of Peter are to have supreme authority over them. It is the conviction of many non-Roman Catholics that the New Testament offers both a variety of belief and a variety of church government. "Oneness" is to be achieved through common allegiance to Christ, and in the common desire to serve humanity in his behalf and in his spirit.

The pope may be a great religious leader. As such, Protestants honor him, as in the case of Pope Leo XIII. But they honor him along with other Christian leaders and not because he claims to be the Vicar of Christ here upon earth. Protestants rebel at the thought of a pope. They get their directives directly from Christ. Anything less than this, from the Protestant viewpoint, is a denial of the fundamental principles of the New Testament.

The Living Word

Protestants establish their authority not upon a human being, nor upon an ecclesiastical position or even upon the visible Church itself, but upon the living Word of God. Thus the

supremacy of the pope is denied and Jesus' words to Peter recorded in Matthew 16:18 and in John 21:15 ("Thou are Peter
and upon this rock I will build my church, and the gates of hell
shall not prevail against it." . . . "Feed my sheep, feed my
lambs.") are not associated with any kind of church organization
whatsoever, but are given an ever-new relationship to Christ, the
spiritual head of the Church.

According to David Schaff, in *Our Fathers Faith and Ours*
(pp. 245-246) the Protestant position in regard to these verses
is stated as follows:

1. In the parallel passages of Mark 8:29 and Luke 9:20 Peter is
not even mentioned.

2. Christ, and not Peter, in every other place in the New Testament
is called the rock, the foundation, the cornerstone of the church. (See
I Cor: 3:11 for example.)

3. The book of Acts is against the theory held by the Roman
Catholic Church. (See Acts 15:4, 14; 8:22, and 10:25.)

4. Paul, when he uses the term "head of the church" in the letters
to the Ephesians and Colossians, always refers to Christ.

5. Peter is never accorded special authority as far as the New
Testament is concerned. He is always co-equal in authority with the
other apostles. (See Matt. 28:19; I Cor. 12:28; Acts 8:14; Rev. 21:14.)

6. Paul's leading place in the early church contradicts the Roman
Catholic contention. (See Gal. 2:17; I Cor. 1:12.)

7. James, rather than Peter, presided at the only church council
which occurred in apostolic times. (See Acts 15:13.)

8. Even the predominant opinion of the Church Fathers concerning
the interpretation of Matthew 16:18 was that Christ rather than Peter
was "the rock." Augustine, for example, was of this opinion.

The revised *Westminster Confession* of 1902 sums up the
Protestant view in regard to the papacy in these words: "There
is no other head of the church but the Lord Jesus Christ and the
claim of any man to be the vicar of Christ and the head of the
church is un-Scriptural, without warrant in fact and is a usurpa-
tion dishonoring the Lord Jesus Christ."

In answer to the question, "What is the Church of God?", the
Standard Catechism of The Methodist Church replies: "It is the
universal society of believers in Jesus scattered throughout the
world, who are nevertheless one in him; because they recognize
him as their only Head; because his Spirit dwells in them; and
because they accept the law of love contained in his Gospel as
the rule of their lives."

Divine Authority of the Word

Protestants find their authority in the Scriptures, for they believe the Bible to be the Word of God. It speaks to them with divine authority. They believe it and accept it as the most precious and binding authority because they are convinced that through the Book God speaks directly to the human soul. "God is a Spirit: and they that worship him must worship him in spirit and truth" (John 4:24). Worshipers are told to "come boldly unto the throne of grace" (Heb. 4:16). And it is pointed out in Ephesians 2:18 that we have direct access to God through Christ.

Based upon the New Testament, the faith of the Protestant has no need for any ecclesiastical authority or intercessor. No church organization, council, or pope has the right to assume the rights and authority which alone belong to Christ (Rom. 10:4, 9).

In II Timothy 3:16-17, Paul places Scripture, and not the Church, as the supreme authority, saying, "All scripture is given by inspiration of God, and is profitable for doctrine, for reproof, for correction, for instruction in righteousness; that the man of God may be perfect, thoroughly furnished unto all good works."

Protestants not only encourage Scripture reading, but also the daily practice of the teachings of the Bible. They take seriously the words of the Book of Revelation (1:3): "Blessed is he that readeth, and they that hear the words of this prophecy, and keep those things which are written therein."

PROTESTANT REFERENCE BOOKS: *The Quest for Christian Unity* by Robert S. Bilheimer, pp. 66 ff.; *Communism, Democracy and Catholic Power* by Paul Blanshard; *A Protestant Manifesto* by Winfred E. Garrison; *Protestant Panorama* by Clarence W. Hall and Desider Holisher; *Protestantism's Challenge* by Conrad Henry Moehlman; *Primer for Protestants* by James Hastings Nichols, Part II; *Our Fathers Faith and Ours* by David Schaff; *Creeds of Christendom* by Phillip Schaff; *The Reformation* by Williston Walker.

5

Ten Commandments
and Six Precepts of the Church

The firm basis of morality, and the day-by-day practice of basic Christian principles, of the Roman Catholic Church are grounded in a realistic acceptance of the Ten Commandments and what are known as the six Precepts of the Church. The Ten Commandments are God's laws and must be obeyed as duties directly to God. The Precepts are the commandments of the Church and are equally binding, although not on the same level. Roman Catholics believe that the Church, being the divine representative of Christ, has the right to make laws, and naturally gives her laws the highest possible sanction of binding in conscience under sin. Her laws, however, cease to bind when the Catholic has a valid reason for not observing them, like severe illness or extreme distance from a church.

The Ten Commandments, as expressed by the Catechism of the Council of Trent, bind the conscience of all mankind, manifesting God's will, and through their observance everlasting salvation may be attained. They are as follows:

I. I am the Lord thy God. Thou shalt not have strange gods before Me.
II. Thou shalt not take the name of the Lord, thy God, in vain.
III. Remember thou keep holy the Sabbath day.
IV. Honor thy father and thy mother.
V. Thou shalt not kill.
VI. Thou shalt not commit adultery.
VII. Thou shalt not steal.
VIII. Thou shalt not bear false witness against thy neighbor.
IX. Thou shalt not covet thy neighbor's wife.
X. Thou shalt not covet thy neighbor's goods.

As will be seen later in this chapter, the Church places a Roman Catholic interpretation on each of these commandments. It will also be seen that Protestant numbering and Catholic numbering of the commandments differ. Roman Catholics divide the last commandment; Protestants divide the first. Therefore the Catholic's second commandment becomes the Protestant's third, and so on.

The Roman Catholic Church, "having the deposit of faith to preserve and make known," has the power to make rules for its members. These commandments, or six Precepts of the Church, are as follows:

1. To hear Mass on Sundays and holy days of obligation.
2. To fast and abstain on the days appointed.
3. To confess at least once a year.
4. To receive the Holy Eucharist during the Easter time.
5. To contribute to the support of the Church.
6. Not to marry persons who are not Catholics, or who are related to us within the third degree of kindred, nor privately without witnesses, nor to solemnize marriage at forbidden times.

These Precepts of the Church supplement the Ten Commandments by giving additional detailed guidance for personal conduct. Because Catholics consider the Church's laws as really God's laws, these precepts are equally binding.

THE ROMAN CATHOLIC POSITION

The First Commandment

The Roman Catholic Church forbids idolatry and commands Catholics to worship God and God alone. It forbids Catholics to give any creature or image the honor which belongs to God. According to the teaching of the Church, "a Catholic sins against faith by infidelity, apostasy, heresy, indifferentism, and by taking part in non-Catholic worship." (*Baltimore Catechism*)

"A Catholic sins against faith by taking part in non-Catholic worship because he thus professes belief in a religion he knows is false." (*A Catechism of Christian Doctrine*, p. 171)

A Catholic sins by superstition when he attributes to a creature a power that belongs to God alone, as when he makes use of charms or spells, believes in dreams or fortune-telling, or goes to spiritists. He also sins by sacrilege when he mistreats sacred persons, places, or things.

This commandment forbids the worshiping, not the making, of images.

Roman Catholics *adore* God and *venerate,* that is, show special respect for, the saints. The first commandment, according to the Church, does not forbid giving honor to the saints, including the Virgin Mary, as chosen friends of God. The crucifix, statues, and images are used to put Catholics in mind of the persons they represent. They have no power in and of themselves. "The first commandment does not forbid us to honor the saints in heaven, provided we do not give them the honor that belongs to God alone. When we pray to the saints we ask them to offer their prayers to God for us. We do not pray to the crucifix or to the images and relics of the saints, but to the persons they represent." (*Baltimore Catechism*)

"In venerating relics, statues, and pictures of Our Lord and the saints we must not believe that any divine power resides in them, nor should we put our trust in them as though they had the power of themselves to bestow favors. We place our trust in God and the intercessory power of the saints." (*A Catechism of Christian Doctrine,* p. 181)

The Second Commandment

Roman Catholics, by this commandment, are obliged always to speak of God, and the saints and holy things, with respect and reverence. They honor God in a special way when an oath, meaning a solemn statement made with God as witness of its truth, is lawful, and when they keep a promise made to God (a vow). But they dishonor God by taking his name in vain, by blasphemy (which is using insulting words about God, or the saints, or holy things), by cursing, that is, by wishing evil on any creature of God, by taking an unlawful oath, and by not keeping any vow made.

"By taking God's name in vain is meant that the name of God or the Holy name of Jesus Christ is used without reverence; for example, to express surprise or anger." (*Baltimore Catechism*)

Catholics are not allowed to join societies which require an absolute oath of secrecy which supersedes the welfare of Church or State.

The Third Commandment

Catholics are commanded to keep Sunday as the Lord's Day, because it was on Sunday that Christ rose from the dead, and the Holy Ghost came down upon the apostles. They are strictly obliged on Sundays to "assist" at the Holy Sacrifice of the Mass, and to keep from doing any bodily labor that is not necessary.

"If we are really sick (not an ordinary headache or toothache) on Sunday, we are excused from the obligation to go to Mass. But we are not excused just because we are going on a Sunday trip or excursion and want to start early.

"The law of the Church obliges us to be present from the very beginning of the Mass to the very end of it. We are guilty of venial sin if we miss a little part of the Mass due to our own fault. But if we miss a great part of it due to our own fault, we shall be guilty of a mortal sin. We are obliged to assist at another Mass if we have missed a great part of the first one we went to." (Father McGuire's comments on *The New Baltimore Catechism and Mass*,[1] p. 107)

The Fourth Commandment

Catholics are commanded, by the fourth commandment, "to respect and love our parents, to obey them in all that is not sinful, and to help them when they are in need. Besides our parents, the fourth commandment obliges us to respect and to obey all our lawful superiors. Parents must provide for the spiritual and bodily welfare of their children; superiors, according to their varying degrees of responsibility, must care for those entrusted to them." (*Baltimore Catechism*)

The fourth commandment also obliges Catholics to love their country and to indicate an interest in its welfare by voting honestly and without selfish motives, by paying just taxes, and by defending their country when necessary.

The Church forbids parents to send their children to non-Catholic or secular schools in which the Catholic religion is not taught, "unless the bishop of a diocese grants permission because of particular circumstances." (*A Catechism of Christian Doctrine*, p. 198)

The Fifth Commandment

By this commandment, Catholics are commanded to take proper care of their own spiritual and bodily well-being, and that of their neighbors. "The fifth commandment forbids murder and suicide, and also fighting, anger, hatred, revenge, drunkenness,

---

[1] This is the No. 2 Official Revised Edition, based on *A Catechism of Christian Doctrine*—Revised Edition of the *Baltimore Catechism* No. 2. Used by permission of the Confraternity of Christian Doctrine.

and bad example." (*Baltimore Catechism*) Abortion is considered murder, and those who practice contraception "are branded with the guilt of grave sin." (Pope Pius XI in encyclical "Christian Marriage")

A nation may wage a just war under certain circumstances such as self defense. A person who commits suicide will not be given a Christian burial. Excessive eating and drinking are sinful because they injure the health of a person and often lead to other sins.

The Sixth Commandment

Catholics, by this commandment, are obliged to be pure and modest in their behavior. "The sixth commandment forbids all impurity and immodesty in words, looks, and actions, whether alone or with others. The chief dangers to the virtue of chastity are: idleness, sinful curiosity, bad companions, drinking,[2] immodest dress, and indecent books, plays, and motion pictures." (*Baltimore Catechism*)

When there is full deliberation in any sin of impurity it is considered by the Church a mortal sin.[3] Unmarried persons are not to carry on a courtship with those who are not free to marry.

The Seventh Commandment

Roman Catholics are obliged, on the basis of the seventh commandment, to recognize all rights which belong to others, to live up to all business agreements, and to pay just debts. They must return all stolen goods to rightful owners, or their equivalent value. The commandment "forbids all dishonesty, such as stealing, cheating, unjust keeping of what belongs to others, unjust damage to the property of others, and the accepting of bribes by public officials." (*Baltimore Catechism*)

---

[2] "Excessive eating and drinking are sins because they violate the virtue of temperance."—Comment by a Catholic educator.

[3] The word "mortal" means deadly, and "venial" means pardonable. Mortal sin drives out sanctifying grace from the soul; and venial sins do not. Mortal sin is deadly, being a break in God-man relations, while venial sins are not a complete turning from God. Both are pardonable. But unless repented, confessed, and atoned for, mortal sin excludes one from God's grace and friendship, and dooms one to hell. When confession is not possible, a Roman Catholic can rid himself of mortal sin by making an act of perfect contrition, that is, contrition or sorrow based on the love of God for His own sake, above all things.

According to Roman Catholic teaching: to steal secretly is considered a theft, to steal violently is robbery; dishonesty which seriously disturbs public order is always a mortal sin; merchants who use false weights and measures, or who make exorbitant profits, sin; public officials sin when they demand money, or its equivalent, in making appointments.

The Eighth Commandment

This commands Catholics to speak the truth in all things, particularly in what concerns the good name and honor of others. The chief sins against this commandment are: (1) lies; (2) rash judgment (without good reason for believing evil of another); (3) detraction (without some good cause making known the faults of another); (4) calumny or slander, that is, lying about another; and (5) telling secrets which they are obliged to keep. When Catholics have injured another's good name or honor, they must repair, as best they can, the damage done.

"It is sinful to read a letter addressed to another without his permission, or to eavesdrop on private conversation, unless done in order to prevent some grave harm." (*A Catechism of Christian Doctrine*, p. 224)

The Ninth Commandment

By the ninth commandment Catholics are commanded to be pure in thought and desire. "Thoughts about impure things become sinful when a person thinks of an unchaste act and deliberately takes pleasure in so thinking, or when unchaste desire or passion is aroused and consent is given to it." (*Baltimore Catechism*)

When Catholics confess deliberate impure desires, as they must do, they must tell the priest their object, that is, whether a married or a single person, whether of the same or opposite sex, since the circumstances change the nature of the sin.

The Tenth Commandment

"The tenth commandment forbids all desire to take or to keep unjustly what belongs to others, and also forbids envy at their success." (*Baltimore Catechism*) It is, of course, permissible for Catholics to seek material prosperity if they do so honestly and do not expose themselves to the proximate dangers of sin.

Notes on the Precepts of the Church

1. "A Catholic who through his own fault misses Mass on a Sunday or holyday of obligation commits a mortal sin." (*Baltimore Catechism*)

The holydays of obligation in the United States are: Christmas, The Circumcision (January 1), Ascension Thursday (40 days after Easter), The Assumption (August 15), All Saints' Day (November 1), and The Immaculate Conception (December 8).

2. The Church commands Catholics to fast and to abstain in order that they may control their desires of the flesh, raise their minds more fully to God, and make satisfaction for sin. It makes Friday a day of abstinence from meat to remind Catholics of Christ's death on Good Friday.

3. If Catholics have committed a mortal sin they are strictly obliged to confess it within the year. They are, however, encouraged to go to confession frequently as a means to a better Christian life. Catholics in the state of mortal sin, and who are in danger of death, are obliged to receive the sacrament of Penance.

4. Every Catholic is strictly obliged under pain of mortal sin to receive Holy Communion worthily during the course of the Easter Season. If for some reason he misses it during this period, he is obliged to receive the Holy Eucharist as soon thereafter as possible.

5. The Catholic, according to the law of the Church, "is obliged to bear his fair share of the financial burden of the Holy See, of the diocese, and of the parish."

Father McGuire, commenting on this requirement in *The New Baltimore Catechism and Mass*, says: "No Catholic can have true peace of conscience unless he is doing his share of paying for the expenses of his Church. Every Catholic, as a member of the Mystical Body of Christ, is strictly obliged, as far as his means allow him, to help the Church, at home and throughout the world, to preach the Gospel, to build and keep up the thousands of churches, schools, hospitals, and other religious works in which the Church is engaged."

"Mass stipends are given to the priest, not in payment for the spiritual benefits received, but as a means of his support." (*A Catechism of Christian Doctrine*, p. 240)

6. The ordinary law of the Church is that "a Catholic can contract a true marriage only in the presence of an authorized

priest and two witnesses." [4] (*A Catechism of Christian Doctrine,* p. 241)

Catholics are forbidden to contract marriage with a non-Catholic (except under certain rigid exceptions), and marriage with a second cousin, or with any other relative closer than a second cousin.

"The Church forbids Catholics to marry non-Catholics because mixed marriages often bring about family discord, loss of faith on the part of the Catholic, and neglect of the religious training of the children."

"For grave reasons the Church sometimes permits mixed marriages or marriages between close relatives; such a permission is called a dispensation." (*Ibid.,* p. 242)

According to the law of the Roman Catholic Church the non-Catholic party must promise in writing not to endanger the faith of the Catholic; both parties must promise in writing that all the children born of the marriage will be baptized in the Catholic Church alone and educated solely in the Catholic religion. Moreover, the Catholic party must promise to strive for the conversion of the non-Catholic party by prayer and good example.

"The Church allows Catholics to marry during Lent and Advent, provided they do so quietly and without much ceremony; a Nuptial Mass is forbidden during these seasons."

"A Nuptial Mass is a Mass which has special prayers to beg God's blessing on the married couple." (*Ibid.,* p. 244)

The Roman Catholic position on divorce will be considered in Chapter 12.

---

[4] Two exceptions: "The first case occurs when one (at least) of the parties desiring to be married is in danger of death. The other case occurs when they are so situated that they can prudently foresee that the services of an authorized priest cannot be secured for a month. In either of the cases the couple can be married by merely giving and receiving the conjugal consent in the presence of two witnesses."—Francis J. Connell, C.SS.R., S.T.D., in *Matrimony,* pp. 28-29.

THE PROTESTANT POINT OF VIEW
On the Relationship of Faith to Good Works

Protestantism cannot accept the official precepts of the Roman Catholic Church because it believes the Christian conscience, and not ecclesiastical requirements, should control the conduct and allegiance of all members of the Church.

Protestants unite with Roman Catholics in accepting the Ten Commandments as a basic moral code. They do not, of course, place peculiar interpretations upon these commandments such as are found stated in this chapter. This they freely grant, however, is the privilege of Roman Catholics.

Protestants, however, are troubled in regard to some of the precepts of the Roman Catholic Church. They do not like, for example, to be considered more or less as pagans as far as marriage is concerned. They insist upon being acknowledged as Christians equal in every respect and treated as such. Today there is need for a clearer understanding and a greater practice of the moral codes of the Christian Church. Whatever Christians as a whole can do to strengthen morality will not only benefit individual members and the Church itself, but also the nation and the world. Protestants therefore join Roman Catholics in the promotion of the moral values inherent in the Ten Commandments and desire, on an equal basis, to work with them in carrying them to fulfillment in modern life.

As for the precepts of the Roman Catholic Church in relation to its own members, Protestants have "no comment," since this is strictly internal business of the Roman Catholic Church. They wonder how these precepts can have such a hold upon its members, and why it has such a bias against Protestants. Yet as far as the right to hold such precepts is concerned, Protestants agree that the Roman Catholic Church, in its internal affairs, has total jurisdiction. It is when it begins to apply the precepts to general conditions *outside* its own organization that Protestants feel that they must object.

Protestant Stress upon Righteousness

Martin Luther, although believing in justification by faith, did not fail to stress the works of righteousness. In his tract on "Good Works" he says: "To train up children to the service of God, parents have their hands full and, in doing so, they are doing good works enough. To teach them to trust and fear God, to provide for them meat and drink, to set before them by word and act a good example, and to take care of the hungry and the naked, the imprisoned and the sick, and to make one's dwelling a hospital for those in need—to do all this, is to do the good works which God requires. . . . He who would serve God should remain where people are and do them good so far as he may be able. If you have a wife, child, servants, neighbors—amongst them you will find opportunity enough to be good and in doing them good you are serving God best."

Protestants have been emphatic in their insistence upon keeping the Ten Commandments. They have created an entirely new moral and ethical atmosphere by their observance not only of the letter but also of the spirit of the moral principles established by Jesus and Paul. John Calvin declared: "It is true that we deny that good works have any share in justification, but we claim that full responsibility rests upon the righteous to do good works." Commenting upon the words of Hosea 6:6, he said, "Faith by itself cannot please God, for it can never exist without love to our neighbor." The *Formula of Concord* (1577) declared that "true faith is never alone but always has with it love and hope," while the *Westminster Confession* (1647) maintained that "the moral law binds all justified persons as well as others to the obedience thereof."

At the World Conference on Faith and Order at Lausanne in 1927, and reaffirmed by the Jerusalem Meeting of the International Missionary Council, it was declared: "Sympathizing with the anguish of our generation, with its longing for intellectual sincerity, social justice, and spiritual inspiration, the Church in the eternal Gospel meets the needs and fulfils the God-given aspirations of the modern world. Consequently, as in the past so also in the present, the Gospel is the only way to salvation. Thus, through His Church, the living Christ still says to men, 'Come unto me! . . . He that followeth me shall not walk in darkness, but shall have the light of life.' "

Directly to the Bible

Protestants go directly to the Bible for their moral and social principles. Beginning with the Ten Commandments (Exod. 20:3-18) and the teachings of the prophets, they proceed to the principles of The Sermon on the Mount and to Christ's new commandments: "Thou shalt love the Lord thy God with thy whole heart, and with thy whole soul, and with thy whole mind. This is the greatest and the first commandment. And the second is like it, Thou shalt love thy neighbor as thyself. On these two commandments depend the whole Law and the Prophets" (Matt. 22:35-40).

In the Scriptures all Protestants are commanded to practice love, even to one's enemies (I Cor. 13; Rom. 12:9-19); to bear one another's burdens (Gal. 6:1-2); to support the weak (I Thess. 5:14-15); to help orphans and widows (Jas. 1:27); to convert sinners from their evil ways (Jas. 5:19-20); and to love in deed and truth (I John 3:18). While Protestants believe that there is no supernatural merit in good works, they nevertheless take seriously the conditions laid down by Christ in the Last Judgment scene, as in Matthew 25: "Then shall the King say unto them on his right hand, 'Come, ye blessed of my Father, inherit the kingdom prepared for you from the foundation of the world! For I was a-hungered, and ye gave me meat: I was thirsty, and ye gave me drink: I was a stranger, and ye took me in: naked, and ye clothed me: I was sick, and ye visited me: I was in prison, and ye came unto me.' Then shall the righteous answer him, saying, 'Lord, when saw we thee a-hungered, and fed thee? or thirsty, and gave thee drink? When saw we thee a stranger, and took thee in? or naked, and clothed thee? Or when saw we thee sick, or in prison, and came unto thee?' And the King shall answer and say unto them, 'Verily I say unto you, Inasmuch as ye have done it unto one of the least of these my brethren, ye have done it unto me.'"

PROTESTANT REFERENCE BOOKS: *The Recovery of Ideals* by Georgia Harkness; *Christian Ethics and Modern Problems* by W. R. Inge; *The Principles of Christian Ethics* by Albert C. Knudson; *Social Religion* by Douglas Clyde Macintosh; *Primer for Protestants* by James Hastings Nichols, Chap. IX; *An Interpretation of Christian Ethics* by Reinhold Niebuhr; *Personalities in Social Reform* by G. Bromley Oxnam; *According to Paul* by Harris Franklin Rall, Chap. 10; *The Higher Happiness* by Ralph W. Sockman; *Christian Ethics in History and Modern Life* by Alban C. Widgery.

6

Special Ministry
of the Seven Sacraments

Roman Catholics and Protestants differ greatly when it comes to the "sacraments." Many Protestant bodies do not call them sacraments. Whereas Roman Catholics have seven, Protestants have only two. The other five are repudiated. Moreover, even on the basis of the two held more or less in common—baptism and the Lord's Supper (The Eucharist)—there is a great difference. There is much disagreement about them within Protestant circles. Probably more misunderstandings and divisions have occurred over these two rites than over all the other doctrines of the Church.

Roman Catholics believe that the sacraments are not merely rituals, but visible signs, instituted directly by Christ, signifying and producing sanctifying grace in the soul.

The larger part of the ritual and practice of the Catholic Church revolves about the sacraments. They are considered, by Catholics, as gifts from God. As Fathers Noll and Fallon say in *Father Smith Instructs Jackson:* "Grace in general is a gift which enables man to save his soul. It is in no way due to us and could be withheld by God without injustice to us. When it is received, it comes to us as a favor, not as something to which we have a right." (p. 134)

THE ROMAN CATHOLIC POSITION

The Grace of God

Because God could not expect men to do the impossible He gave Adam and Eve a supernatural gift known to Roman Catholics as "sanctifying grace." This gift enabled them to share in His own life. That is, this gift would transform the ordinary actions of the parents of the human race into supernatural value and they would thus merit a reward in heaven. God had intended this sanctifying grace for all mankind, but due to the sin of Adam and Eve it was lost. Original sin, according to the Roman Catholic Church, has deprived every human being destined to enter this world (except the Virgin Mary) of sanctifying grace.

Christ, by his death on the Cross, restored grace to men. Moreover, every thought, word, and action of the Saviour during his earthly life "merited infinite grace for men." Thus through the merits of Christ the possibility of grace was re-established. But in order that a person's actions may possess supernatural value two things are necessary: (1) the person must be in a state of sanctifying grace, meaning free from mortal sin, and (2) a person must perform all actions with purity of intention, with the motive of honoring and pleasing God. (*Religion: Commandments, Precepts and Sacraments* by Rev. William J. Cavanagh, M.A., and the Sisters of St. Joseph)

As given in *A Catechism of Christian Doctrine* some of the basic points in relation to grace are as follows: (1) Grace is not merely the absence of sin but rather a spiritual quality infused by God into the soul; (2) Grace is a free gift from God; (3) Man cannot attain eternal life by powers that are only natural. He must have constantly "the impulse of God" to merit eternal life.

According to the Roman Catholic Church, there are two kinds of grace: sanctifying grace and actual grace. The first, a sharing of the life of God, confers new life on souls. It is necessary for salvation. It is lost only through mortal sin. The second, actual grace, is "a supernatural help of God which enlightens our mind and strengthens our will to do good and to avoid evil." It is a divine impulse which moves a person to perform acts above his natural powers. Actual grace is necessary, according to *A Catechism of Christian Doctrine*, for all Roman Catholics who have attained the use of reason, because without it "we cannot long resist the power of temptation or perform other actions which merit a reward in heaven."

In addition to prayer, the principal way to receive grace is through sacraments, especially the Eucharist. Baptism and Penance give grace to those who do not possess it. The other sacraments increase it in those who are already in a state of grace.

What the Church Teaches About the Sacraments

According to *Apologetics and Catholic Doctrine*, a textbook used in Roman Catholic schools and colleges, "The Church teaches solemnly: (1) that there are seven Sacraments, neither more nor less, *viz.*, Baptism, Confirmation, Eucharist, Penance, Extreme Unction, Holy Orders, and Matrimony; (2) that all the Sacraments were instituted by Christ Himself; (3) that they truly cause grace in him who is fit to receive them; (4) that the Sacraments of Baptism, Confirmation, and Holy Orders imprint a *character*, or indelible mark, on the soul, and that, therefore, they cannot be received more than once; (5) that, to confer a Sacrament validly, the minister must intend to do what the Church does, but it is not necessary that he be in the state of grace." (p. 126)

Definition of Sacrament

"A sacrament is an outward sign instituted by Christ to give grace. . . . Each of the sacraments also gives a special grace, called sacramental grace, which helps one to carry out the particular purpose of that sacrament." (*A Catechism of Christian Doctrine*, pp. 245, 249)

Exact Moment

Christ gave the sacraments, according to the Roman Catholic Church, in order that men might receive grace through the instrument of divine power and love, and also that men might know, with certainty, just the exact moment when his grace is received. Everything is worked out carefully and in order, following a divine pattern, in the Roman Catholic Church. There is no guesswork. Every act has a reason, and every doctrine a basis of Scripture or tradition. The Catholic Church leaves nothing to chance.

Instituted by Christ

The Roman Catholic Church teaches that Christ Himself instituted all seven of the sacraments,[1] although some in a more general sense than others, "because He earned by His Passion, and marked off, the grace which each should confer, and because He personally appointed the several sacramental rites—in detail for Baptism and the Blessed Eucharist, and in general outline for the rest." (*Apologetics and Catholic Doctrine*, p. 127)

---

[1] "The Council of Trent defined that the seven sacraments of the New Law were instituted by Christ (Sess. VII, Can. i). This settles the question of fact for all Catholics."—*The Catholic Encyclopedia.*

Sacraments Signify the Grace They Confer

According to the Roman Catholic Church the sacraments signify, or indicate, the grace they confer. This is true "(1) because, in each, words are used which clearly point to the spiritual effect produced, e.g., 'I baptize thee . . .'; 'I absolve thee from thy sins . . .'; and (2) because, in each case, the meaning of the words is enforced or illustrated by the ceremony itself."

"In Baptism, Confirmation, Extreme Unction, and Holy Order, the words are accompanied by an appropriate action or gesture: thus, in Baptism, the washing with water signifies the spiritual cleansing; in Confirmation, the anointing signifies strengthening, and in Extreme Unction, healing; in Holy Order, the imposition of hands signifies the giving of the Holy Ghost. In the Blessed Eucharist, the bread and wine over which the priest utters the words of consecration, suggest the spiritual food into which they are to be changed. In Penance, the whole ceremony has the appearance of an act of reconciliation; the sorrowful confession of guilt at the tribunal of mercy presaging and pointing to the absolution that is to follow. Matrimony signifies grace, not exactly from the words used or any action accompanying them, but because, as we are taught by the Holy Spirit, speaking to us through the lips of St. Paul, Christian marriage is a figure of the union, so fruitful in spiritual gifts, of Christ with His Church." (*Apologetics and Catholic Doctrine,* p. 128)

The Minister of the Sacrament

The minister of the sacrament must be qualified for his office. For all the sacraments, except Baptism and Matrimony, he must be in Holy Orders. Baptism may be administered, in case of necessity, by a layman—even by a non-Catholic. Matrimony is conferred by the parties to the sacred contract, each giving the sacrament to the other. The minister must employ the proper words (or words of the same meaning). He must perform the prescribed action. He must use the prescribed things (water in the case of Baptism and oil in the case of Extreme Unction). He must intend to do what the Church does. It is not at all essential that the minister be in the state of grace, or even believe in the efficacy of the sacrament. The condition of his soul does not affect the validity of his act; the virtue of what he does comes from Christ and not himself.

Valid Reception of the Sacraments

In order to receive a sacrament validly it must be received not merely in appearance, but in reality. It must be received really and truly. Adults cannot receive any Sacrament validly without first having the proper intention or will to receive it. For infants no intention is required for the valid reception of Baptism. Those who have not received the sacrament of Baptism are incapable of receiving the other sacraments.

The Living and the Dead

The seven sacraments are divided into two sections: Baptism and Penance for the dead; and the other five for the living. The former give sanctifying grace to the soul devoid of it; [2] the latter augment it in a soul already possessing it. The sacraments of the dead raise the soul from death to life; sacraments of the living presuppose the presence in the soul of spiritual life—and then augment or intensify it.

For the worthy reception of the sacraments of the dead, the adults require faith, hope, and at least attrition [3] for grave sin committed; for sacraments of the living they must be in a state of grace.

The following official Roman Catholic definitions of the sacraments are taken from "A Catechism of Christian Doctrine."

Baptism

Roman Catholics believe that Baptism is the sacrament that gives our souls the new life of sanctifying grace by which we become children of God and heirs of heaven. By means of sanctifying grace received in Baptism we are spiritually reborn; we become members of the family of God, who becomes our Father in the supernatural order.

Baptism takes away original sin; and also actual sins and all the punishment due to them, if the person baptized be guilty of any actual sins and truly sorry for them. The effects of the char-

---

[2] "Baptism and Penance are called 'sacraments of the dead,' because they give life, through sanctifying grace . . . to those who are spiritually dead by reason of original or actual sin."—*The Catholic Encyclopedia*.

[3] Detestation of sins arising from supernatural motives inferior to charity, e.g., fear of the punishment of hell or fear of the loss of heaven.

acter imprinted on the soul by Baptism are that those baptized become members of the Church, subject to its laws, and capable of receiving the other sacraments.

The priest is the usual minister of Baptism, but if there is danger that someone will die without Baptism, anyone else may and should baptize. In case of necessity even a heretic or an unbaptized person can validly and licitly baptize. The sacrament of Baptism may be validly administered: *first,* by immersion; *second,* by pouring; *third,* by sprinkling.

Baptism is necessary for the salvation of all men except martyrs. Those who through no fault of their own have not received the sacrament of Baptism can be saved through what is called baptism of blood (martyrdom) or baptism of desire (when he loves God above all things and desires to do all that is necessary for his salvation). Children should be baptized as soon as possible after birth, because Baptism is necessary for salvation. Infants who die without baptism of any kind do not suffer the punishments of those who die in mortal sin. They may enjoy a certain natural happiness, but they will not enjoy the supernatural happiness of heaven.

Confirmation

Roman Catholics believe that Confirmation is the sacrament through which the Holy Ghost comes in a special way and enables those in grace to profess faith as strong and perfect Christians and soldiers of Jesus Christ.[4] The word "confirmation" means "a strengthening." The bishop is the usual minister of Confirmation. The bishop extends his hands over those who are to be confirmed, prays that they may receive the Holy Ghost, and, while laying his hand on the head of each person, anoints the forehead with holy chrism (a blessed mixture of olive oil and balm) in the form of a cross, saying, "I sign thee with the sign of the Cross, and I confirm thee with the chrism of salvation, in the name of the Father, the Son, and the Holy Ghost." Confirmation increases sanctifying grace, gives its special sacramental grace, and imprints a lasting character on the soul. All Catholics

---

[4] "Confirmation is to Baptism what growth is to generation. Now it is clear that a man cannot advance to a perfect age unless he has first been born; in like manner, unless he has first been baptized he cannot receive the Sacrament of Confirmation."—(St. Thomas Aquinas, *Summ. Th.,* III, Q. lxxii, a.6).

are confirmed in order to be strengthened against the dangers to salvation and to be prepared better to defend their Catholic faith.

The Holy Eucharist [5]

The Holy Eucharist is a sacrament and a sacrifice. In the Holy Eucharist, under the appearance of bread and wine, the Lord Christ is contained, offered, and received.

Christ instituted the Holy Eucharist at the Last Supper, the night before He died. When Our Lord said, "This is My body," the entire substance of the bread was changed into His body; and when He said, "This is My blood," the entire substance of the wine was changed into His blood.

After the substance of the bread and wine had been changed into Our Lord's body and blood, there remained only the appearance of bread and wine. By the appearances of bread and wine we mean their color, taste, weight, shape, and whatever else appears to the senses. The change of the entire substance of the bread and wine into the body and blood of Christ is called Transubstantiation. Jesus Christ is whole and entire both under the appearances of bread and under the appearances of wine. This change of bread and wine into the body and blood of Christ continues to be made in the Church by Jesus Christ, through the ministry of His priests. Only ordained priests have the power of changing bread and wine into the body and blood of Christ. When they consecrate, they act in the person of Christ, through the power received in the sacrament of Holy Orders.

Penance

The teaching of the Roman Catholic Church is that Penance is the sacrament by which sins committed after Baptism are forgiven through the absolution of the priest who is granted this power by a competent authority, usually his bishop. Through mortal sin the soul is deprived of its supernatural life. The sacrament of Penance raises the soul from death to supernatural life. The priest has the power to forgive sins from Jesus Christ, who said to His apostles and to their successors in the priesthood; "Receive the Holy Spirit; whose sins you shall forgive, they are forgiven them; and whose sins you shall retain, they are retained."

No man, by his own power and authority, could possibly for-

---

[5] Holy Communion and the Mass will be considered together in Chap. 13.

give sins. Only God can do that, because sin is an offense against Him. But the priest, as God's representative, can forgive sins because God has given him the power to do so.

The effects of the sacrament of Penance, worthily received, are: *first,* the restoration or increase of sanctifying grace; *second,* the forgiveness of both mortal and venial sins; *third,* the remission of the eternal punishment, if necessary, and also of part, at least, of the temporal punishment, due to our sins; *fourth,* the help to avoid sin in future; *fifth,* the restoration of the merits of our good works if they have been lost by mortal sin.

To receive the sacrament of Penance worthily, we must: *first,* examine our conscience; *second,* be sorry for our sins; *third,* have the firm purpose of not sinning again; *fourth,* confess our sins to the priest; *fifth,* be willing to perform the penance the priest gives us.[6]

Extreme Unction

Extreme Unction is the sacrament which, through the anointing with blessed oil by the priest, and through his prayer, gives health and strength to the soul and sometimes to the body when we are in danger of death from sickness, accident, or old age. In administering Extreme Unction the priest anoints with his thumb, moving in the form of a cross, the eyes, the ears, the nostrils, the lips, the hands, and, if convenient, the feet of the sick person. When the priest judges that there is not sufficient time for multiple anointings, he can administer the sacrament by a single anointing, preferably on the forehead.

Roman Catholics believe that those who are in danger of death should welcome the sacrament of Extreme Unction. It cannot harm them, and it often helps them physically. A person does not actually have to be dying in order to receive Extreme Unction. It suffices that there is probable danger of death through some infirmity actually afflicting the body. While anointing the different senses the priest says the prayer: "Through this holy anointing, and His most tender mercy, may the Lord forgive you whatever sins you may have committed by sight" (by hearing, etc.).

Extreme Unction takes away mortal sin when the sick person is unconscious or otherwise unaware that he is not properly disposed, but has made an act of imperfect contrition. Preparation to receive Extreme Unction is made by a good confession, by

---

[6] The confessional will be considered in Chap. 16.

acts of faith, hope, charity, and, especially, by resignation to the will of God. Only the parish priest, or a priest authorized by him or his bishop (except in cases of extreme necessity) can administer this sacrament. The oil used is olive oil, exorcised by a bishop, or by a priest with papal-delegated authority.

In case of sudden or unexpected death, absolution and Extreme Unction can be given conditionally for some time after apparent death. We are not certain of the moment when the soul leaves the body; the soul may remain united to the body for some time after apparent death. The sacraments of Penance and Extreme Unction can be administered conditionally for several hours after signs of life have ceased, because of the possibility that the soul may still be united with the body.

Holy Orders

Holy Orders is the sacrament through which men receive the power and grace to perform the sacred duties of bishops, priests, and other ministers of the Church.

According to the Roman Catholic Church, the distinction between clergy and laity is of divine origin, for *first,* Christ chose the twelve apostles from among His disciples; and in a special way deputed and consecrated them for the exercise of spiritual ministration; and, *second,* the apostles, who could not mistake the will of Christ, administered the sacrament of Holy Orders by consecrating bishops and by ordaining priests and deacons.

That a man may receive Holy Orders worthily it is necessary: *first,* that he be in the state of grace and be of excellent character; *second,* that he have the prescribed age and learning; *third,* that he have the intention of devoting his life to the sacred ministry; *fourth,* that he be called to Holy Orders by his bishop.

Without a special dispensation, no one may be ordained a priest until he is twenty-four years of age. Ordinarily the prescribed learning consists of four years of high school, four years of college, and four years of theology completed in a seminary. The chief supernatural powers of the priest are: to change bread and wine into the body and blood of Christ in the Holy Sacrifice of the Mass, and to forgive sins in the sacrament of Penance.

Roman Catholics show reverence and honor to the priest because he is the representative of Christ Himself and the dispenser of His mysteries.

The bishop is the minister of the sacrament of Holy Orders.[7]

---

[7] Please see Chap. 7 on "Functions of the Catholic Priest."

Matrimony

Matrimony is the sacrament by which a baptized man and a baptized woman bind themselves for life in a lawful marriage and receive the grace to discharge their duties. Though unbaptized persons can be truly married, only validly baptized persons, both Catholic and Protestant, can be united in the sacrament of Matrimony and receive the graces of this sacrament.

Roman Catholics maintain that marriage was made a sacrament by Our Lord sometime during His life on earth. They cite Ephesians 5:32: here Protestant Bibles use the word "mystery" and Roman Catholic, "sacrament."

The sacrament of Matrimony is administered by the contracting parties, each of whom confers the sacrament on the other.

The bond of the sacrament of Matrimony lasts until the death of husband or wife because Christ has said: "What therefore God has joined together, let no man put asunder." Once a baptized man and a baptized woman are completely united in the sacrament of Matrimony, they remain truly husband and wife until the death of either of them. A separation, a divorce, or an attempted marriage with another person does not destroy the marriage bond.

The laws of the Church require a Roman Catholic to be married in the presence of the parish priest, or the bishop of the diocese, or a priest delegated by either of them, and before two witnesses.[8] The marriage of a Catholic before a minister or a civil official, such as a judge, a justice of the peace, a squire, or any clerk of court, is not really a marriage. Catholics who live together after such a marriage are living in sin just as much as if they had never gone through such a ceremony. Catholics who attempt marriage in this fashion commit a mortal sin and incur other punishments of the Church.[9]

---

[8] However, under extreme circumstances, such as imminent death, or when a competent priest is unavailable, and will not be available within a month (as in missionary countries), a valid marriage contract and sacrament may be effected before two witnesses (who should be, but do not have to be, Roman Catholics). See *Marriage* by Francis J. Connell, C.SS.R., S.T.D., p. 18.

[9] Marriage and divorce, along with the home and the family, will be further considered in Chap. 12.

THE PROTESTANT POINT OF VIEW
On the Meaning of Baptism and the Lord's Supper

Protestantism does not accept the seven sacraments as required by the Roman Catholic Church, because it finds only two, Baptism and the Lord's Supper, demanded by the teachings of Scripture.

Protestant churches accept not seven, but two sacraments. While agreeing upon the number they do not agree upon the nature, form, or functions of the sacraments. Some reject the belief in the "real presence" in any physical form; others believe that Christ is present along with the elements. All believe that Christ is present at the Communion service in a real spiritual sense.

Protestants have several interpretations of baptism, ranging from a channel of redeeming grace and the basis for church membership, to acceptance of it only as an "ordinance" without any special significance of and by itself. The form of baptism is being re-examined; some theologians feel that infant baptism does not represent, even in symbolism, the spirit and teaching upon the subject as found in the New Testament; they feel that it tends to weaken the basis of active church membership.

Protestants refuse to believe that Confirmation, Holy Orders, Penance, Matrimony, or Extreme Unction have any scriptural basis for being called sacraments. If Roman Catholics are better Christians for having these five extra "sacraments," Protestants have no objection. But, they do not want these designated as fundamental requirements for *all* Christians. Protestants feel that baptism and the Lord's Supper are sufficient when used in accordance with the spirit and teachings of Christ.

Before being too critical of the Roman Catholic position in regard to the sacraments, some Protestants may need to re-examine their own beliefs and practices concerning the Lord's Supper and baptism. Do they truly manifest, as now believed and practiced, the will of Christ? In their present form, can they divide more than unite? Protestant leaders must especially find some formula which will give both fellowship and freedom of interpretation before the Lord's Table. As the Willingen missionary conference concluded: "Division in the church distorts its

witness, frustrates its mission, and contradicts its own nature."
It is therefore imperative that Protestantism join forces around
the essentials which are held in common.

Baptism and the Lord's Supper

While some churches, like the Baptists, consider baptism and
the Lord's Supper merely as ordinances, most of the other
churches, as was agreed at the Lund Conference in Sweden in
1952, consider that in the administration of these two sacraments
"God offers us His grace, imparts saving knowledge of Himself
and draws us into communion with Himself." While Protestants
have not yet solved the problem of intercommunion, most
churches are in agreement that "when controlled by the words
of institution," they are "real means of grace through which
Christ gives Himself to those who in fact receive the appointed
elements of bread and wine."

The word "sacrament" does not appear in the New Testament.
Protestants accept baptism and the Lord's Supper because they
are specifically instituted by Christ (Matt. 3:11-17; Mark 1:8-11;
Luke 3:15-16; Matt. 26:26-30; Mark 14:22-26; Luke 22:14-20; I
Cor. 10:16, 17, 11:23-29). Their position is stated officially in the
Thirty-nine Articles as follows: "There are two sacraments ordained by Christ. The five commonly called sacraments, that is,
confirmation, penance, order, marriage, and extreme unction, are
not to be counted for sacraments of the Gospel. They have no
visible sign or ceremony ordained of God."

According to the *Westminster Shorter Catechism*, "the sacraments become effectual means of salvation, not from any virtue
in themselves or in him who does administer them but only by
the blessing of Christ and the working of his Spirit in them that
by faith receive him." Baptism is not, with most Protestants, necessarily a condition of salvation. The *Westminster Confession*
puts it this way. "It is a sin to condemn or neglect baptism, nevertheless grace and salvation are not so inseparably annexed unto
it as that no person can be regenerated or saved without it."

The form of baptism differs among Protestants: some accepting only adult baptism by immersion; others practicing infant
baptism. Some Protestant churches practice both sprinkling and
immersion. The *Lutheran Common Service Book* contains the
prayer that "God may of his goodness receive the child by baptism into the church of the Redeemer and make it a living member of the same." The *Book of Common Prayer* says: "Seeing that

this child is regenerate and grafted into the body of Christ."
Confirmation usually follows infant baptism, when the child
reaches the years of understanding, but it is treated as an ecclesiastical ordinance and not as a sacrament.

Concerning the theory of transubstantiation, the *Thirty-nine
Articles* have this to say: "Worthy receivers do inwardly by faith,
really and truly, yet not carnally and corporally but spiritually,
receive and feed upon Christ crucified and all the benefits of his
death." Transubstantiation, as a miracle, is repudiated by Protestants.

At Lund, the delegates from Protestant churches all over the
world agreed that they all had a common experience at the
Lord's Table. "Whatever may be our various opinions on the
nature and efficacy of ritual acts," they declared, "we are all
agreed that *Deus non alligatur sacramentis,* and that (in the
words of the Gospel) 'the Spirit bloweth where He listeth.' We
record in thankfulness that we have reached in our discussions
a measure of understanding which none of us could ever have
anticipated on the problem of the sacrificial element in Holy
Communion. The mystery of the love of God, which we celebrate
at the Lord's Table, surpasses human expression. But in our attempts to describe that mystery we have the warrant of Holy
Scripture for using sacrificial language. 'Behold the Lamb of
God.'" While Protestants differ widely as to the interpretation
of Christ's presence at the Lord's Table—from a memorial service to a sacramental ritual—they all believe that the true worshiper really meets Him there.

What the Scriptures Say

Protestants find authorization in the New Testament for only
two sacraments: baptism and the Lord's Supper. Since there is
authorization for only two, they believe that they are conscience
bound to abide by the Bible, rather than by tradition or ecclesiastical decrees. Here are the exclusive New Testament sacraments or ordinances:

"And Jesus came and spake unto them, saying, 'All power is
given unto me in heaven and in earth. Go ye therefore, and teach
all nations, baptizing them in the name of the Father, and of the
Son, and of the Holy Ghost'" (Matt. 28:18, 19). This is based
upon Jesus' own example of being baptized by John (Matt. 3:13-
17), and the practice of baptism in the early church (Acts 2:41).

At the Last Supper it is recorded in Mark 14:22-24, "And as

they did eat, Jesus took bread, and blessed, and brake it, and gave to them, and said, 'Take, eat: this is my body.' And he took the cup, and when he had given thanks, he gave it to them: and they all drank of it. And he said unto them, 'This is my blood of the new testament.' " Matthew adds: "Do this in remembrance of me."

No mention is made of the changing of the bread and wine into Christ's actual flesh and blood. Protestants believe that Christ was not here performing a miracle, but establishing a spiritual fellowship around the Lord's Table.

After giving the members of the church at Corinth a warning not to abuse the Lord's Supper, Paul adds (I Cor. 11:26-28) to the words of institution this comment: "For as often as ye eat this bread, and drink this cup, ye do show the Lord's death till he come. Wherefore, whosoever shall eat this bread, and drink this cup of the Lord, unworthily, shall be guilty of the body and blood of the Lord. But let a man examine himself, and so let him eat of that bread, and drink of that cup."

Regarding baptism, Paul says, "Know ye not, that so many of us as were baptized unto Jesus Christ were baptized unto his death? Therefore we are buried with him by baptism unto death: that like as Christ was raised up from the dead by the glory of the Father, even so we also should walk in newness of life. For if we have been planted together in the likeness of his death, we shall be also in the likeness of his resurrection" (Rom. 6:3-5).

PROTESTANT REFERENCE BOOKS: *The Teaching of the Church Regarding Baptism* by Karl Barth (translated by Ernest A. Payne); *The Quest for Christian Unity* by Robert S. Bilheimer, pp. 63 ff.; *The Divine-Human Encounter* by Emil Brunner, pp. 183 ff.; *The One Church* by Clarence Tucker Craig, Chaps. V and VI; *The Lord's Supper* by Harold E. Fey; *Faith and Order,* the Lausanne Conference Report; the official report of the Third World Conference on Faith and Order, Lund, 1952.

7

Functions of the Catholic Priest

Pope Pius XI in his encyclical letter *Ad Catholici Sacerdotii,*
written to the priests of the Roman Catholic Church in December, 1935, points up vividly the birth to death functions of the
priesthood and, at the same time, without attempting to do so,
draws a distinction between Catholic and Protestant beliefs and
practices concerning the clergy.

"The Christian, at almost every important stage of his mortal
career," writes Pope Pius XI, "finds at his side the priest with
power received from God, in the act of communicating or increasing that grace which is the supernatural life of his soul.

"Scarcely is he born before the priest, baptizing him, brings
him a new birth to a more noble and precious life, a supernatural
life, and makes him a son of God and of the Church of Jesus
Christ.

"To strengthen him to fight bravely in spiritual combats, a
priest invested with special dignity makes him a soldier of Christ
by holy Chrism.[1]

"Then, as soon as he is able to recognize and value the Bread
of Angels, the priest gives It to him, the living and life-giving
Food come down from Heaven.

"If he falls, the priest raises him up again in the name of God,
and reconciles him to God with the Sacrament of Penance.

"Again, if he is called by God to found a family and to collaborate with Him in the transmission of human life throughout the
world, thus increasing the number of the faithful on earth, and
thereafter the ranks of the elect in Heaven, the priest is there to
bless his espousals and unblemished love; and when finally, arrived at the portals of eternity, the Christian feels the need of
strength and courage before presenting himself at the tribunal of
the Divine Judge, the priest with the holy Oils anoints the fail-

---

[1] Blessed olive oil and balm.

ing members of the sick or dying Christian, and reconsecrates and comforts him.

"Thus the priest accompanies the Christian throughout the pilgrimage of this life to the gates of Heaven. He accompanies the body to its resting place in the grave with rites and prayers of immortal life. And even beyond the threshold of eternity he follows the soul to aid it with Christian suffrages, if need there be of further purification and alleviation. Thus, from the cradle to the grave the priest is ever beside the faithful, a guide, a solace, a minister of salvation and dispenser of grace and blessing."

The distinctions between the Protestant and Catholic clergy constitute a basis for some of the most serious misunderstandings between the two faiths. In this chapter we shall present the Catholic position and then point out the chief differences in relation to the Protestant point of view.

THE ROMAN CATHOLIC POSITION

Teachings of the Council of Trent

The Council of Trent (1545–63), which defined the position of the Roman Catholic Church in regard to the priesthood, declares: "If anyone says that Order [Holy Orders], or Sacred Ordination, is not truly and properly a Sacrament instituted by Christ the Lord; that it is a kind of human figment devised by men unskilled in ecclesiastical matters; or that it is only a sort of rite for choosing ministers of the word of God and the Sacraments; let him be anathema."

It observes that Holy Orders is proved to be a Sacrament "on the testimony of the Scriptures, the Apostolic tradition, and the unanimous consent of the Fathers." The Council of Trent teaches that there is in the Catholic Church a divinely instituted hierarchy consisting of bishops, priests, and deacons, and that bishops are superior to priests, having the power of confirming and ordaining.

Use of the Title "Father"

Roman Catholics call their priests "Father" because they are the ordinary ministers of baptism which, according to Catholic doctrine, gives them the new birth of supernatural grace, and also in his care for them the priest is the spiritual father of the faithful.

Clerical Celibacy

Celibacy is not a divine law of the Roman Catholic Church. But it is an obligatory law of the Western Church, imposed very largely for practical reasons. After long experience the Church has learned that a celibate clergy can do more effective work for God's people than a married clergy.[2] For example, an unmarried priest is freer and far more independent than a minister with a wife and family. Besides, the specified duties of a priest would leave him little time for a family.

Roman Catholics believe that God helps the priest to remain chaste. Although they think of marriage as having a sacramental character, they also feel that there is special merit in a virgin life by one who gives his life to God for full-time service. In the early church married men were sometimes ordained priests. Peter himself was married. But as Father Conway points out in *The Question Box,* "Whether St. Peter was married or not is utterly irrelevant, for clerical celibacy is not a divine law, but a Church law, dating only from the fourth century. It does not depend on precedent; it is founded on the Church's estimate of the more perfect following of Christ by her clergy." (p. 317)

The Priest's Prayer Book

Priests are often seen using a small prayer book. It is known to Catholics as the Priest's Breviary. It contains the various prayers, in Latin, that every priest is obliged to say every day of the year. It takes about an hour to say all that is required.

The Breviary consists of Psalms, Scripture readings, and prayers arranged according to feast days and the seasons of the year. It is therefore the priest's Bible as well as prayer book, since in it he reads once a year portions of every book of the Bible.

Exclusive Rights

Priests become part of a holy order, with exclusive rights, through the sacrament of Holy Orders (see Chap. 6). It is the solemn teaching of the Roman Catholic Church that (1) Holy Orders is a sacrament instituted by Christ; (2) it imprints an indelible mark or character on the soul;[3] (3) through this sacra-

---

[2] This, of course, is not the only reason. Another is the imitation of Christ (I Cor. 7:32 ff.).

[3] The recipient of this sacrament remains for good or ill "a priest for ever," though he be so unfortunate as subsequently to fall from grace, or even to apostatize from the faith of Christ.

ment there is set up a hierarchy consisting of bishops, priests, and ministers (deacons); (4) the episcopate is superior to the priesthood and the bishop has the power to confirm and ordain; and (5) the priest has the power to consecrate and offer the Holy Eucharist and to forgive sin. The subject of these exclusive rights may be any baptized person of the *male sex*. The sacrament is conferred by the bishop by the imposition of hands and prayer, indicating that power is being given and that it is a sacred power.

Protestant Clergy Excluded

In 1896, Pope Leo XIII rejected the validity of the Anglican priesthood. The Roman Catholic Church, therefore, denies that the Anglican Church, or any other Protestant Church, has a valid ecclesiastical system and a properly ordained ministry. No one can be admitted to the Roman Catholic Church unless and until he accepts the infallibility and supremacy of the Vicar of Christ, the pope. Every minister, or priest, of a Protestant Church must be re-ordained. The Roman Catholic Church will not accept, under any conditions, the ordination rites and authority of non-Roman Catholic churches.[4]

This decision of Pope Leo XIII concerning the Anglican priests is irrevocable. He spoke for the Church infallibly. No Anglican clergyman, nor any other Protestant minister who would enter the Roman Catholic Church and desire to function as a clergyman, can officiate in the Roman Catholic Church without first being ordained by a Catholic bishop.[5]

When a Priest Is Ordained

The ordination of a priest in the Roman Catholic Church is a very solemn, impressive matter. The ceremony, presided over by the bishop, is observed either at a solemn pontifical Mass or at a low Mass. In his address to those who are being consecrated to the office of the priesthood, the bishop says:

---

[4] Generally speaking, the Roman Catholic Church recognizes the validity of the Orders of the schismatic Eastern Orthodox Church, and of those Protestants occasionally ordained or consecrated by Orthodox bishops. If converted to the Roman Catholic Church, these men would be re-ordained only *conditionally* ("If thou art not validly ordained . . .") for the sake of sureness.

[5] See *Are Anglican Ministers Catholic Priests?* by Francis Woodlock, Paulist Press, p. 8.

"Wherefor, dearly beloved sons, whom the voice of our brethren has chosen that you may be consecrated as our helpers, let your conduct at all times be the outcome of a chaste and holy life. Consider what you do, imitate that which you handle; and as you celebrate the Mysteries of the Lord's Death, be earnest in ridding your members by mortification of all vices and lusts. Let your teaching be a spiritual remedy for God's people; let the fragrance of your lives be a delight to the Church of God, that both by preaching and by example you may build up the house—that is, the family of God, so that neither we may deserve to be condemned of the Lord for promoting you to so sublime an office, nor you for taking it upon yourselves, but rather that He may reward us all. May He of His grace grant us this."

Indulgences for Attending Mass of Newly Ordained Priest

At the end of the booklet, *The Ordination of a Priest,* the following indulgences are listed:

For Attending the First Mass of a Newly Ordained Priest
and for Kissing His Hands

"(1) To all the faithful who devoutly assist at the first Mass of any priest, an indulgence of seven years is granted; a plenary indulgence is granted if they are blood relatives of the priest to the third degree inclusive, and if they have obtained pardon for their sins, received Holy Communion and prayed for the intentions of the Pope.

"(2) To those who on the day of priestly ordination and on the day of the first Mass devoutly kiss the palms of the hands of the new priest, there is granted an indulgence of one hundred days." (*Preces et Pia Opera,* 629)

THE PROTESTANT POINT OF VIEW
On the Position of the Christian Minister

Protestantism rejects the functions of the Roman Catholic priest because Christ refused to establish a separate priesthood with exclusive powers but did create a "priesthood of all believers."

Protestants believe in the "priesthood of all believers," and not in a divinely appointed priesthood entirely separated from the regular members of the church. They ordain men, and in some instances women, to the Christian ministry, but they do not believe, in most cases, that the clergy is thereby given any peculiar spiritual powers all its own. The clergy is looked upon as a sacred calling, and clergymen are trained to perform certain Christian functions. They are leaders and are expected to set an example in faith and morals. Protestants, in most cases, make no distinction between the clergy and the rest of the membership as far as the constituency of the church is concerned. They are one, and on the same level. In many churches ecclesiastical government is not in the hands of the clergy, but of the laity. Here the clergy is called by the laity to serve the church in a special way, but it is still subject to the total membership.

Celibacy is a voluntary matter as far as Protestantism is concerned. Most churches like to have a married man in the pulpit. But many successful pastors are unmarried. It is entirely a personal matter.

Luther declared in his address to the German Nobles that "It is a pure myth that popes, bishops, priests and monks are to be called the spiritual estate. All Christians are the spiritual estate." It should be pointed out that Protestants base their arguments for the right of the clergy to marry upon Christ's honoring marriage by his presence at the wedding at Cana; by the fact that Peter was married (Matt. 8:14 speaks of his mother-in-law); that Philip, one of the seven deacons, was married (Acts 21:8); and that Paul commends clerical marriage (I Cor. 7:9; I Tim. 3:2; Titus 1:6).

A Cardinal Principle of Protestantism

Although one of the cardinal principles of Protestantism is the "priesthood of all believers," most Protestant churches believe in a specially called and trained ministry. There is a distinct feeling that clergymen are men of God, set apart for extraordinary Christian service. They are not only expected to live upright lives but also to be pastors, administrators, personal counselors, and sometimes prophets.

Protestantism has no single theory of the Christian ministry. In some communions the clergyman is considered merely as a regular member of the church who has been called of God to render ecclesiastical services; in other communions a valid clergy consists of those who have been properly ordained by a bishop in line of apostolic succession.

The whole problem of the episcopally ordained clergy, and of the "apostolic succession," is a real issue within the Protestant churches. This has been called into special focus by the formation of The Church of South India, a united church which is now trying to work out a valid ministry which will be fully acceptable to all Protestant churches, including those churches (like the Anglicans) which insist on a historic, unbroken succession in the ministry. While progress is being made in the area of Protestant fellowship and co-operation, "intercommunion" waits upon the agreement of some churches to recognize the right of non-episcopal clergymen to administer the elements at the Lord's Supper.

At the Lund Conference it was agreed that "most of our Churches believe that our Lord has called forth in His Church a stated ministry. To this ministry alone the leadership of certain acts of worship is restricted. This raises for us the question of the basis of this restriction. For some of us this restriction rests upon the belief that the Church by the guidance of the Holy Spirit calls some of its members to this or that function. For others it is based upon the belief that the Holy Spirit gives to some members of the Church the appropriate grace of holy order. Again, some churches emphasize the ministerial priesthood as definitely distinct from the priesthood of all believers."

While the theological aspects of "intercommunion" are being restudied, most Protestants in youth, laymen's, and women's conferences are finding it possible to worship together in Christian love and to meet at the Lord's Table on the basis of the "priesthood of all believers." In this respect the rites of the Church are making way for the unity of Christian experience in Christ.

Protestants and the Bible

Protestants base their trust in a universal priesthood of all believers upon Scripture. They believe that since every Christian is in Christ, and that Christ is as close as breathing, there is no difficulty in direct communication and that there is therefore no need of an extra person or priest to bring Christ near. "Like living stones be yourselves built into a spiritual house to be a holy priesthood, to offer spiritual sacrifice to God through Jesus Christ" (I Pet. 2:5).

Instead of establishing a hierarchy of the priesthood, Protestants declare that every Christian is called by Christ to be a minister, a servant of Christ (Acts 2:18). In the early church there were apostles and deacons (Act 6:1-6) but there were also prophets, teachers, workers of miracles, healers, helpers, administrators, evangelists, pastors (I Cor. 12:28; Eph. 4:11). As far as the record shows there is no evidence in the New Testament church that there were any officials known as "priests." Christ alone is "a great high priest" (Heb. 4:14) for all believers. Moreover in Matthew 23:1-10, Jesus specially says, "Call no man your father on earth, for you have one Father, who is in heaven." Writing to a group of ordinary Christians, Peter says, "You are a chosen race, a royal priesthood" (I Pet. 2:9).

PROTESTANT REFERENCE BOOKS: *Imperialistic Religion and the Religion of Democracy* by William Adams Brown, Chap. IV; *Our Protestant Faith* by William R. Cannon, Jr., Chap. VI; *The One Church* by Clarence Tucker Craig, pp. 15, 20, 69, 70; *A Protestant Manifesto* by Winfred E. Garrison, pp. 115 ff.; *Primer for Protestants* by James Hastings Nichols, Chap. VII; *Our Fathers Faith and Ours* by David Schaff, Chap. XXI; *Why I Am a Protestant* by Roy L. Smith, leaflet, pp. 13-14.

8

Place of the Laity
in the Roman Catholic Church

In the Roman Catholic Church there is a sharp separation between the clergy and the laity. It seems to most Protestants that the Catholic Church is the clergy in action and that the laity has little or nothing to do but to obey. This is far from the truth. The individual members of the Catholic Church not only "assist," that is, follow or participate in the Mass, they take a very active part in the Mass and in Catholic Action and in the Confraternity of Christian Doctrine. Besides all this, there are an increasing number of Catholic organizations to keep the individual members well occupied.

The development, during the past few years, of the lay apostolate is most interesting from a Protestant point of view. It must always be kept in mind, however, that no matter how far the Catholic Church plans to go in creating a militant laity, and the current evidence indicates that it is going a long way, back of it all is the guidance of the hierarchy. Everything essential in the Roman Catholic Church must pass the test of the clergy. Faith and morals are under the "infallible guidance" of the Church. And the ultimate authority, passing from priest to bishop, is the Holy Father at Rome.

THE ROMAN CATHOLIC POSITION

Meaning of the Laity

A *Catholic Dictionary*, edited by Donald Attwater, gives this account of the meaning of the Catholic laity: [1] "Those who have membership in the Church without authority. The distinction of clergy and laity is of divine institution, although not all grades

---

[1] Also see Chap. XIX of *The Catholic Church in Action* by Michael Williams, The Macmillan Co.

of clergy are divinely instituted. Lay persons cannot exercise the power of orders or jurisdiction, but they may be religious and rule their brethren in religion with dominative power, which is not jurisdiction.

"The laity have the right, legally enforceable, to receive from the clergy those spiritual aids to salvation due to them in accordance with ecclesiastical discipline. They are exhorted to join approved associations, and are forbidden to belong to condemned or dangerous societies. No lay association has any ecclesiastical status unless erected or at least approved by the competent ecclesiastical authority.

"Non-Catholics may not be members of a Catholic association which has a religious significance or implication, or which claims ecclesiastical sanction."

The Faithful

The membership of the Roman Catholic Church is known as "the faithful." This indicates that individual members are to be absolutely faithful in regard to the faith and practice of the Church. It also means that together, in the mass, Roman Catholics constitute the faithful. Obedience is a central obligation. Duty is a privilege. Every Roman Catholic has a list of "musts" to which he has to adhere. But, surprising as it may seem to most Protestants, there is a large measure of willing, creative participation on the part of the Catholic laity.

Although the clergy governs the Roman Catholic Church, it is the laity which is the hope of the Church. Increasingly they are being encouraged not only "to assist" the priest at the Mass, that is, to follow actively as a participant every phase of the service, but also to apply Catholic principles to daily life. Roman Catholicism can no longer be charged with being negative as far as the laity is concerned.

Young and old, and all in between, are being challenged to help bring peace, charity, justice, to nations and to individuals. It is the contention of the Roman Catholic Church that the zealous apostolate of laymen will aid the salvation of the world. The faithful are being organized, locally, nationally, and internationally, to be missionaries, in a very special sense, for the Faith.

The Call of the Popes to Catholic Action

Pope Pius XI is known as "the Pope of Catholic Action," because he, more than any other Catholic, challenged the "faithful," that is, the laity, to specific Catholic action. This call has been re-emphasized by Pope Pius XII. Catholic Action is now a vast lay movement within the Church which has taken, as we shall see in this chapter, many different forms. It is, in a very special sense, The Church at work.

The call of the popes to Catholic action on the part of the laity follows: "Of all forms of the Church's apostolate, Catholic Action most conforms to the needs of the times. It is more efficacious than all other modes of action. The restoration of the Kingdom of Christ is connected indissolubly with Catholic Action. All must co-operate in this new and indispensable apostolate. Catholic Action is a universal and harmonious action of all Catholics, without exception as to age, sex, social condition, or culture." (Pope Pius XI)

"Let the clergy see in Catholic Action an impelling necessity to organize collaborators among the laity, and let them use the method of Catholic Action ready at hand and well-tested for their formation and their organization.

"Special courses of study are to be arranged to prepare religious for this new work, so that through their preaching (and teaching) and their manifold activities, the faithful may be inspired and trained for the apostolate of Christian Action.

"The time for reflection and planning is past. Now is the time for action. Are you ready?" (Pope Pius XII)

The Meaning of Catholic Action

Basic to Catholic Action is the burning desire, on the part of Roman Catholics, to restore the social order to Christ. Action therefore takes the form not only of deeds of mercy and the building of a better world order, in some cases involving political and economic structures, but also activity on the part of the laity in winning converts to the Roman Catholic faith. This is the essential basis of Catholic Action. Lay participation in the Confraternity of Christian Doctrine is an important phase of this work. Catholic Action, on the part of Roman Catholics, centers in the local parish—although it does not end there.

Archbishop Richard J. Cushing of Boston, in *The Call of the Popes to the Laity*, makes the participation of every member of every parish exceedingly clear: "Nothing could be more fundamental, nothing more Catholic, than the apostolate. The salvation of the world will not come by a miracle; it can only come by

patient work, work by us all—prelates, priests and people."
(p. 17)

Catholic Action, according to Pope Pius XI, is "the participation of the Catholic laity in the apostolate of the hierarchy."

The Program of Catholic Action

Since Catholic Action is more a broad, general program than a specific organization, it is difficult to define. It does have two universal principles: (1) the salvation of souls, and (2) the organization, under the direction of the hierarchy (priest, bishop, and pope) of group action. Specific organization, once these basic principles are accepted, varies from place to place, from country to country. The fact that St. Francis of Assisi is the patron saint of these groups explains a great deal about their spiritual and social character.

Perhaps the best way to understand how Catholic Action functions in a definite area, is to look at the organization in the United States. At the heart of Catholic Action in this country is the National Catholic Welfare Conference, with headquarters at 1312 Massachusetts Ave., N.W., Washington, D.C. A voluntary association of the bishops of the nation, it was established in 1919 for the purpose of unifying, co-ordinating, and organizing the efforts of Roman Catholics throughout the country in education, social welfare, immigrant aid, and other activities of a national character. It is not a council or legislative assembly, but rather a clearing house regarding activities of Roman Catholics.

The administration of the National Catholic Welfare Conference is under an Administrative Board of the archbishops and bishops. All U.S. cardinals are *ex officio* members. Eight departments function under the members of this board:

Executive Department: Bureau of Immigration, The Confraternity of Christian Doctrine, Bureau of Information, the monthly publication *Christian Action*, Publications office, Bureau of International Affairs, Inter-American Bureau, and the office of UN Affairs.

Education Department: Information Services, Statistics, Teachers' Registration, Library, and Educational Liaison.

Press Department: with many weekly news, feature, editorial, and telegraphic services, letters, special translations, etc.

Social Action Department: Catholic Conference on Industrial Problems, Family Life Bureau, National Catholic Conference on Family Life, Catholic Association for International Peace, and the Bureau of Health and Hospitals.

Legal Department: collects documents and data, and keeps abreast of current developments in federal and state legislatures and with actions in courts interpreting legislation touching the interests of the Catholic Church; handles religious and social matters which need to be discussed with the administrative officials of the federal government in Washington; explains Catholic attitude on current legislation before Congressional committees.

Catholic Action Study: an exchange for Catholic Action on an international basis.

Youth Department: The National Council of Catholic Youth, and the National Catholic Camping Association.

Lay Organization Department: The National Council of Catholic Men (some 3,000 local, diocesan, regional, and national organizations), The National Council of Catholic Women (federation of 6,000 U.S. Catholic women's organizations with more than 6,000,000 members). Prominent in the work of the former is the weekly Catholic Hour over the National Broadcasting Company network. The National Council of Catholic Nurses also comes within the scope of this general department.

War Relief Services (NCWC) was established in January, 1943, to administer a program of relief and assistance to refugees, prisoners of war, displaced persons, and merchant seamen. It has set up such special agencies as the National Catholic Resettlement Council and the Bishops' War Emergency and Relief Collection.

Other NCWC organizations include the National Catholic Community Service, the Mission Secretariat, which provides assistance to U.S. religious societies sending missionaries to foreign lands, and many Bishops' Special Committees.

The Confraternity of Christian Doctrine

One of the best means of lay participation through Catholic Action is in the Confraternity of Christian Doctrine, to be established in every parish by the law of the Church. Organized on a local parish level, its work is "the spread of knowledge and practice of the Faith by the following means: religious training of Catholic elementary school children not attending Catholic schools, by instruction classes during the school year and in vacation schools; religious instruction of Catholic youth of high school age not attending Catholic schools, in study clubs and by other methods; religious discussion clubs for adult groups; religious education of children by parents in the home; instruction of non-Catholics in the teaching and practices of the Catholic Faith." (*National Catholic Almanac*, p. 427)

Active members serve at least one hour a week, or a minimum of fifty hours during the year. They may serve in the following ways: as *Teachers* who assist priests and sisters in catechetical work; as *Fishers* who serve as home visitors to encourage children to attend instruction classes and adults to join discussion clubs; as *Helpers* who provide facilities for classes and clubs, materials and transportation; as *Discussion Club Leaders;* as *Parent-Educators* who co-operate with the parent-education programs of the Confraternity; and as *Apostles of Good Will* who assist in the program for non-Catholics.

Great stress is placed upon this phase of Catholic Action in the local parish. For example, Pope Pius X declared, "In each and every parish the society known as the Confraternity of Christian Doctrine is to be canonically established. Through this Confraternity, the pastors, especially in places where there is a scarcity of priests, will have lay helpers in the teaching of the Catechism, who will take up the work of imparting knowledge both from a zeal for the glory of God and in order to gain the numerous Indulgences granted by the Sovereign Pontiffs." (*Acerbo NIMIS*)

In its various parish activities the Confraternity of Christian Doctrine engages, prepares, directs the faithful in the lay apostolate. The CCD thus constitutes "a living Rosary," working and praying to restore all things in Christ. Here is, according to the Most Reverend Amleto Giovanni Cicognani, Apostolic Delegate to the United States, the "royal priesthood" of the Catholic Church; a body of laity which assist the bishops and pastors, co-operating with the hierarchy in the winning of souls.

Other Agencies for the Laity

Just to list a few of the many Roman Catholic agencies for the laity will give some evidence of the great stress which the Church is placing upon lay activity: Catholic Order of Foresters, Catholic Boy Scouts, Junior Catholic Daughters of America, Girl Scouts under Catholic Auspices, Catholic Youth Organization, Christ Child Society, National Federation of Catholic College Students, Newman Club, Catholic Students' Mission Crusade, National Catholic Alumni Federation, various fraternities and sororities, specialized Catholic Action (Young Christian Workers, League of Christian Workers, Young Christian Farmers, Summer School for Christian Action), the Legion of Mary, the Narberth Movement (a neighborhood apologetic movement), the Christopher Movement, Catholic Campaigners for Christ, the Catholic Evidence Guild, the Catholic Interracial Movement, the National Council of Catholic Nurses, the Catholic Maternity Guild Apostolate, the Family Life Movement, the National Catholic Community Service, the Knights of Columbus, the Cooperative Movement, the National Catholic Rural Life Conference, the Catholic Dramatic Movement, Blackfriars Guild, the Catholic Actors Guild of America, Inc., and the various laymen's retreat movements.

Catholic Lay Evangelism

Roman Catholic laymen in large numbers are being asked to undertake a program of evangelism. This type of lay apostolate takes many forms including street preaching, conducting of Catholic information centers, winning the non-Catholic of mixed marriages, mass communications, and personal evangelism. This "sharing of the Faith" movement is directed toward the hundred million non-Catholics in the United States. The Catholic laity is being enlisted, and trained, to win America, and the world, to the faith and practice of the Roman Catholic Church.

The convert movement in 1947 reached the 100,000 mark in the U.S.A. That year the Church received 115,214 converts. The present gains through conversions, according to Professor John A. O'Brien of the University of Notre Dame in his book, *Sharing the Faith*, "are not merely reduced but are more than nullified by a leakage, steady, stealthy and persistent." (p. 9)

In view of the fact that the task of winning converts to the Roman Catholic Church is traveling only "at a snail's pace"[2] in the United States, and is not making great strides in membership gains, the Roman Catholic Church is now trying to enlist laymen in a national campaign to win the 80,000,000 churchless people of the country. In order to accomplish this, the annual convert rate will have to reach the million mark.

Roman Catholics fully realize that their Faith cannot be confined within their churches if this goal is to be achieved. And it cannot be done by the 43,000 priests. They need the active support of 29,000,000 lay members, who will take the Faith out into the highways and byways of life, using all kinds of methods of

---

[2] *Sharing the Faith,* p. 9.

mass communication. A new meaning and emphasis is being placed upon the Catholic laity. Non-Catholics, Negroes, the working class, are targets. The gap which has existed between priest and people is being gradually closed.

Professor O'Brien sums up the matter this way: "Christ, the Apostles, the pontiffs and bishops are summoning our laity to abandon their passive attitude of reticence and to throw themselves fearlessly into the mighty task of winning the world for Christ. . . . Until that is accomplished we shall limp along with the pathetic average of 2.7 converts per priest per year, while the mountain of churchless people grows ever larger, threatening to obscure the sun. Until the search for the sheep that are lost, strayed or stolen becomes the daily concern of pastors, nuns, adults and youth, we shall continue to average but one lone convert a year for 250 Catholics." (*Sharing the Faith,* p. 198)

THE PROTESTANT POINT OF VIEW
On the Lay Leadership in the Christian Church

Protestantism will not accept the place of the laity as distinguished by the Roman Catholic Church because in the New Testament there is to be found a fellowship in which not merely the Christian leaders, but all men and women, have the right of full participation.

Protestantism exalts its laymen. Protestantism would be hopelessly crippled if all the positions of real authority were taken away from the laity. The situation in the Roman Catholic Church is entirely different. There would be no change in the Church if every layman should lose his position of responsibility—largely because top official positions are held by the clergy. To be sure, there are laymen serving the Church under the authority of the hierarchy, but their authority is limited and delegated.

Increasingly the Roman Catholic Church is beginning to realize, what Protestants have maintained from the beginning, that lay leadership is absolutely necessary in order to develop a sense of participation and an enthusiastic evangelistic movement. The clergy can lead and officiate, but it is not numerous enough to do the work of evangelism which a strong, virile Church must have.

Protestants cannot accept the position of the Roman Catholic

Church which insists that Christ instituted a priesthood and gave to it particular powers, such as the power to forgive sins. The evidence of the New Testament indicates that Christ selected laymen as his disciples, and that these were never ordained by him. Later the local churches did set apart laymen for special services. Here again Protestants and Roman Catholics will understand each other a little better if, instead of formulating their own rules and regulations, they turn directly to the New Testament for a fresh directive on this important matter.

Protestantism's Great Strength

Protestantism's great strength lies in the active participation of its lay forces—men, women, and young people. There is no sharp distinction made between the laity and the clergy in most Protestant churches. Laymen are given positions of heavy official responsibility; they not only serve as elders, trustees, and deacons, but also teach and preach and in some churches may administer the sacraments. Young people take upon themselves important Christian projects at home and abroad. Protestant women have been noted, along with the men, for their missionary zeal and programs. Having strong national lay movements in most of the denominations, this vast endeavor is now co-ordinated for many denominations through the General Divisions of United Men and United Women in the National Council of the Churches of Christ in the U.S.A.

Luther in his *Address to the German Nobility,* and the *Babylonian Captivity,* was one of the first champions of lay leadership in the Christian Church. In these documents he denounced the exclusion of laymen from church control, the pope's claim to be the sole interpreter of the Bible, and the pope's exclusive right to call a church council. All these had a bearing upon the new position of the laity under Protestantism.

David Schaff declares in *Our Fathers Faith and Ours:* "Protestantism exalts the layman and puts every believing man into the hierarchy. Christian merit follows devotion to duty, public and private, in the family and on the street. Fidelity, not vocation, determines the honor a person shall receive. A long list of laymen, women and men in Protestant lands, in these recent days has put society under a debt for the social and moral changes which they carried through, and of the like of which the mediaeval Crusaders never dreamt." (p. 626)

As Elmer G. Homrighausen points out in the Interseminary

Series, Book Three, *The Gospel, the Church and The World*
(p. 189), the Reformers lifted church membership to a vocation.
Every Christian layman was called to a task. The Reformers did
not limit a Christian's vocation to the ministry. Calvin, for example, believed that every Christian had a vocation, not merely
because he is called by God to a life of fellowship with Him,
but also because he is called to serve God in whatever work he
is engaged in. Therefore the Protestant conception is that the
whole round of common tasks is directly related to the Christian's life with Christ. The glory of God can thus be made manifest, besides at the altar, in the family, at the daily tasks, and in
everyday life.

At the first meeting of the World Council of Churches at
Amsterdam, in 1948, great stress was placed upon the significance
of the laity in the Church. It declared that "in the laity the
Church has a body of men and women in which the real daily
meeting of the Church and the world on its own ground takes
place. This implies that the Church must see the great significance
of giving guidance to her laity, trying to understand where
exactly the intellectual, moral and religious issues lie which they
have to face, and so giving them by these efforts the certainty
that they are not isolated individuals, but are sustained by the
experience of living and working as members of the living Body."

The Scriptural Principle

Founded upon the Scriptural principle of the priesthood of all
believers, Protestants have emphasized another New Testament
principle—the Christian vocation of the laity (I Pet. 2:9). Not
only is the Christian his own priest; he is his brother's priest also
(I Pet. 4:10). Together they constitute the Christian community
in which every person, without exception, is called to witness for
Christ (Heb. 10:24-25).

All Christians belong to the Body of Christ. The church is a
fellowship of those who have dedicated themselves to Christ
(I Cor. 1:2). Therefore Protestantism teaches that laymen are
called to specific Christian service within their own vocations,
whether they are farmers, business men, scientists, or politicians.
In every phase of occupation the Christian layman is called upon
to inject the Christian principles of honesty, unselfishness, and
love (Eph. 5 and 6).

In the early church both men and women were active par-
ticipants (Rom. 16:1-6). In spite of Paul's famous admonition

that women ought to keep silent in church (I Cor. 14:34) they apparently have been, ever since Mary and Martha, active spiritual and practical promoters of the Christian cause.

A good example of this lay participation is found in the case of Tabitha. "Now there was at Joppa a certain disciple named Tabitha, which by interpretation is called Dorcas: this woman was full of good works and almsdeeds which she did" (Acts 9:36). Paul in Galatians 3:26-28 points up the comprehensive nature of the church: "For ye are all the children of God by faith in Jesus Christ. For as many of you as have been baptized into Christ have put on Christ. There is neither 'Jew' nor 'Greek,' there is neither 'bond' nor 'free,' there is neither 'male' nor 'female': for ye are all one in Christ Jesus."

Lay participation in the early church is mentioned frequently in the New Testament, as in the case of I Corinthians 16:19, "The churches of Asia salute you. Aquila and Priscilla salute you much in the Lord, with the church that is in their house."

PROTESTANT REFERENCE BOOKS: *God and the Common Life* and *God and the Day's Work* by Robert L. Calhoun; *Our Protestant Faith* by William R. Cannon, Jr., Chaps. VI and VIII; *The Christian at His Daily Work* by Cameron Parker Hall; *Protestant Panorama* by Clarence W. Hall and Desider Holisher, Chaps. III and IV; *Christian Faith and My Job* by Alexander Miller; *We Have This Ministry*, edited by John Oliver Nelson; *Our Fathers Faith and Ours* by David S. Schaff; *Laymen Speaking* and *What On Earth Are You Doing?*, edited by Wallace C. Speers; *Your Other Vocation* by Elton Trueblood.

PART III
The Beliefs of Roman Catholics

9

What Roman
Catholics Are Required to Believe

Roman Catholics must believe official creeds and dogmas of the Church. There is no question of compromise at this point. If they are to remain within the Church, and receive the benefit of its sacraments and blessings, there are specific beliefs which each member has to accept. These will be pointed out in this chapter.

Protestants are likely to go far astray in this area. They assume that Roman Catholics have a rigid system of belief in which there is no flexibility and no freedom. This is certainly so. Yet when certain dogmas are accepted, Catholics are quite free to believe, to argue, to search, as they please, about other things. This is true in the field of science. And to a certain extent, where the proposition has not been defined by the Church, it is also true in the area of theology. Catholic theologians are by no means in full agreement at every point.

But on the essential basis of faith and morals they are of one mind. What the Roman Catholic Church teaches all believe, no matter where they live or what language they speak. It is this fundamental, defined, official deposit of belief with which we are dealing in this chapter.

THE ROMAN CATHOLIC POSITION

The Basis of Faith

The Roman Catholic definition of faith, from the objective standpoint, is "the object of belief; the sum of the truths taught by the Catholic religion" (*A Catholic Dictionary*, p. 186). The

97

Faith, from this standpoint, is the system of belief and conduct taught as revealed truth by the Roman Catholic Church. It is a way of learning God's truths on the word and authority of God who teaches them through, what Catholics believe to be, the infallible Church.

Roman Catholics place great stress upon the intellect and the will as far as faith is concerned. It is not an emotional matter. There is a firm intellectual basis for every single belief. "While Catholics accept all Catholic truths as the word of Christ who taught them, they also learn the *why* of everything, because the Catholic religion is the most reasonable in all its teachings." (*How To Become A Catholic* by D. J. Corrigan, C.SS.R., p. 9)

Outside of certain supernatural faith, which must be accepted as a gift from God, Roman Catholics take great pains to prove their faith by reference to the Bible, the Creeds, and to Tradition.[1] No new doctrines are ever created by the Church; it merely explains or interprets what has already been given by the three original sources of faith and doctrine: the Bible, the Creeds, and Tradition.

Revealed Truth

Roman Catholics accept, as revealed truth, the Apostles', the Nicene and the Athanasian creeds. They also accept the Creed of Pope Pius IV, which affirms all the articles of the Nicene creed, the traditions of the Apostles, the sacraments, the sacrifice of the Mass, Purgatory, indulgences, the invocation of saints, and the Holy See. In teaching, and in worship, the Apostles' Creed is by far the most common in the Roman Catholic Church. According to *A Catholic Dictionary*, "The articles of this creed are binding upon the belief of Catholics under pain of heresy." (p. 28)

As given in the new *Baltimore Catechism*, forming the first section of the catechism, the Apostles' Creed is as follows:

> "I believe in God, the Father Almighty, Creator of heaven and earth; and in Jesus Christ, His only Son, Our Lord; who was conceived by the Virgin Mary, suffered under Pontius Pilate, was crucified, died, and was buried. He descended into hell; the third day He rose again from the dead; He ascended into heaven, sitteth at the right hand of God, the Father Almighty; from thence He shall come to judge the living and the dead. I believe in the Holy Ghost, the Holy

---

[1] Tradition means the official teaching of the Roman Catholic Church, and not merely the view of the Church Fathers.

Catholic Church, the communion of saints, the forgiveness of sins, the resurrection of the body, and life everlasting. Amen."

Distinctive Roman Catholic Features

Along with most other Christians, Roman Catholics believe in God as the Supreme Being who made all things; in the Trinity; in a literal heaven and hell; in sin, the forgiveness of sins, the incarnation, the Church, the Holy Spirit; in redemption of the soul; in the communion of saints, judgment, the resurrection of the body, and life everlasting.

It is interesting to note the following interpretations based upon the Apostles' Creed, taken from the *Baltimore Catechism*, which are distinctly Roman Catholic:

"The Blessed Virgin Mary was free from original sin, and this favor is called her Immaculate Conception."

"There are two kinds of actual sins: mortal sin and venial sin. Mortal sin is a grievous offense against the law of God. Venial sin is a less serious offense against the law of God."

"When we say that Christ descended into hell we mean that, after He died, the soul of Christ descended into a place or state of rest, called limbo, where the souls of the just were waiting for Him."

"The Holy Ghost dwells in the Church as the source of its life and sanctifies souls through the gift of grace."

"The principal ways of obtaining grace are prayer and the sacraments, especially, the Holy Eucharist."

"The Church is the congregation of all baptized persons united in the same true faith, the same sacrifice, and the same sacraments, under the authority of the Sovereign Pontiff and the bishops in communion with him."

"Christ did not intend that the special power of chief teacher and ruler of the entire Church should be exercised by Saint Peter alone, but intended that this power should be passed down to his successor, the Pope, the Bishop of Rome, who is the Vicar of Christ on earth and the visible head of the Church."

"The one true Church established by Christ is the Catholic Church."

"We know that the Catholic Church is the one true Church established by Christ because it alone has the marks of the true Church."

"The chief marks of the Church are four: It is one, holy, Catholic or universal, and apostolic."

"The chief attributes of the Catholic Church are authority, infallibility, and indefectibility."

"All are obliged to belong to the Catholic Church in order to be saved." (Please see page 7.)

"By 'the communion of saints' is meant the union of the faithful on earth, the blessed in heaven, and the souls in purgatory, with Christ as their Head."

"The faithful on earth, through the communion of saints, can relieve the sufferings of the souls in purgatory by prayer, fasting, and other good works, by indulgences and by having Masses offered for them."

"By the special privilege of her Assumption, the body of the Blessed Virgin Mary, preserved from corruption, was raised from the dead [2] and taken into heaven."

"The rewards or punishments appointed for men after the particular judgment are heaven, purgatory, or hell."

"Those are punished for a time in purgatory who die in the state of grace but are guilty of venial sin, or have not fully satisfied for the temporal punishment due to their sins."

"Those are punished in hell who die in mortal sin; they are deprived of the vision of God and suffer dreadful torments, especially that of fire, for all eternity."

"Those are rewarded in heaven who die in the state of grace and have been purified in purgatory, if necessary, from all venial sin and all debt of temporal punishment; they see God face to face and share forever in His glory and happiness."

Acceptance of the Trinity

The doctrine of the Trinity is classified by the Roman Catholic Church as a supernatural mystery which cannot be fully understood. Roman Catholics, not being able to understand this truth through natural reason, accept it as a teaching of the Church. It is accepted on faith. Revelation, not reason, confirms the Roman Catholic's belief in one God who is three divine Persons— the Father, the Son, and the Holy Ghost.

According to the *Catechism of Christian Doctrine,* what Roman Catholics believe about the Trinity is that "the three divine Persons are really distinct from one another," yet they are not distinct in nature. They are all perfectly equal to one another, because all are one and the same God, all having one and the same divine nature, the same perfections, and the same external works. "But in order that we may better know the three divine Persons, certain perfections and works are attributed to each Person; for example, omnipotence and the works of omnipotence, such as creation, to the Father; wisdom and the works of wisdom, such

---

[2] It is interesting to note that Pope Pius XII, in defining the dogma of the Assumption, did not imply that Mary died.

as enlightment, to the Son; love and the works of love, such as sanctification, to the Holy Ghost."

Principal Heresies

Heretics, according to Catholic Canon Law, are those "baptized persons who, while retaining the name of Christian, obstinately deny or doubt any of the truths proposed for belief by the divine and Catholic faith." Those who separate themselves from the authority of Rome, or the Supreme Pontiff, are schismatics. The Eastern Orthodox Church is an example of schism. Such separation is wrong not only in fact, but leads definitely to errors concerning dogmatic truths.

Here are some of the principal heresies condemned by the Roman Catholic Church, and its own basis for condemnation:

Anabaptism (16th century): because it proposed to re-establish "primitive" Christianity, to make the Bible the sole rule of faith, and rejected infant baptism.

Anglicanism (beginning with Henry VIII and Archbishop Cranmer): because it set up an independent national church, transferred supreme authority from the pope to the Crown, declared Scripture as the only rule of faith, denied the Real Presence and Mass, changed the rite of ordination, and rejected invocation of the Virgin Mary and the saints.

Arianism (Arius, 280-336): because it attempted to rationalize the Trinity, making Christ a mere creature.

Baptists (John Smyth in England, died 1612; Roger Williams in America, died 1683): because they reject infant baptism and consider only immersion valid; accept baptism and the Lord's Supper only as "symbols," not sacraments; make Scripture the only rule of faith; allow private interpretation of the Bible; and reject all nonscriptural doctrines and duties.

Calvinism and Presbyterianism (John Calvin, 1509–64): because, among other things, it stresses predestination, denies the Real Presence and free will. Calvinism was condemned at the Council of Trent (1545–63).

Christian Science (Mary Baker Eddy, 1821–1910): because it contains "the error of both pantheism and philosophic idealism."

Congregationalism (Robert Browne, 1550–1633): because it teaches the freedom of the individual soul and the independence of the local church.

Gnosticism (beginning in the 2nd century): because its fundamental errors consisted in placing reason above faith and disregarding all ecclesiastical authority.

Lutheranism (Martin Luther, 1483–1546): because the twofold principle of invincible concupiscence, and justification by faith alone, constitutes the fundamental error according to the Roman Catholic Church. Besides, Luther formulated the principle of private interpretation of the Bible; cast aside the sacrifice of the Mass; ridiculed the doctrine of indulgences; taught that fasting, confession, and mortification were not necessary; denied the supremacy of the pope; and repudiated the celibacy of the clergy. Lutheranism was condemned by the Council of Trent.

Methodism (John Wesley, 1703–91): because its two distinctive doctrines are "witness of the Spirit," to the individual soul, and the consequent assurance of salvation. It admits only two sacraments, holds that baptism does not produce sanctifying grace, and regards the Lord's Supper as only a memorial.

Modernism: because it destroys the validity of religious belief, making it a human product and not a divine revelation; denies the divinity of Christ and the authority of the Church.

Mormonism (Joseph Smith, 1805–44): because it claims direct revelation from an angel from heaven.

Quakerism (George Fox, 1624–91): because its central doctrine is that of the "inner light" communicated to the individual soul by Christ. It also rejects priesthood, exterior ceremony, and authority.

Unitarianism: because it believes in a unipersonal God, and makes the Church autonomous.

Universalism: because it believes in the salvation of all souls.

Waldensianism (beginning in the 12th century): because it claims to practice Christianity in its pristine purity. According to the Catholic Church, its chief "doctrinal errors" are: the denial of purgatory, indulgences, and prayers for the dead; all lying as a grievous sin; refusal to take oaths and considered capital punishment unlawful. The Third Lateran Council (1179) condemned this "heresy."

Wyclifism (John Wyclif, 1320–84): because it made the Bible the sole rule of faith, defended predestination, denied transubstantiation, taught that the pope is not the head of the Church, rejected the hierarchy, declared that confession is useless, and maintained that bishops have no pre-eminence over other priests. The Council of Constance (1414) condemned these doctrines.

The Meaning of Excommunication

Excommunication is an ecclesiastical censure, administered by bishops or the pope, which excludes a baptized person from communication of the faithful, with all the consequent disabilities and deprivations. Those excommunicated lose the right of attending divine service,[3] receiving the sacraments, and have no share

---

[3] But they still have to fulfill the obligations of the Roman Catholic Church. (See p. 103, *A Catechism of Christian Doctrine.*)

in indulgences, public prayer, and Mass. (*A Catholic Diction-ary*, p. 182)

The chief crimes which incur excommunication are as follows:

Throwing away the Sacred Host or otherwise treating it with speci-fied grave irreverence. Laying violent hands on the pope. A priest pretending to absolve his female accomplice in sin. Direct violation of the seal of confession.[4]

Those who, having professed the Catholic faith, apostatize, profess heresy, and go into schism. Appealing from the decision of the pope to an ecumenical council. Deliberately citing a cardinal, apostolic nuncio, or delegate, or one's own ordinary, as defendant before a civil court without permission from the Holy See. Forging apostolic decrees, letters, or other papal documents. Falsely accusing a priest to his superiors of solicitation in the confessional.

Other "crimes" which may incur excommunication are:

Granting or publishing indulgences for money. Joining the Free-masons or other societies which work against the Church or lawful civil authority. Violating the laws of monastic papal enclosure. Con-version of ecclesiastical property to one's own use. Dueling. Attempted marriage by or with a person under a solemn vow of chastity. Simony. Attempt by a Catholic to contract marriage before a non-Catholic minister as such. Agreeing before marriage that all or any of the children shall be brought up outside the Church. Making, selling, and distributing false relics. Laying violent hands on any cleric or religious whatsoever. Procuring abortion. Publishing without permission notes and comments on the Holy Scriptures. Compelling anyone against his will to receive Holy Orders. (*A Catholic Dictionary*, p. 182)

Roman Catholic Dogmas

The common idea of a dogma, meaning some arbitrary doc-trine, imposed and generally believed, is not accepted by the Roman Catholic Church. It is rather a truth directly proposed

---

Conway's *Question Box*, p. 205, says, "Neither excommunication nor anathemas imply the Church's condemning anyone to hell. That is the pre-rogative of God alone."

According to *The Catholic Encyclopedia*, Vol. V, p. 681, "All who have been baptized are liable to excommunication, even those who have never belonged to the true Church, since by their baptism they are really her subjects, though of course rebellious ones."

The power of excommunication, therefore, extends to all baptized per-sons, Roman Catholics and non-Catholics. It may even include entire groups, regions, nations.

[4] These first four are the severest excommunications and are reserved to the pope.

by the Church as an article of divine revelation. It is truth revealed by God, according to Roman Catholic teaching, and therefore must be believed.

In defining a doctrine, making it binding upon all Catholics, the Roman Catholic Church does not create a new teaching. It merely makes clear something which has always been a reality, although not fully understood. Thus in 1854 the dogma of the Immaculate Conception was formulated, and in 1870 the Infallibility of the Pope was made a dogma. Fathers Rumble and Carty explain it this way: "Both doctrines were believed in so far as Catholics believed in the revelation given by Christ, which contained these doctrines *implicitly*. When the Church defined them she merely made *explicit* and of faith what had been hitherto implicit. She gave, not a new truth, but merely made these matters clear by defining these doctrines to be part of the revelation brought to us by Christ." (*Radio Replies*, Vol. I, p. 93)

The dogma of the physical assumption of Mary into heaven, defined in 1950, must be accepted now, without question, by all Roman Catholics. Contained in the Apostolic Constitution, *Munificentissimus Deus*, which "defined the dogma of faith that Mary, the Virgin Mother of God, has been assumed into heaven in body and soul" are these words:

"Hence if anyone, which God forbid, should dare wilfully to deny or to call into doubt that which We have defined, let him know that he has fallen away completely from the divine and Catholic Faith.

"It is forbidden to any man to change a page of this, our declaration, pronouncement, and definition or, by rash attempt, to oppose and counter it. If any man should presume to make such an attempt, let him know that he will incur the wrath of Almighty God and of the Blessed Apostles, Peter and Paul."

Freedom of Belief

Roman Catholics pride themselves on their freedom of belief. They point out that Catholics do not give a blind, degrading obedience to a fallible, human authority. They do not believe without reason. Instead they find their freedom in gladly, and willingly, accepting a divine authority which offers only truth and protects against error.

As Father Conway says in his *Question Box*, "The doctrine of infallibility is indeed opposed to the false freedom of believing error, but not to the true freedom of believing truth. We have no right to believe what is false, any more than we have a right to do what is evil. . . . A prejudiced Protestant may have a false conception of the meaning of an indulgence, or of Papal infallibility; his ignorance of Latin may make him believe that the Jesuits teach that the end justifies the means; his fallacious reasoning may convince him that a Catholic owes civil allegiance to a foreign power, or that birth control is not against the divine law. But he certainly is not to be praised for believing what is not true. We call such freedom of thought error and ignorance. It is unreasonable, unscientific and contrary to the evidence." (p. 97)

THE PROTESTANT POINT OF VIEW
On the Great Historic Creeds

Protestantism repudiates Roman Catholic dogma, definitions, and tradition because it believes that each individual has the divine right to believe as led by the Spirit of Truth.

Protestants, as well as Roman Catholics, have their creeds. And they also have their various tests and norms of correct belief. In order to belong to some Protestant churches a member must accept and not depart from the prescribed creedal position. Protestants, as well as Roman Catholics, have ways of punishing those who depart from orthodoxy. This, of course, is not true of all denominations. Some have no creeds, and only ask of their members acceptance of the New Testament as the basis of faith and life. Not a few churches give perfect freedom to their members to believe as they are led by facts and the spirit of truth. Here the spirit counts for more than the letter.

Laymen, particularly, are making less and less of detailed creedal statements and are stressing the Christian way of life. Some feel free to join the church of their immediate locality, whether it coincides with the faith of their fathers or not. There is a tendency in many denominations to offer "open membership," placing all denominations upon an equal basis. This is not true of Roman Catholicism. It remains absolutely exclusive. Its requirements remain unchanged. In this the Roman Catholic feels a sense of security and points to the conflicting creedal positions of Protestants as a measure of weakness.

In general, however, Protestantism asks that each individual believe the fundamentals of Christianity. Belief, theology, deep convictions, are essential. But Protestants need not agree in every detail with all of their fellow members. Allowance is made for individual differences. Here is the power of Protestantism. In diversity of views, within a central core of faith, there is tremendous strength. In freedom of thought there is a creative foundation for intellectual and spiritual progress.

Personal Liberty

Fundamental to the Protestant position is freedom of conscience, with creedal statements serving more as directives than as hard and fast dogmas. Moreover, most Protestants accept the principle of progressive revelation, believing that while the Scriptures do contain fully the basis for Christian life and doctrine, there are new spiritual insights which break into history through the inspiration of the Spirit of Truth.

Principal creeds and statements of faith held by Protestants, many of them having passed through several revisions, are: the Apostles' Creed; the Nicene Creed; Lutheran, the Augsburg Confession (1530); Reformed, the First Helvetic Confession (1536); Anglican, the Thirty-nine Articles (1571); Presbyterian, the Westminster Confession (1646–47); Congregational, Browne's Statement of Congregational Principles (1582); Baptist, the Philadelphia Confession (1742); and Methodist, the Twenty-five Articles (1784). Most Protestants are familiar with the Apostles' Creed, which represents an accumulation of Christian belief in the second century. It had a development in thought and phrase until in the seventh century it took the form in which we know it today.

This statement concerning baptism is a sample of the *Augsburg Confession:* "Of Baptism they teach that it is necessary to salvation, and that by Baptism, the grace of God is offered, and that children are to be baptized, who by Baptism, being offered to God, are received unto God's favor. They condemn the anabaptists, who allow not the Baptism of children and affirm that children are saved without Baptism."

The *Heidelberg Catechism* gives the following question and answer: "Are infants also to be baptized? (*Answer*) Yes; for since they, as well as their parents, belong to the covenant and people of God, and both redemption from sin and the Holy Ghost, who works faith, are through the blood of Christ promised to them no less than to their parents."

According to the *Thirty-nine Articles* (27th), "Baptism is not only a sign of profession, and mark of difference, whereby Christian men are discerned from others that be not christened, but it is also a sign of regeneration or newbirth, whereby, as by an instrument, they that receive Baptism rightly are grafted into the Church."

Protestant liberty of interpretation, both within those churches which have creeds and those which do not have any creeds, is indicated by the fact that all of them rely upon the Holy Spirit, or the Spirit of Truth, as each individual's guide. Protestants are not bound, in blind allegiance, to historic creeds. They believe in Christ's ever-new revelation. As expressed by the Willingen Conference, "The inner life of the churches depends upon the Holy Spirit who is the source of all new life."

Protestant Interpretation of Scripture

Except in the great central convictions of faith, there is no uniformity of belief among Protestants. This right to believe and interpret Scripture as led by the Spirit of Truth is a fundamental New Testament principle. At the first council of the Christian Church held at Jerusalem, there was a serious difference of opinion (Acts 11 and 15). Paul could not always agree with Peter (Gal. 2:11). There were different views of missions in the early church (Acts 15:36-40). And while Christ called for unity of spirit, he never demanded uniformity of thought.

Protestants maintain that freedom of belief is established in such passages of Scripture as "Ask, and it shall be given you; seek, and ye shall find" (Matt. 7:7); "Whosoever will, let him take the water of life freely" (Rev. 22:17). It is also established in Christ's conversation with the woman at the well (John 4: 7-26), and Paul's stand at Mars Hill (Acts 17:22-34). In the New Testament there is no coercive power outside of that of the Spirit of Truth. Protestants believe that by following Christ's truth they will become free (Gal. 5:1).

It is plainly evident in Galatians 2:11-14 that Paul believed that he had a perfect right to disagree with Peter. In his letter he declared, "But when Peter was come to Antioch, I withstood him to the face, because he was to be blamed. For before that certain came from James, he did eat with the Gentiles: but when they were come, he withdrew and separated himself, fearing them which were of the circumcision. And the other Jews dissembled likewise with him; insomuch that Barnabas also was carried away with their dissimulation. But when I saw that they walked not uprightly according to the truth of the Gospel, I said unto Peter before them all, 'If thou, being a Jew, livest after the manner of Gentiles, and not as do the Jews, why compellest thou the Gentiles to live as do the Jews?'"

Paul not only won this issue, but proved that Peter did not have to be accepted as the final authority of the Church.

PROTESTANT REFERENCE BOOKS: Those who wish a fuller explanation of the historic Protestant statements of faith should turn to *Studies in Religion and Theology* by A. M. Fairbairn; Harnack's *History of Dogma; The Apostles' Creed* by A. C. McGiffert; McGlothlin's *Baptist Confessions of Faith; Protestantism's Challenge* by Conrad Henry Moehlman; *Creeds of Christendom* by Phillip Schaff; *History of Christian Theophagy* by Preserved Smith; *Creeds and Platforms of Congregationalism* by W. Walker.

10

What Roman
Catholics Believe About the Bible

Contrary to common Protestant belief, Roman Catholics read, sell, promote, and display the Bible. At the present time the Roman Catholic Church is waging a vast Bible-reading campaign. There is a Catholic Biblical Association of America; Bibles are displayed for sale in Catholic Book Stores; Catholics have several new translations of the Bible and the New Testament; daily Bible reading is urged upon all Catholics. The Bible is at the heart of Catholic worship.

Of course Roman Catholics do not use Protestant Bibles, nor are they allowed to interpret Scripture as they please. They have the guidance of the Church at this point. What Roman Catholics really believe about the Bible, and how they actually use it, will be the subject of this chapter. They have strong convictions concerning the Bible which are in direct opposition, at many places, to the accepted beliefs of Protestants. One of the chief reasons for the Protestant Reformation is to be found here.

THE ROMAN CATHOLIC POSITION

The Official Teaching About the Bible

The official teaching of the Roman Catholic Church concerning the Bible is found in the *Baltimore Catechism* as follows: "Sacred Scripture, or the Bible, is the word of God written by men under the inspiration of the Holy Ghost, and contained in the books of the Old and the New Testament.

"Inspiration is the act by which God moves and directs the sacred writers faithfully to commit to writing all those things and only those things that He wishes them to write. The sacred writers act as free instruments of God, who is the principal author of Sacred Scriptures."

Church Before Scripture

Roman Catholics, while holding an exalted belief in the Scriptures as the word of God, nevertheless place their Church historically ahead of the Bible. According to them it was the Church which determined that the books of the Old and New Testament contained in the Catholic Bible were inspired and canonical, and which gives the only correct interpretation of the sacred pages. They believe that the Church not only existed before the New Testament, but was the mother of it.

After pointing out that Christ wrote nothing, and did not command that his apostles write anything, Father John A. O'Brien, in *The Faith of Millions*, goes on to say that the Church "is not the child of the Bible, as many non-Catholics imagine, but its mother. She derives neither her existence nor her teaching authority from the New Testament. She had both before the New Testament was born: she secured her being, her teachings, her authority *directly* from Jesus Christ." (p. 146)

Catholics accept the Scriptures as the Word of God, but they do so only because the Church has declared it to be the Word of God. According to James Cardinal Gibbons, in *The Faith of Our Fathers*, "The Church is the divinely appointed Custodian and Interpreter of the Bible. For, her office of infallible Guide were superfluous if each individual could interpret the Bible for himself. . . . God never intended the Bible to be the Christian's rule of faith, independently of the living authority of the Church." (p. 63)

Not the Sole Guide of Faith

The Roman Catholic Church teaches that the Bible is not the sole guide of faith. It adds the divine tradition committed to the Church. And it puts them not merely on an equal basis, but passes both through the divine authority of the Church. According to the *Baltimore Catechism*, "Tradition is the unwritten word of God—that body of truths revealed by God to the apostles, and not committed by them to writing but handed down by word of mouth. These truths, which were later committed to writing, particularly by the Fathers of the Church, have been preserved and handed down to the present day."

Roman Catholics do not find the chief means of salvation in reading the Bible as such, but rather in the sacraments of the Church. But the sacraments are based upon the Scripture and tradition. Catholics take great care in supporting their doctrines with Scripture references.

Verbal Inspiration and Literal Infallibility

It is the teaching of the Roman Catholic Church that Sacred Scripture is the Word of God, but it does not support the view of the verbal dictation of the Bible. Rather it holds that the Bible is everywhere true in the sense intended by the individual sacred writer. (*A Catholic Dictionary*, p. 54)

Fathers Rumble and Carty explain the Catholic position as follows: "If, by verbal inspiration [is meant] a dictation of the very words to the writers by God, as one dictates to a stenographer, Catholics are not obliged to believe in verbal inspiration. But we are obliged to believe that every single word as it left the hands of the original writers was written under the inspiration of God, and infallibly expressed the truth intended by God. . . . Not a word, nor a sentence, belonging to the original writings, could be excluded from the divine influence of God's inspiration. . . . The whole of the Bible is for us the Word of God. We cannot regard the Bible as a mixture of God's Word and merely human thoughts or opinions." (*Radio Replies*, Vol. III, p. 39)

The Original Version

Roman Catholics admit that the original writings of the inspired authors of the Bible have been lost. The Scriptures have, therefore, come down to the faithful in the form of translations or versions. The oldest Hebrew manuscript belongs to the second century B.C., while the principal Greek manuscripts (Sinaitic and Vatican) date back to the fourth century A.D.

The most important ancient translations are the Septuagint and Vulgate; the former Greek version of the Old Testament was begun in the third century B.C. and completed sometime before 100 B.C. The Latin Vulgate was almost entirely the work of St. Jerome, lasting from 383 to about 406 A.D., and undertaken at the command of Pope Damasus. The Council of Trent ordered the Vulgate to be held as "authentic [authoritative] in public readings, disputations, preachings and expositions." Catholics believe that it conforms substantially with the originals and therefore contains no errors in faith and morals.

Roman Catholics Have a Larger Bible

From the Roman Catholic point of view the term "canon" is applied to the list of books of the Bible officially recognized by the Catholic Church as inspired and containing the rule of faith and morals revealed by God. The Council of Trent placed seventy-two books of the Old and New Testaments in the canon. In addition to the books found in Protestant Bibles there were included Tobias, Judith, Wisdom, Ecclesiasticus, Baruch, and the two books of the Maccabees, with additions to the books of Esther and Daniel. These are known as the "deutero-canonical books."

Modern Speech Translations

Roman Catholics also have translations of the Bible in the vernacular. There are, in fact, several translations in English.[1] The best known of these Catholic English versions is what is known as the "Rheims and Douay Version," getting its name because the New Testament was printed at Rheims in 1582, and the Old Testament at Douay in 1609–10. Based upon the Vulgate text, the translations were made by exiled English priests and educators. The Rheims-Douay remained the standard English version for Catholic use until near the time of the American Revolution.

Because of language changes, natural to all living tongues, a more modern version was needed, and Bishop Challoner, of London, met the need by producing, in 1750, a new translation of the entire Bible. He regarded his work, as the title page shows, merely as a revision of the Rheims-Douay.

While improvements were made in the Challoner version by Roman Catholic scholars there was a growing desire, particularly in America, for a better translation. This was finally realized in 1941 with the publication of *The New Testament,* Translated from the Latin Vulgate, A Revision of the Challoner-Rheims Version edited by Catholic scholars under the patronage of the Episcopal Committee of the Confraternity of Christian Doctrine. This text is much more than an attempt to bring the language of Challoner's version into conformity with modern English idiom. As the Preface to the translation points out, "It is a revision in the sense that it goes back to the source upon which Challoner

---

[1] There were several German translations shortly after the Gutenberg Bible.

drew, and reconsiders in a thorough way the accurate rendering of the divine message in the language of our day."

Along with this new version, which has the complete approval of the Biblical Commission at Rome, making it official, there have been these other modern English translations of the Scriptures by Catholics: the Westminster version of the entire Bible, in course of publication in England since 1914; the New Testament by Father F. Spencer, edited by Fathers Callan and McHugh (New York, 1937). These are both translations from the original language. Ronald Knox's translation of the New Testament—undertaken at the request of the English hierarchy—was published in 1944, and the Old Testament in 1950.

Catholic scholars, encouraged by Pope Pius XII (in the encyclical *Divino Afflante Spiritu*) to take recourse to the original languages and the application of recognized principles of textual criticism, are now working on an English version of the Old Testament. The first eight books have already been published. The remaining volumes of the Old Testament will be published in three yearly intervals, followed by a direct translation of the New Testament.

No Private Interpretation

While every Roman Catholic is encouraged to read the Bible, no Catholic has the right of private, individual interpretation—unless it agrees with the teaching of the Roman Catholic Church, which serves as a Supreme Court. It is the interpretation of the Church which must be accepted. The Church alone, Catholics believe, can give the true, authentic interpretation.

The Council of the Vatican confirmed the decree of the Council of Trent which declared: "In matters of faith and morals pertaining to the building up of Christian doctrine, that is to be held as the true sense of Sacred Scripture which Holy Mother Church has held and does hold, to whom it belongs to judge of the true sense and interpretation of Holy Scripture, and therefore that it is permitted to no one to interpret the said Scriptures against this sense or, likewise, against the unanimous consent of the Fathers."

With the Church as an infallible interpreter of Scripture, every Catholic is absolutely sure that the interpretation is correct.[2] This saves Catholics from the "errors" of many different interpreta-

---

[2] "The authentic text, legitimately promulgated, is a source and rule of faith, though it remains only a means or instrument in the hands of the

tions, contradicting each other, such as is in evidence among the Protestant denominations.

Bible Reading Encouraged

Roman Catholics do not fear the Bible, or what is within the Sacred Book. They are encouraged to practice it, as well as to read it. After his ordination every priest is obliged to devote at least an hour every day in reading the Word of God. And Catholics believe that what is good for the clergy is also good for the laity.

Father Conway, in his *Question Box,* says, "They [Catholics] are not forbidden but encouraged to read the Bible. The Catholic Church, as the guardian and interpreter of the Scriptures, must needs prevent her people from being led astray by false translations of the Bible, which are often accompanied by glosses and notes destructive to the Catholic faith. But she never has prohibited versions in the vernacular which have been approved by the Bishops of the various countries, and have been edited with explanatory notes by Catholic scholars." (pp. 83-84)

Pope Leo XIII, in his encyclical on the Bible (1893), wrote: "The solicitude of the Apostolic office naturally urges, and even compels us, not only to desire that this great source of Catholic revelation should be made safely and abundantly accessible to the flock of Jesus Christ, but also not to suffer any attempt to defile or corrupt it. . . . [By reading the Scriptures] the intelligence will be illuminated and strengthened . . . and at the same time the heart will grow warm, and will strive with ardent longing to advance in virtue and divine love."

The present pope, Pius XII, says: "We firmly hope that in the future reverence for, as well as the use and knowledge of, the Sacred Scriptures will everywhere more and more increase for the good of souls."

The current Apostolic Delegate to the United States, the Most Reverend Amleto Giovanni Cicognani, said in an address to the Seventh National Congress of the Confraternity of Christian Doctrine in 1941: "The New Testament is the code of love and salvation. It carries the word of God, the revelation of our Lord through His teachings. It is of utmost importance, for every age, not least for our own, to hear it with the same clarity, vividness

---

teaching body of the Church, which alone has the right of authoritatively interpreting Scripture."—*The Catholic Encyclopedia.*

and comprehension with which it was first pronounced by our Lord."

Indulgence for Bible Reading

In the front of the revision of the Challoner-Rheims version of the New Testament are found these words:

"Pope Leo XIII granted to the faithful who shall read for at least a quarter of an hour the books of the Sacred Scripture with the veneration due to the Divine Word and as spiritual reading, an indulgence of 300 days."—(*Preces et Pia Opera*, 645)

Catholics do not have to read the Bible, for the Church takes care in various ways to give it to the faithful through liturgy and the sacraments. But in this granting of a 300-day indulgence, the Roman Catholic Church offers a practical inducement in order to make its members Bible readers.

THE PROTESTANT POINT OF VIEW
On the Bible—All-Sufficient Rule of Faith and Life

Protestantism rejects the Roman Catholic conception of the Bible because it believes that each individual Christian has the God-given right to interpret the Holy Scriptures to the best of his ability.

Protestants and Roman Catholics agree that the Bible is the Word of God, that it is inspired, and that it is the basis for the Christian way of life. But, Protestants depart from Roman Catholic belief in the acceptance of the Church as the infallible interpreter of the Bible. Protestants reject this position both on historical grounds and on the basis of personal experience. They believe that the New Testament preceded and paved the way for what we know today as the Church. If it had not been for the letters of Paul, the Gospels, and the Book of Revelation, there might have been no Church at all, since a variety of churches were held together by the inspiration and admonitions of the various letters and messages.

On the basis of personal experience, Protestants know that the *Word* speaks to them from the pages of the Scriptures. There is no need of an official interpreter. As the New Testament books were written directly to the early Christians, in the vernacular, so should they be received today. The Bible is a great source of spiritual power for Protestants. It has brought them hope, comfort, courage, peace of soul, and salvation. It has convicted them of sin and sent them to their knees in prayer.

The Bible as All-Sufficient

Protestants believe that the Bible is all-sufficient as a rule of faith and life. They accept it as God's Word and encourage its reading. Today, the Bible is the "best seller" of all books, religious or secular. To Protestants it contains inspiration and guidance, the revelation of the Son of God, the way to eternal salvation. John Wyclif stated the Protestant view when he said, "the sacred Scriptures contain all truth, all philosophy, all logic, all ethical teaching." The *Thirty-nine Articles* declare that "Holy Scripture containeth all things necessary to salvation, so that whatsoever is not read therein nor may be proved thereby, is not to be required of any man that it should be believed as an article of the faith or to be thought requisite or necessary to salvation." The *Westminster Confession* declares "that the whole counsel of God, covering all things necessary for His own glory, man's salvation, faith and life, is either expressly set down in Scripture or by good and necessary consequence may be deduced from Scripture, unto which nothing at any time is to be added, whether by new revelations of the Spirit or traditions of men."

John Wyclif put it this way: "Believers should ascertain for themselves what are the true matters of their faith by having the Scriptures in a language which all may understand for the laws made by prelates are not to be received as matters of faith unless founded on the Scriptures." Tyndale's position was that "In this way [that translations might cause rebellions against kings, etc.] they all be agreed to drive you from the knowledge of Scripture and that you shall not have the text in the mother tongue, and to keep the world in darkness to the intent they might sit in the consciences of the people through vain superstition."

In answer to the question, "What authority has Holy Scripture?", the *Standard Catechism* of The Methodist Church replies, "Holy Scripture containeth all things necessary to salvation: so that whatsoever is not read therein, nor may be proved thereby, is not to be required of any man, that it should be believed as an article of faith, or be thought requisite or necessary to salvation. The Bible is thus the only rule, and the sufficient rule, both of our faith and practice."

Bible Christianity

Protestantism rests its case upon the Bible. It has a Bible Christianity. Its final court of appeal is the Holy Scriptures. Here again Protestants are not being different just to be difficult, but they are following specific New Testament directives. Jesus quoted the Bible as being of special spiritual importance. "Search the scriptures; for in them, ye think ye have eternal life; and they are they which testify of me" (John 5:39).

"All scripture is given by inspiration of God, and is profitable for doctrine, for reproof, for correction, for instruction in righteousness; that the man of God may be perfect, thoroughly furnished unto all good works" (II Tim. 3:16, 17).

"Blessed is he that readeth, and they that hear the word of this prophecy, and keep these things which are written therein" (Rev. 1:3).

Protestants believe that the Bible should come first because it is truly the Word of God. No man or institution, no matter how great, can supersede the Word. For Protestants it is the Living Word.

The Word of God is made very real in John 17:14-17, "I have given them thy word; and the world hath hated them, because they are not of the world, even as I am not of the world. I pray not that thou shouldest take them out of the world, but that thou shouldest keep them from the evil. They are not of the world, even as I am not of the world. Sanctify them through thy truth: thy word is truth."

"Jesus saith unto him, If I will that he tarry till I come, what is that to thee? Follow thou me. Then went this saying abroad among the brethren, that that disciple should not die: yet Jesus said not unto him, He shall not die; but, If I will that he tarry till I come, what is that to thee? This is the disciple which testifieth of these things, and wrote these things: and we know that his testimony is true. And there are also many other things which Jesus did, the which, if they should be written every one, I suppose that even the world itself could not contain the books that should be written" (John 21:22-25).

PROTESTANT REFERENCE BOOKS: *An Introduction to the Old Testament* by Harlan Creelman; *Introduction to the Literature of the Old Testament* by S. R. Driver; *A Guide to Understanding the Bible* by Harry Emerson Fosdick; *A Protestant Manifesto* by Winfred E. Garrison, pp. 116 ff.; *How to Read the Bible* by Edgar J. Goodspeed; *The*

Making of the English New Testament by Edgar J. Goodspeed; *History and Interpretation in the Gospels* by R. H. Lightfoot; *Primer for Protestants* by James Hastings Nichols, Chap. VIII; *Literature of the New Testament* by Herbert R. Purinton; *The Validity of the Gospel Record* by Ernest Findlay Scott.

11

Veneration of the Virgin Mary

About the only time in the course of the entire year when Protestants hear about or take any special notice of Mary, is at Christmas time and Easter. Then it is only incidental to the birth of Christ: as part of the Christian story, the Cross, and the resurrection of Christ. But in the Roman Catholic Church great prominence is given to Mary every day of the year. She is greatly honored as the "Mother of God," but Roman Catholics maintain that the *veneration* shown Mary is not the same as their *worship* of God.[1]

This chapter will describe Roman Catholic devotion and veneration of the Virgin Mary. Some of the honors given to her may be sanctioned by Protestants. But in respect to the Immaculate Conception, the Assumption, and the various alleged appearances (which Catholics do not have to believe) of the Virgin, Protestants cannot agree.

Roman Catholics feel that they are fully justified in their veneration of Mary. They give what are for them valid reasons for their belief and practices. Because there is so much misunderstanding concerning the Roman Catholic attitude toward Mary, we will discuss in detail what they do, and do not, believe about her.

THE ROMAN CATHOLIC POSITION

The Incarnation

It is the teaching of the Roman Catholic Church that after the fall of Adam mankind was not abandoned by God. He promised to send a Saviour to free man from all his sins and to reopen to him the gates of heaven. This promise was fulfilled in the com-

---

[1] The authoritative *National Catholic Almanac*, however, does equate Christ with Mary and the saints in the words "a pious practice in honor of Our Lord, the Blessed Virgin, the angels or saints."

ing of Jesus Christ to the world—as God in the flesh. Only through the merits of Christ can salvation be found.

Roman Catholics believe that Christ is God, being the only Son of God and having the same divine nature as His Father. He is "the second Person of the Blessed Trinity, who from eternity proceeds by true spiritual generation from the Father." (*A Catechism of Christian Doctrine*, p. 58)

Other Roman Catholic beliefs concerning Christ, according to this same source, are as follows: He is a man because he was born of the Virgin Mary and had a human body and soul, human intelligence and free will. In spite of the fact that his conception and birth were miraculous, he came into the world as an infant like other men. Being man, he was the most perfect of all men, being free from all ignorance and error, from all sin and imperfection. His human soul, however, could suffer along with that of his body. It is heresy to deny the divine nature of Christ, merely accepting him as a man; it is also heresy to deny his human nature along with that of the divine. The defined teaching of the Church (Leo IX, April, 1053) is: "I also believe in the Son of God, the Word, begotten of the Father in eternity, before all time . . . born in time of the Holy Ghost from Mary, ever Virgin; born with a rational soul; having two nativities, one eternal of the Father, the other in time, of His Mother."

Mother of God

According to the Roman Catholic Church, Mary is the mother of Christ. Christ is God. Therefore Mary is the mother of God. This is the reasoning of Roman Catholics concerning the Virgin Mary. Of course this reasoning does not stop here and, besides, it is supported all the way along by quotations from Scripture, tradition, and the Church Councils. It is the official teaching of the Roman Catholic Church that:

"The Son of God was conceived and made man on Annunciation Day, the day on which the Angel Gabriel announced to the Blessed Virgin Mary that she was to be the Mother of God.

"The miraculous privileges accorded the Blessed Virgin Mary by Almighty God testify to her position as the most exalted of God's creatures.

"Because of her consent to accept the office of Mother of the Redeemer, and also because of her merits in intimately sharing the sufferings of her Divine Son for the salvation of mankind, the

Blessed Virgin is given the title of Co-Redemptrix of the human race." (*A Catechism of Christian Doctrine,* p. 65)

No Other Child

Some Protestants are of the opinion that Mary had other children besides Jesus, her first-born; but not so Roman Catholics. They believe that "Mary, the Mother of God, remained a virgin not only in the conception of Christ but also in His birth and during the rest of her life." (*Baltimore Catechism*)

The Immaculate Conception

Roman Catholics not only believe in the Virgin Birth, but also in the Immaculate Conception. While they are related in general through the person of Mary, they are considered, by the Roman Catholic Church, to be two entirely separated doctrines. The first relates primarily to Christ and the Incarnation. The second refers entirely to Mary and relates to the condition of her *soul* at conception. It must also be understood that Catholics do not believe that Mary's own physical birth was supernatural—as in the case of the virgin birth of Jesus. She was born physically as any other person—only without the taint of original sin. The teaching of the Roman Catholic Church on this point is that "the Blessed Virgin Mary was preserved from original sin in view of the merits of her Divine Son; and this privilege is called her Immaculate Conception." (*Baltimore Catechism*)

This dogma of the Roman Catholic Church, proclaimed to the world by Pope Pius IX in 1854, went through a long and exhaustive process of development.[2] In his Bull, *Ineffabilis Dei,* in which he defines the dogma of the Immaculate Conception of Mary, the pope is most careful not only to declare the "proofs of Mary's Immaculate Conception," but to reveal the long process of investigation through which it passed. He cites Scripture, tradition, and the unanimous voice of Catholic scholars, bishops, and the cardinals. A special congregation of investigators was appointed by the pope. They all asked Pope Pius IX "with the same alacrity and zeal for the definition of the Immaculate Conception of the Mother of God."

After proceeding with great prudence the pope declared: "So

---

[2] It was during this period that Franciscan opposed Dominican, and Jesuit opposed Jansenist, regarding the desirability of making the Immaculate Conception a dogma of the Church. After the dogma had once been defined, they all had to agree at this point.

by His inspiration, for the honor of the Holy and Undivided Trinity, for the glory and adornment of the Virgin Mother of God, for the exaltation of the Catholic faith and for the increase of the Catholic religion, by the authority of Jesus Christ Our Lord, of the Blessed Apostles Peter and Paul, and by Our own, *We declare, pronounce and define that the Most Blessed Virgin Mary, at the first instance of her Conception was preserved immaculate from all stain of original sin, by the singular grace and privilege of the Omnipotent God, in virtue of the merits of Jesus Christ, the Savior of mankind, and that this doctrine was revealed by God, and therefore, must be believed firmly and constantly by all the faithful.*"

Thus every Roman Catholic has to believe that Mary, unlike every other human being, was endowed with God's grace at conception, instead of being conceived and born in original sin. What every Roman Catholic receives at baptism—redemption from the sin of Adam—Mary received at conception. She thus became the New Eve, free from all sin.

Mary's Body Taken to Heaven

Along with the Immaculate Conception of Mary, and closely related to it, is the dogma of the Assumption of Mary's physical body to heaven. While this seems like a new dogma, being defined by Pope Pius XII in 1950, it has existed and has been believed implicitly, according to the Roman Catholic Church, from the very beginning.

Here again Mary is unique among human beings. In the ordinary course of events death comes to every man as the result of original sin. Christ overcame sin and death on the Cross, and those who through baptism are born again have also, through Christ, conquered sin. Nevertheless, even the bodies of the just are corrupted and only at the Last Day are joined again with their redeemed souls. But not so with Mary. As Pope Pius XII explains it, "Now God has willed that the Blessed Virgin Mary should be exempted from this general rule. She, by an entirely unique privilege, completely overcame sin by her Immaculate Conception, and as a result she was not subject to the law of remaining in the corruption of the grave, and she did not have to wait until the end of time for the redemption of her body."

Having listed in great detail many "proofs" of incorruption of Mary's body and its assumption into heaven, Pope Pius XII solemnly declares the following as a doctrine of the Roman Catholic Church: "We pronounce, declare, and define it to be a divinely revealed dogma: that the Immaculate Mother of God, the ever Virgin Mary, having completed the course of her earthly life, was assumed body and soul into heavenly glory.

"Hence if anyone, which God forbid, should dare wilfully to deny or to call into doubt that which We have defined, let him know that he has fallen away completely from the divine and Catholic Faith."

The Veneration of Mary

According to Roman Catholic teaching, the First Commandment does not forbid giving honor to Mary, provided that the honor given does not belong to God alone. Thus Mary can be venerated, but not worshiped.[3]

As the *Catechism of Christian Doctrine* points out: "The veneration paid to the saints in heaven differs essentially from the adoration of God. The saints are creatures and are not to be given the supreme worship due to the Creator alone. The supreme honor given to God only is adoration in the full and strict sense of the word. The veneration given to the Blessed Mother and to the saints is an act of respect and honor of an entirely different nature. The veneration given to the Blessed Mother of God surpasses that given to the saints and angels." (p. 177)

"Our motive in commemorating Mary's name," says Cardinal Gibbons (*The Faith of Our Fathers,* p. 150), "is not merely to praise her, but still more to keep us in perpetual remembrance of our Lord's Incarnation, and to show our thankfulness to Him for the blessings wrought through that great mystery in which she was so prominent a figure. There is not a grain of incense offered to Mary which does not ascend to the throne of God Himself."

Thus the statues, the Angelus, the Rosary, the shrines, special processions, reference to her in the Eucharist, are all honors which bring the faithful nearer to God.

Mary's Intercession

Do Roman Catholics pray to Mary? Catholics direct their prayers to Mary. They ask her for help. And they seek her intercessory aid in carrying appeals to Christ himself. In this sense

---

[3] Note on page 119 also applies here.

it can be said that Catholics pray to Mary, not as to God, but as an intermediator.

Catholics believe that Christ alone can redeem mankind. He alone can reconcile a person to God, making him a partaker of His grace now and in the hereafter. Moreover, they believe that no divine gift can reach an individual except through Christ and the merits of His sacrifice on the Cross.

Father Conway therefore explains the position of Mary in his *Question Box*, "Every prayer we pray, and every prayer in heaven of the Blessed Virgin, the angels and the saints, have their efficacy only through Jesus Christ our Lord. The saints simply add their prayers to ours, and, although specially pleasing to God because of their greater holiness, they aid us only through the merits of the One Mediator." (p. 370)

Mary being no ordinary person or saint, and being so close to her Son, Jesus Christ, is in an especially good position to intercede for the faithful. Catholics naturally take full advantage of this relationship. They believe that when she asks for something for them, Christ will hardly deny it.

Millions of Roman Catholics every day speak to Mary in the prayer of the Hail Mary:

> "Hail Mary, full of grace! the Lord is with thee! blessed art thou amongst women; and blessed is the fruit of thy womb, Jesus. Holy Mary, Mother of God, pray for us sinners, now and at the hour of our death. Amen."

Miracles of Mary

Roman Catholics believe in miracles, and certainly in the miracles associated with Mary:[4]

"No sooner had Pius IX proclaimed that we must believe by Catholic faith that Mary was free from the original stain, than the Virgin herself began those wonderful manifestations at Lourdes. It was then that those vast and magnificent temples to the Immaculate Mother of God were built, in which miracles are performed daily through the prayer of the Mother of God." These are the words of Pope Pius X in his encyclical letter *Ad Diem Illum* (1948).

Catholics believe that Mary not only gives them special blessings, performs miracles and distributes heavenly gifts, but also

---

[4] Mary can perform miracles only as the instrument of God; not through her own power.

that, at certain times, she reveals herself to the faithful. Some of her most recent alleged visits to earth occurred at the following places, according to the *National Catholic Almanac:*

Our Lady of Guadalupe, 1531, Mexico: "In the year 1531 the Blessed Virgin appeared to a fifty-five-year-old neophyte, the humble Indian, Juan Diego, who was hurrying down Tepeyac hill to hear Mass in Mexico City. She instructed him to convey to the Franciscan Bishop Zumarraga her wish that a church be built on the spot. When the Bishop prudently asked for a sign to prove her identity, the Lady told Juan to gather roses on Tepeyac hill. This he did, though it was winter. On his return, the Virgin rearranged the flowers in his mantle and bade him keep them undisturbed till he reached the Bishop. As he unfolded his mantle and the roses fell out, the Bishop and his attendants dropped on their knees. A life-size figure of the Virgin, just as Juan had described her, had miraculously been painted on his mantle."

Our Lady of the Miraculous Medal, 1830, France: "Three times in 1830, antedating by twenty-four years the solemn definition of the dogma of her Immaculate Conception, the Virgin Mary appeared to Catherine Laboure, a twenty-four-year-old novice of the Daughters of Charity of St. Vincent de Paul. . . . In the late afternoon of November 27, the Lady commissioned Catherine to have made, and to spread devotion to, the medal of the Immaculate Conception, now known throughout the world as the Miraculous Medal." [5]

Our Lady of La Salette, 1846, France: The Virgin Mary appeared to two peasant children at this mountain site in southeastern France. She was weeping. Later, when the people of the village came to the place, "they found there the now famous fountain of La Salette." It is now a center for pilgrimages, ceremonies, and miracles of healing.

Our Lady of Lourdes, 1858, France: Bernadette Soubirous, a poor, fourteen-year-old girl, in 1858, had eighteen appearances from the Virgin Mary. On February 25, Mary told Bernadette to drink of the water of the spring which miraculously gushed forth when she, before an amazed crowd, scratched the dry earth. The Virgin requested that a chapel be built and this was done, after rigid examination to prove the credibility of the apparition, in 1862. "Most of the cures occur when the sick are blessed with the Sacred Host after the traditional profession of the Blessed Sacrament, though baths in the spring water or visits to the shrine have proved efficacious. The water has been found by analysis to contain no curative properties. The miracles can in no wise be explained on any natural basis."

---

[5] The name of the Miraculous Medal comes from its origin, rather than the graces which were promised to those who wear it. Various indulgences may be gained by those who wear the medal, provided it has been blessed by a priest having the proper authority.

Our Lady of Fatima, 1917, Portugal: [6] On May 13, 1917, the Virgin Mary appeared to three shepherd children, Lucia dos Santos, ten, and her cousins, Francisco and Jacinto, nine and seven, in a field called Cova da Iria, near Fatima, a Portuguese village north of Lisbon. During this, and subsequent visits, she recommended frequent recitation of the rosary, and that Russia be consecrated to her Immaculate Heart.

According to Lucia, the only one living of the three children, who reported her secret twenty-five years after the event, the Virgin Mary said to her:

> "I come to ask the consecration of Russia to My Immaculate Heart and the Communion of Reparation on the First Saturdays. If they listen to my requests, Russia will be converted and there will be peace. If not she will scatter her errors through the world, provoking wars, and persecutions of the Church. Many good people will be martyred, the Holy Father will have much to suffer, many nations will be annihilated.
>
> "In the end My Immaculate Heart will triumph. The Holy Father will consecrate Russia to me, and a certain period of peace will be granted to the world."

Pilgrimages bring hundreds of thousands to Fatima, and in one five-year period 215 miraculous cures were reported. Pope Pius XII in 1942, on the closing of the silver jubilee celebration of the apparitions at Fatima, made a broadcast and consecrated the world, with special reference to Russia, to the Immaculate Heart of Mary.

Our Lady of Beauraing, 1932–33, Belgium: The Virgin Mary appeared here to four girls and a boy, telling them that she wished a chapel erected and pilgrimages made in her honor. Cures, the conversion of sinners and fallen-away Catholics, have been reported in connection with the shrines and pilgrimages.

Our Lady of Banneux, 1933, Belgium: Between January 15 and March 2, 1933, Mary appeared eight times to an eleven-year-old peasant girl, Mariette Beco, in the village of Banneux, near Liége. Mary announced herself as "Virgin of the Poor," and said, "I have come to bring relief to the sick." She pointed out a spring close by which she asked to be dedicated to her for the sick of all nations. The fame of "the Virgin of the Poor" has spread throughout the world; thousands have journeyed to the shrine for spiritual and physical healing. Today the International Union of Prayer, intimately associated with devotion to Mary, has a membership of over 700,000.[7]

---

[6] A movie has recently been based on this "miracle."

[7] All of the above "notable apparitions" have the approbation of the Roman Catholic Church, and each apparition, according to the *National*

Mary and the Rosary

Many forms of ceremonies and organizations have grown up around the Virgin Mary. One organization, popular in Europe, is known as the Guard of Honor of the Immaculate Heart of Mary. Its members are banded together "like a heavenly army," in order to have "an extraordinary devotion to the Pure Heart of the Mother of God, to cultivate and imitate her virtues, and to make reparation for the injuries inflicted upon the Mystical Body of Christ. The Holy See endowed this Pious Union with indulgences." (From a brief of Pope Pius XII, December 17, 1951)

The Angelus is a devotion in honor of the Incarnation. It consists of three short verses, each followed by a "Hail Mary," and concludes with a special prayer. The purpose of this devotion is to remind the faithful of how Christ's coming to earth was made known through Mary, and how, on her giving her assent to be the Mother of God, the Incarnation actually took place. This devotion was introduced by the Franciscans in 1263.

The Rosary is one of the most popular, universal devotions of the Catholic Church. It is a form of prayer in honor of Mary. Its outward form is a string of beads. Its inner form is a series of ten "Hail Marys," or decades, each beginning with the "Lord's Prayer," and at the conclusion of these saying the Doxology ("Glory be to the Father"). The complete rosary is made up of fifteen decades, and each five decades is devoted to meditation on certain mysteries of redemption: joyful, sorrowful, and glorious. It is used by all classes, by rich and poor alike, and from the peasant to the pope.

"A plenary indulgence is granted to all who after confession and Holy Communion say five decades of the rosary in a church or chapel where the Blessed Sacrament is reserved." (*National Catholic Almanac*, p. 299)

Rosary beads have been designed as an aid in counting the prayers. Their usual form is a chaplet of five decades, with crucifix, and four beads on which at the beginning of the rosary are said the Apostles' Creed, one Lord's Prayer, three Hail Marys, and one Glory be to the Father. At the completion of the rosary a "Hail, Holy Queen" is said as follows:

Catholic Almanac, "has been accompanied or followed by extraordinary graces and blessings." But there is no obligation on individual Catholics to believe with faith that any of these are miracles. The approbation of the Church simply means that these can be piously believed.

"Hail, holy Queen, Mother of Mercy! our life, our sweetness, and our hope! To thee do we cry, poor banished children of Eve; to thee do we send up our sighs, mourning and weeping in the valley of tears. Turn, then, most gracious Advocate, thine eyes of mercy toward us; and after this our exile show unto us the blessed fruit of thy womb, Jesus; O clement, O loving, O sweet Virgin Mary."

"Pray for us, O holy Mother of God."

"That we may be made worthy of the promises of Christ."

The Rosary may be recited under most of the circumstances of life. It may be recited walking, sitting, or kneeling; at any time of the day; in the street, at home, while riding to work; in trains, automobiles, boats, airplanes; or it can be used as morning or evening prayers. It is a communion which unites words of meditation with mental spiritual exercises and holy silence.

October is dedicated to the Rosary, and a feast has been instituted in honor of it on the seventh day of October each year.

THE PROTESTANT POINT OF VIEW
On the Significance of Mary the Mother of Jesus

Protestantism does not venerate the Virgin Mary because, on scriptural grounds, it accepts Mary not as the "Mother of God," but as the human mother of Christ.

Protestants are at an absolute loss when it comes to appreciating the Roman Catholic attitude in regard to the Virgin Mary. They can understand how Roman Catholics might honor her and love her; but they cannot appreciate the so-called veneration of Mary, praying to her, requiring that all believe in her immaculate conception, and her alleged bodily assumption into heaven. Where in the Scriptures, they ask, can such dogmas find the slightest foundation of verification?

If Roman Catholics find Mary helpful in their worship of God, without taking from him all due honor, then that is their privilege. But they should not insist that others are failing in true worship if they do not do likewise. Protestants exalt Mary and the Holy Family at the Christmas season. They worship with her during Holy Week at the foot of the Cross. They expect to meet her in heaven. Protestants think of Mary as the ideal mother, but never as the "Mother of God." Considerate Protestants will say that her alleged appearances, miracles, and special blessings verge on the side of superstition—if they are taken in any literal sense, as they are by many in the Roman Catholic Church.

The Place of Mary in Protestantism

Protestants read in Acts 1:14 that "These all continued with one accord in prayer and supplication with the women and Mary the mother of Jesus and his brothers." They still retain this basis of fellowship and association with the mother of Jesus. She remains to them the model of motherhood and they hold her in esteem every time they recite in the Apostles' Creed the words, "born of the Virgin Mary." Protestants, in creating their estimation of Mary, turn to the Scriptures where they find the following verses referring to her. In Luke 1:47 Mary claims God as her Saviour. Elizabeth, in Luke 1:42, calls her "blessed among women." Christ, we find in Luke 2:51, was subject to his parents. In John 2:4 and Matthew 12:46-52 we find that Jesus places Mary on the same level as any other mother, while placing his own mission above family ties. Brothers and sisters of Jesus are mentioned in Matthew 12:56.

The Protestant position is stated by David Schaff in *Our Fathers Faith and Ours*: "For Protestants, the Roman figure of Mary, is an ecclesiastical fiction which has grown with the centuries until it was turned into a dogma by the arbitrary utterance of Pius IX, that she was born without sin. Mariology may have its historical significance during the age of chivalry in exalting womanly purity but the Scriptures have no syllable to justify it. . . . Sinners do not need Mary's mediation to reach their Saviour and through him to reach God, for they 'have an advocate with the Father, even Jesus Christ the righteous, who is the propitiation for our sins and also for the sins of the whole world.'—I John 2:1." (pp. 458-459)

Scripture References to Mary

The following New Testament passages refer to Mary the mother of Jesus:

"Now the birth of Jesus Christ was on this wise: when as his mother Mary was espoused to Joseph, before they came to-

gether, she was found with child of the Holy Ghost" (Matt.
1:18; also Luke 2:1-16).

"And Joseph and his mother marvelled at those things which
were spoken of him" (Luke 2:33).

"And when they saw him [in the Temple] they were amazed;
and his mother said unto him, 'Son, why hast thou thus dealt with
us? Behold, thy father and I have sought thee sorrowing!'"
(Luke 2:48).

"And he said unto them, 'How is it that ye sought me? wist
ye not that I must be about my Father's business?' And they
understood not the saying which he spoke unto them. And he
went down with them, and came to Nazareth, and was subject unto them: but his mother kept all these sayings in her
heart" (Luke 2:44).

"Now there stood by the cross of Jesus his mother. . . .
When Jesus therefore saw his mother, and the disciple stand-
ing by whom he loved, he saith unto his mother, Woman, be-
hold thy son! Then saith he to the disciple, Behold thy mother!
And from that hour that disciple took her into his own home"
(John 19:25-27).

"And when they [the Apostles] were come in, they went
up into an upper room. . . . There all continued with one
accord in prayer and supplication, with the women, and Mary
the mother of Jesus, and with his brethren" (Acts 1:13-14).

In none of these Scripture passages is there the slightest indication of the Immaculate Conception, the Assumption, or Mary
as the "Mother of God." Mary is pictured as being rebuked by
Jesus (John 2:4) and not sure of her own role (Luke 2:50).
Protestants accept the New Testament version of Mary. This
would include her beautiful song:

"My soul doth magnify the Lord. And my spirit hath rejoiced
in God my Saviour. For he hath regarded the low estate of his
handmaiden: for, behold, from henceforth all generations shall
call me blessed. For he that is mighty hath done to me great
things; and holy is his name. And his mercy is on them that fear
him, from generation to generation. He hath showed strength
with his arm: he hath scattered the proud in the imagination of
their hearts. He hath put down the mighty from their seats and
exalted them of low degree. He hath filled the hungry with good
things and the rich he hath sent empty away. He hath holpen
his servant Israel, in remembrance of his mercy; as he spake to

our fathers, to Abraham, and to his seed for ever" (Luke 1:
46-55).

PROTESTANT REFERENCE BOOKS: *Jesus of Nazareth* by George A.
Barton, Chap. X; *American Freedom and Catholic Power* by Paul
Blanshard (note pages in Index listed under Virgin Mary); *Lord of
All Life* by A. Ian Burnett, Chap. I; *The Jesus of History* by T. R.
Glover, Chap. II; *A Life of Jesus* by Edgar J. Goodspeed, Chap. I;
The Life and Teachings of Jesus by Charles Foster Kent, pp. 43-48;
The Story of Jesus Christ by Elizabeth Stuart Phelps, first section
called "Presage"; *Our Fathers Faith and Ours* by David S. Schaff,
Chap. XXIV.

12

Marriage, Divorce,
the Family, and Birth Control

Marriage, in the Roman Catholic Church, is a holy thing, and is raised to the position of a sacrament. The family gets its inspiration from Mary and the Holy Family. Because marriage is such a sublime matter in the eyes of Catholics—involving their co-operation with God in the propagation of the human race—divorce is not allowed and birth control is forbidden.

Protestants and Roman Catholics agree very largely on the purpose and aims of marriage. They agree that the family is the basis of national life, and is of particular significance to the Christian Church. But in theory at least, and many feel in practice also, they disagree upon the feasibility of divorce and the right to use birth control information.

Whether the Roman Catholic family is better morally and spiritually than the Protestant family is a matter of opinion and debate. But not so with the Catholic marriage laws and regulations. They are clear, rigid, and binding. They are spelled out by the Church in great detail. While it is not possible to develop here every doctrine and ruling in regard to marriage, divorce, the family, and birth control, we shall report on those aspects which are of special interest and concern to Protestants.

THE ROMAN CATHOLIC POSITION

The Marriage Contract

Thousands of men and women are being married every day. Outside of the Roman Catholic Church these marriages are on the basis of a civil contract, plus in many cases a religious ceremony. The Roman Catholic Church recognizes these couples as truly married; it even considers the marriage of baptized non-

Catholics as a sacrament. And to Catholics the contract and the sacrament are inseparable—if the parties have been baptized.

As a contract marriage is a pact, or a mutual agreement, whereby a man and a woman give to each other the rights of sexual relations and other normal conditions of married life, such as cohabitation and co-operation in common needs and interests. Therefore one who is permanently impotent is barred from marriage, and one who is devoid of reasoning powers cannot marry. And one who does not know what is involved in the marriage contract is not truly married, nor is a person who does not intend to fulfill the obligations of marriage.

A true marriage contract must have the following features:

1. It must be freely given.
2. It must be expressed externally or publicly.
3. It must, in order to become absolutely indissoluble, be consummated.

The public authority for the baptized is the Church; for non-baptized, it is the civil government.

Matrimony as a Sacrament

According to the Roman Catholic Church, as defined by the Council of Trent: (1) matrimony is a sacrament instituted by Christ; (2) a Christian is forbidden by divine law to have several wives at the same time; (3) the Church has power to create impediments making it unlawful or impossible for people to contract marriage in certain circumstances; (4) the marriage bond cannot be broken by adultery; (5) the marriage bond cannot be broken by heresy, ill-temper, or desertion; (6) the Church has the power to grant a separation, but not to contract a new marriage while both parties are still living; (7) clerics in Holy Orders, and others who have taken a solemn vow of chastity, cannot contract a valid marriage; (8) marriage not consummated can be dissolved by the solemn religious profession of either party.

According to *A Catechism of Christian Doctrine*, "Matrimony is the sacrament by which a baptized man and a baptized woman bind themselves for life in a lawful marriage and receive the grace to discharge their duties.

"Though unbaptized persons can be truly married, only baptized persons can be united in the sacrament of Matrimony and receive the graces of the sacrament.

"God instituted marriage when He made Eve as a helpmate for Adam in the garden of Eden.

"We know from the constant tradition of the Church that marriage was made a sacrament by Our Lord sometime during His life on earth.

"The outward sign in the sacrament of Matrimony is the external expression by the man and woman of their mutual consent to give themselves to each other as husband and wife.

"The sacrament of Matrimony is administered by the contracting parties, each of whom confers the sacrament on the other."

In Order to Be Truly Married

In answer to the question, "In whose presence do the laws of the Church require a Catholic to be married?", the *Baltimore Catechism* gives the following answer: "The laws of the Church require a Catholic to be married in the presence of the parish priest, or the bishop of the diocese, or a priest delegated by either of them, and before two witnesses.

(a) The marriage of a Catholic before a minister or a civil official, such as a judge, a justice of the peace, a squire, or any clerk of court, is not really a marriage.

(b) Catholics who live together after such a marriage are living in sin just as much as if they had never gone through such a ceremony.

(c) Catholics who attempt marriage in this fashion commit a mortal sin and incur other punishments of the Church."

How to Have a Successful Marriage

From the Roman Catholic position a successful marriage is insured if the following conditions are met: first, careful preparation for marriage and, second, the receiving of God's blessing for the marriage.

The Roman Catholic Church gives this counsel to those preparing to enter the holy bond of matrimony: seek God's guidance in the choice of a mate; secure the advice of parents and confessors; practice the virtues, particularly chastity; receive frequently the sacraments of Penance and Holy Eucharist. It is bold to say that sinful and unhappy marriages very often result from the company-keeping of Catholics with non-Catholics. "Catholics who are eligible and who intend to marry should keep company only with Catholics" is the subsequent advice given in *A Catechism of Christian Doctrine* (p. 367). The Roman Catholic Church tells the faithful that the best way to obtain God's blessing for marriage is by being married at a Nuptial Mass and by receiving Holy Communion devoutly.

Mixed Marriages

Marriage to a non-Catholic is forbidden by the Church, and is tolerated only on the basis of a specific dispensation. According to the *Baltimore Catechism*, "the Church forbids Catholics to marry non-Catholics because mixed marriages often bring about family discord, loss of faith on the part of the Catholic, and neglect of the religious training of the children."

When, for grave reasons, the Roman Catholic Church grants permission for a mixed marriage by means of a dispensation, it demands that all danger to the faith of the Catholic party be removed; that the non-Catholic party must promise, in writing, that he will not interfere with the faith of the Catholic, and both must promise that all the children born of the marriage will be baptized in the Roman Catholic Church alone and be educated solely in the Roman Catholic religion. On the other hand, the Catholic party must promise to strive for the conversion of the non-Catholic by prayer and good example.

No Divorce

Under no circumstances will the Roman Catholic Church grant a divorce. In fact it does not recognize such a thing as divorce by any *human* power. This does not mean "that *God* cannot grant divorces for sufficient reasons." (Father Connell in *Matrimony*, p. 20) It is the teaching of the Church that "once a man and woman are completely united in the sacrament of Matrimony, they remain truly husband and wife until the death of either of them. A separation, a divorce, or an attempted marriage with another person does not destroy the marriage bond." (*Baltimore Catechism*)

Due to this union in marriage, any other sexual union during the life of either party is considered adultery. Moreover, the Church declares that laws which permit remarriage during the life of husband or wife are contrary to the laws of God. According to *A Catechism of Christian Doctrine*, "Even though civil law may permit remarriage, such a marriage is sinful and not really a marriage at all, but rather an adulterous union." (p. 362)

While the Roman Catholic Church does not believe in divorce, it does believe in separation and annulment under certain conditions. It sometimes grants a separation of husband and wife because of cruelty or adultery, but will not permit either of them to marry again during the lifetime of the other. (In *Apologetics and Catholic Doctrine,* page 261, these other causes justify a decree of separation: joining a non-Catholic sect; giving the children a non-Catholic education; living a criminal and ignominious life; causing grave danger to soul or body of the partner.)

After detailed examination the Holy See may reach the conclusion that a marriage which appears to be valid is, in reality, no true marriage.[1] Such a decision is not a dissolution of the marriage bond; it is a declaration that as a matter of fact there never existed, even from the beginning, any real marriage.[2] Some of the chief reasons for an annulment are:

"A Marriage is invalid, if entered into because of violence or grave fear, inflicted unjustly and from without, to escape which one is forced to choose Marriage." (*Canon Law 1087*) "If either party or both by a positive act of the will exclude the marriage itself . . . or any essential property of marriage, the contract is invalid." (*Canon Law 1086,* No. 2) Other causes for annulment [3]

---

[1] "Annulment—a declaration by ecclesiastical or civil authorities that a reputed marriage never was a marriage, i.e., valid, because owing to some known or hidden invalidating impediment it was not contracted validly and is therefore null and void."—*The Catholic Encyclopedia.*

[2] *The Pauline Privilege*—"According to a passage in St. Paul's First Epistle to the Corinthians (7:12-15), if two unbaptized persons have been married, and later one of them embraces the Christian faith and is baptized, and the other refuses to dwell with the convert, or renders the practice of religion very difficult to him or her, or is an occasion of sin—in such a case the Christian party is permitted to contract another marriage (with a Christian), thus dissolving the previous marital bond. According to Church law, there must be formal *interpellations* or questioning before this may be done—that is, the Christian party must ask the non-Christian if he or she is willing to be converted also, or at least to co-habit peacefully. This is called the Pauline Privilege."—Francis J. Connell, C.SS.R., S.T.D., *Matrimony,* p. 21.

[3] The full list of impediments is given under the topic of "Marriage" in *The Catholic Encyclopedia.*

Technically a couple are married when they make the contract, and the essence of marriage, from the Roman Catholic point of view, consists in the contract which cannot be dissolved by merely human authority. If the marriage is not consummated, it can, for serious reasons, be *dissolved* by the pope, by divine authority which Roman Catholic tradition maintains he has from God. Likewise, by divine authority, according to the Roman

are failure to consummate marriage; previous marriage; boys under the age of sixteen and girls under fourteen; relationship in
the third degree of consanguinity, and impediment of spiritual
relationship (when not covered by proper dispensations); the
marriage having been performed in the absence of the parish
priest and the required two witnesses. (Note exceptions on p.
57.)

In the matter of annulment, the Church has the same laws
for rich and poor alike. History proves that the powerful have
been refused annulments as well as the weak. Pope Pius VII,
for example, refused to grant a decree to Napoleon's brother,
who had in 1803 married Miss Patterson, a Protestant girl of
Baltimore. He wrote, in part, to Napoleon, "Your Majesty will
understand that upon the information thus far received by us
it is not in our power to pronounce a sentence of nullity. We
cannot utter a judgment in opposition to the rules of the Church,
and we could not, without laying aside those rules, decree the
invalidity of a union which, according to the Word of God, no
human power can sunder."

The Roman Catholic Family

To Roman Catholics the family is a holy institution. The chief
purpose of marriage is the propagation of the human race. But
it is also for the purpose of "bringing forth of children for the
Church, fellow-citizens with the saints, and the domestics of
God; so that a people might be born, and brought up for the
worship and religion of the true God and our Savior Jesus
Christ." (Pope Leo XIII in encyclical letter *Arcanum Divinae
Sapientiae*)

In the home the husband is the chief of the family and head
of the wife. The wife must be subject to her husband and obey
him, not as a servant, but as a companion. The relationship of
husband and wife is that of Christ and his Church, the husband
representing Christ and the wife the Church. Children are required to submit to their parents and obey them, and to give
them honor for conscience's sake. Parents, on the other hand, are

---

Catholic Church, a non-consummated marriage is dissolved by solemn religious profession of one of the parties. The *dissolution* of the marriage in
the "Pauline Privilege" case is also by divine authority. These are not annulments (since in these cases there is a true marriage), but real *dissolutions*
of the marriage bond.

bound to give every possible care and watchful thought to the education of their children in the Catholic faith.

While the burdens of the Catholic home are not always light, it can count on the strength which comes from the sacrament of Matrimony. Thus the Catholic home is a holy place, which has as its model the Holy Family. It is far more than a human relationship. The contracting parties are joined in both body and soul, which raises them above the union of animals and the haphazard unions of men. Home, to the Roman Catholic, is a divine institution and must be regarded as such. The enemies of the home are the enemies of God.

Birth Control

The Roman Catholic Church considers birth control as one of the principal enemies of marriage and the home. Roman Catholics are opposed to any form of birth control which violates the natural purpose of sexual intercourse. They do, however, permit couples to limit offspring by means of abstinence and continence. In other words, Catholic married couples are not required to have children to the utmost capacity of the mother for childbearing. (Father Conway, *Question Box,* p. 339)

Nor are Roman Catholics forbidden to have sexual intercourse except for the sake of having children. This is its main purpose. But if it brings closer spiritual unity between husband and wife, even at times when conception is not likely to take place, it is allowed. The periodic method falls into this natural category. As Pope Pius XI has said (Encyclical letter on Christian Marriage, 1931), "Married people do not sin if they make use of their marital privileges in the proper manner, although at a time when, because of natural reasons either of time or of certain other defects, new life cannot be conceived, or is less likely to be conceived."

It is, however, considered unlawful and sinful for either husband or wife to prevent birth by use of any kind of chemical, mechanical, or other artificial means.

Pope Pius XI makes this very plain, in the same encyclical letter quoted above, when he says, "Any use whatsoever of marriage exercised in such a way that the act is deliberately frustrated in its natural power to generate life is an offense against the law of God and of nature, and those who indulge in such are branded with the guilt of grave sin."

The Roman Catholic Church is dead-set against birth prevention. As is stressed in the *National Catholic Almanac* (p. 581), under no circumstances whatsoever will the Church modify or destroy the fundamental natural law of morality which forbids the practice of contraception. It is against unnatural birth control in every form, whether by interrupted intercourse, the use of preventive measures, or artificial sterilization.[4]

Not only does the Roman Catholic Church oppose birth control because it is alleged to be contrary to God's moral law, but because of its "evil consequences." Father Dominic Pruemmer in his booklet entitled *Birth Control*, published by the Paulist Press and bearing the Imprimatur of the late Patrick Cardinal Hayes, takes the following positions:

"Birth control leads necessarily to moral and religious degeneracy" (p. 12). "Birth control is nothing else than mutual masturbation or unnatural lust" (p. 13). "The unnatural fear of conception leads to the hatred of the child" (p. 13). "The one-and-two-children system is a deadly foe of good education" (p. 14).

"Birth control also exerts a pernicious influence on the common good and produces economic decay. . . . The unparalleled economic development of the United States would be unthinkable but for the rapid increase of population during the last decades" (pp. 14 and 15). "Birth control also impairs the personal welfare of the couple . . . since it violates the natural law, and every violation of the natural law must be expiated by the person guilty of the violation" (pp. 15 and 16). "Birth control is a devastating plague which threatens death and ruin for all modern society. . . . Birth control is nothing but unchaste lust exercised by man and woman, and is thus a perversion of sex. But when such sexual perversity is practiced by many, it gradually develops into a universal social evil which spreads like a raging conflagration" (pp. 17 and 18).

Pope Pius XI sums up the attitude of the Roman Catholic Church regarding birth control when he says (in the same encyclical), "Since, therefore, the conjugal act is destined primarily by nature for the begetting of children, those who in exercising it deliberately frustrate its natural power and purpose sin against

---

[4] For a study of the "rhythm method," which is permitted by the Roman Catholic Church, since it is natural and does not employ artificial means to prevent birth, see *The Rhythm of Sterility and Fertility in Women* by Leo J. Latz, M.D., published with ecclesiastical approbation and having an introduction by a member of the Society of Jesus.

nature and commit a deed which is shameful and intrinsically vicious."

The Sin of Abortion

Abortion, according to Roman Catholic teaching, is a murderous attack on the life of the unborn child. While birth control *prevents* human life, abortion *destroys* life. (Both are serious sins, according to the Roman Catholic Church.) All those who perform, or even assist in any way, an abortion are guilty of a crime to which the Church attaches the penalty of excommunication. (*Father Smith Instructs Jackson*, p. 100; also *Canon Law 2350*) Miscarriage, artificially produced, is also a grave sin and carries the penalty of excommunication. (*A Catholic Dictionary*, p. 3)

Pope Pius XI, in his encyclical letter *Casti Connubi*, 1930, gives the official position of the Church on what he calls a "very grave crime," when he says, "However much we may pity the mother whose health and even life is gravely imperilled in the performance of the duty allotted to her by nature, nevertheless what could ever be a sufficient reason for excusing in any way the direct murder of the innocent? This is precisely what we are dealing with here. Whether inflicted upon the mother or upon the child, it is against the precept of God and the law of nature: 'Thou shalt not kill.' The life of each is equally sacred, and no one has the power, not even the public authority, to destroy it."

THE PROTESTANT POINT OF VIEW
On Marriage, Divorce, and Planned Parenthood

Protestantism differs with Roman Catholicism on marriage, divorce, and birth control because in these areas it believes that the spirit, rather than the letter of the law, should be the guiding principle.

Protestants cannot agree with Roman Catholics concerning marriage, divorce, the family, and birth control; they do not agree entirely among themselves in regard to these matters. Although they do not consider marriage a sacrament, they do consider it a holy and sacred bond. While most denominations permit divorce, and the remarriage of the innocent party, this does not mean that they encourage divorce. Quite the contrary. They seek to have a strong, solid family life. And while they do not oppose birth control, on moral or religious grounds, they believe that common sense, founded upon morality, should control its practice.

Protestants are in complete agreement with Roman Catholics that everything possible should be done to strengthen Christian family life and link it more closely to the Church. America needs homes which are rooted in Christian principles. What troubles Protestants is not the strong moral teachings of the Roman Catholic Church concerning marriage and family life, but the attempted control by the Roman Catholic Church of non-Roman Catholic private lives and thinking. This is particularly true in the case of birth control. Some Protestants are against birth control; others are not. They desire, however, to be free from the dictates of the Roman Catholic Church in such a matter. When it tries to legislate for all citizens, when it forces doctors to withhold birth control information, when it condemns international peace organizations which may advocate artificial regulation of population, then Protestants feel that the Roman Catholic Church is stepping beyond its rightful authority. It can control the individual lives of its own members; but it has no right to insist that the rest of the world community shall behave as Roman Catholics.

"Not Inadvisedly or Lightly"

Protestants follow the statement of Bishop Latimer when he declared in a sermon preached at Stamford, England, that "they cannot deny marriage by any Scriptures, but that the marriage of priests is as good and godly as the marriage of any other man, for wedlock is honorable among all men and the wedding bed undefiled." The *Thirty-nine Articles* declared that "it is lawful for bishops, priests and deacons, and for all other men to marry at their own discretion," while the *Westminster Confession* maintained that "monastical vows of perpetual single life, far from being a dogma of higher perfection, are a superstitious and sinful snare in which no Christian may entangle himself." From the Protestant point of view, marriage is a permanent union and, according to the *Book of Common Prayer*, "it is not to be entered into inadvisedly or lightly, but advisedly, soberly and in the fear of God."

Protestants, taking into account Christ's words as recorded in

Matthew 19:9, while often denouncing the "divorce evil," do not declare legal divorces invalid. The Protestant Episcopal Church in general refuses to admit to communion persons who have re-married after divorce—but each case is left to the discretion of the Bishop. The *Westminster Confession* lists willful desertion as proper grounds for divorce. While various churches, and cler-gymen, have different ways of interpreting the teaching of the New Testament regarding divorce, all of them make their deci-sions upon the basis of real happiness, personally and in the home, and in regard to the relationship of the couple to the church and to society in general. The family, particularly where children are involved, is a sacred institution to Protestants. The family, the home, the church, and the community are all of one piece. They are interrelated and when one suffers all the others suffer with it.

Birth control is not a theological issue in Protestant churches or homes. It is discussed upon practical, as well as scientific and medical grounds. The former Federal Council of Churches, on the basis of answers to a questionnaire sent out from Johns Hop-kins Medical School, endorsed the right of married couples to receive birth control counsel from their physicians. On the whole, Protestant churches, while giving warnings and stressing limita-tions, take a favorable attitude toward the practice of "planned parenthood."

Dr. G. Bromley Oxnam, Methodist Bishop of Washington, D.C., states the case this way: "When we make available to mothers sound scientific information which is used for the high moral objective of bringing to our families healthy, happy children, we are wisely using scientific means for moral ends. Religious leaders are awake to the dangers of family life which planned parenthood can help to correct. Communities which fail to pro-vide proper marriage counseling, sex education, and child-spac-ing service are recreant to their trust." [5]

Turning to the Bible

Protestants turn to their Bibles to secure guidance for mar-riage, divorce, and family life. Jesus blessed the marriage at Cana with his presence (John 2:1-11). The home of Jesus serves as the model for the Christian family (Luke 2:51-52). And the

---

[5] *Planning Your Family* by Herbert Yahraes, Public Affairs Pamphlet No. 136, p. 11.

home of Mary and Martha was a place of spiritual refreshment for the Master.

The New Testament teaching on divorce (Matt. 5:31-32), where Christ permits a writ of divorce, in the case of adultery, is accepted by most Protestants as providing scriptural grounds for divorce.

Protestants can find no moral law against birth control in the Bible.

In regard to husband and wife relations Paul has much to say (Rom. 7:1-3; I Cor. 7:8-15, 39-40; Col. 3:18-19). The essence of Paul's teaching is that a man and wife should honor the marriage bond, lead pure lives, establish Christian homes in which children will be nurtured in the love of God.

PROTESTANT REFERENCE BOOKS: (Two leaflets which may be secured from the Joint Department of Family Life, National Council of Churches, are recommended: *If I Marry a Roman Catholic,* and *Christian Marriage.*)   *The Fine Art of Living Together* by Albert W. Beaven; *Thinking About Marriage* by Roy A. Burkhart; *A Social Theory of Religious Education* by George A. Coe; *Youth and the Homes of Tomorrow* by Edwin T. Dahlberg; *Religion and Social Justice* by Sherwood Eddy; *The Reconstruction of Religion* by Charles A. Ellwood, Chaps. VI-VIII; *American Marriage and Family Relationships* by Ernest R. Groves and William F. Ogburn; *Readings in the Family* by Ernest R. Groves and Lee M. Brooks; *Wholesome Marriage* by Ernest R. Groves and Gladys H. Groves; *The Fate of the Family* by Arthur E. Holt; *Christian Ethics and Modern Problems* by W. R. Inge, p. 283; *The Modern Family and the Church* by Regina Westcott Wieman, pp. 333 ff.; *Foundations of Happiness in Marriage* and *Pastoral Counseling in Family Relationships* by Leland Foster Wood; *This Man and This Woman* by F. W. Brink.

13

Miracle of the Mass

Protestants and Roman Catholics are probably farther apart in the celebration of the Mass than at any other point. For here, as manifested in the Protestant Reformation, there is a clash of conviction on essential principles. To the Roman Catholic the Mass is the very epitome of his faith; to the Protestant it is something to be repudiated.

Most Protestants, although understanding many features of the Roman Catholic faith with some measure of appreciation, are usually at a total loss when it comes to the Mass. (The exception would be high churchmen of the Episcopal Church.) For many Protestants the Mass seems to be superstition placed in a colorful setting and accompanied by strange incantations in a foreign tongue. Catholics understand it, appreciate it, and find spiritual life through it. The all-important functions of their Church center about it.

Every single day throughout the world, Mass is offered to tens of thousands of the faithful on thousands of altars. Here, at what they think of as the great Sacrifice, they find strength for their daily cares, and grace to fight the battle of faith. All Roman Catholic conventions begin with Mass. When a conclave of cardinals is called to elect a new pope, it opens with Mass. At marriage and at death the Mass plays an all-important part.

In this chapter we shall see why the Mass plays such a vital part in the life of the Roman Catholic Church.

THE ROMAN CATHOLIC POSITION

Definition of the Mass

"The Mass is the Sacrifice of the New Law in which Christ, through the ministry of the priest, offers Himself to God in an unbloody manner under the appearance of bread and wine," is

144

the official definition as given in *A Catechism of Christian Doctrine.* (p. 281)

The name "Mass" comes from the latin word *Missa,* meaning dismissal. In the early church it was the signal, with the singing of the *Ite Missa Est,* that the entire sacrifice had been completed. The sacrifice of the Mass is, according to Roman Catholic teaching, the same sacrifice as the one on the Cross because the victim is the same, and the principal priest is the same, both being Jesus Christ. Christ, though invisible, is the principal minister, offering Himself in the Mass. The actual priest is the visible, and secondary minister, who offers Christ in the Mass.

Different Parts of the Mass

Consecration is the most important part of the Mass. For in the Consecration, according to Roman Catholic belief, the bread and wine are changed into the body and blood of Christ, who then becomes actually present on the altar. The other important parts of the Mass are the Offertory and the Communion. During the Offertory the priest offers to God the bread and wine that Catholics believe are to be changed into the real body and blood of Christ. It is this body and blood of Christ which the priest and the people receive in the Communion.

In this eucharistic sacrifice, with its liturgy of prayers and ceremonies, the purposes for which the Mass is offered are these:

1. To adore God as our Creator and God.
2. To thank God for his many favors.
3. To ask God to bestow his blessings on all men.
4. To satisfy the Justice of God for the sins committed against Him.

Besides these purposes are the fruits of the Mass which consist of "the blessings that God bestows through the Mass upon the celebrant, upon those who serve or assist at it, upon the person or persons for whom it is offered, and also upon all mankind, especially the members of the Church and the souls in purgatory." (*A Catechism of Christian Doctrine,* p. 286)

Various Kinds

There are four types of Mass,[1] each equally true and a proper offering of the sacrifice, from the Roman Catholic viewpoint.

---

[1] For an exposition on the music of the Mass the reader is referred to the *Catholic Encyclopedia* under the topic "Music of the Mass."

They are (1) Pontifical Mass (of which Papal Mass is a special form); (2) Solemn Mass; (3) High Mass; and (4) Low Mass.

The first is celebrated by the pope, a bishop, or by certain other prelates. The second, or Solemn Mass, is celebrated by a priest who is immediately assisted by a deacon and a subdeacon, and in which certain portions are sung by the priests and other parts by the choir. In the third, or High Mass, the celebrating priest sings certain parts of the Mass while other parts are sung by the choir. Low Mass is a modified form of High Mass in which the priest speaks all the parts, and is the most common way in which Mass is celebrated. The celebrant is assisted usually by one server or acolyte who is generally a layman or a boy, and there is no choir or incense. Low Mass is sometimes accompanied by the singing of Latin or vernacular hymns or chants and even by the recitation of prayers aloud. These, however, are extra-liturgical and do not belong to the Mass *per se*. Any of these Masses can be a Requiem Mass, or one which is offered for the dead. In this Mass the celebrant wears black vestments and reads or chants special prayers for the dead. A votive Mass is one that the priest offers according to his own wish, or that of the person requesting it. The votive Masses most frequently offered are the Mass of the Dead, and the Nuptial Mass.

Assisting at Mass

Roman Catholics, when they go to Mass, are expected to participate in it, or "assist at Mass." Even more, they actually offer Mass with the priest. Going to Mass is therefore not a passive or negative matter. All of the faithful are supposed not only to understand all that is taking place at the altar, but to follow Christ through the Mass, from His incarnation to his ascension.

While the priest uses Latin, the faithful now have translations which they follow in the missal. The priest, in the prayers, uses "we," indicating that the people are included, and the server, a layman, represents the laity at the altar. The priest also asks God to accept the confession of the congregation, and at a certain point turns and salutes the people. By kneeling, standing, or, while being seated, by partaking of the Communion, by making the sign of the Cross, by reciting the Rosary, and by striking the breast three times, the faithful actively participate in the Mass. "The best way of assisting at Mass is to unite with the priest in offering the Holy Sacrifice, and to receive Holy Communion." (*A Catechism of Christian Doctrine*, pp. 290-291)

Here are a few of the directives given to the people in connection with the Mass:

"The Priest returning to the middle of the altar, begins the 'Kyrie,' a cry for mercy to the Blessed Trinity. With him plead with God, the Father, with God, the Son, and with God, the Holy Ghost to have mercy on you and on all."

"The Offertory is the First Principal part of the Mass. Up to now you have been preparing yourself so that you may Participate in the Holy Sacrifice. And now the priest offers to God the bread and wine which he will soon change into Our Lord's Body and Blood for the remission of our sins and the sins of the whole world. Unite yourself in sentiment with the Priest and offer to God a Gift most pleasing to Him, a heart pure, humble, and contrite."

"We have now reached the Second Principal part of the Mass. The bell rings to warn us that the coming of the Lord is at hand. Make a short act of contrition at this solemn moment and with bowed head pray with the Priest."

"The bell rings as the Priest genuflects, again as he elevates the Host, and again when he genuflects.

"Your head was bowed in reverence during the consecration. But now lift it up, and look upon your Lord, saying:

    'My Lord and My God.'"

"(For saying this aspiration at this time an indulgence is granted.)" [2]

Symbols and Aids to the Mass

The Mass is a most colorful and dramatic service, with many symbolic features and many different kinds of accessories. To go into detail concerning all these would in itself require a book.[3] The best we can do here is to outline some of the more important elements.

The Altar: This is the first thing that strikes your attention upon entering a Catholic Church. In every chapel, church, or cathedral there is an altar. It is basic to the all-essential rite of the Church, that is, the sacrifice of the Mass. It is the place where the sacrifice of Christ takes place and symbolizes the long narrow table at which Christ and the apostles sat on the night of the Last Supper. Altars may be made either of wood or of marble. The altar-stone, at the center, contains relics and is consecrated by a bishop or by a prelate having authority. This special part is truly the altar, and no matter how elaborate the supports, sepulchre, or tabernacle may be, this simple consecrated stone is the one essential part.

---

[2] *Within the Sanctuary, The Mass, With Manual of Prayers,* pp. 17-36.

[3] See *The Ceremonies of the Mass* by the Reverend Carroll C. Smyth, The Paulist Press, New York.

The Tabernacle: Built in the center of the altar, usually covered by a canopy. In it the consecrated Host is reserved.

Altar Cross: High above the altar, where it may be seen by all, is the image of Christ nailed to the Cross. It is a reminder that the sacrifice about to be offered is the same as was offered on Calvary.

Candles: The candles, made of beeswax, symbolize the pure flesh of Jesus received from his Virgin Mother. The wick typifies the soul of Christ, the flame his divinity. These candles must be lighted during the Mass.

Sanctuary Lamp: The lamp, suspended from the ceiling, is kept burning night and day where the Blessed Sacrament is kept. The oil used in the sanctuary lamp is vegetable oil, representing purity, peace, and godliness.

Altar Cloths: The altar must be covered with three linen cloths. The reason for this is, according to Church law, "to have the altar cloths absorb the Precious Blood before It reaches the altar stone, if perchance any should be spilled." (*The Ceremonies of the Mass*, p. 7)

Vestments: The priest, before he celebrates Mass, clothes himself with vestments which signify the dignity of the solemn office which he is to perform. The amice, alb, cincture, maniple, stole, and chasuble are a reminder of the sufferings of Christ. Moreover, they cover the personality of the priest as much as possible, since, according to Catholic belief, he is taking the place of Christ.

Colors of the Vestments: White is worn on most of the feasts of Christ and the Virgin Mary, feasts of the other virgins, and of confessors. It is a symbol of purity. *Red,* a symbol of blood and fire, is worn on Pentecost and on the feasts of martyrs. *Green,* indicating hope, is used on ordinary Sundays between Epiphany and Septuagesima, and between Trinity Sunday and Advent. *Violet,* the sign of penance, is used during Lent and Advent, on ember days, as well as on the vigils of some of the greater feasts. *Black* is used on Good Friday and in Masses for the dead. *Gold* is sometimes substituted for white, red, and green.

Altar Wine: The validity of the Mass depends upon the genuine quality of the wine. It must be the pure juice of the grape, naturally and properly fermented.

Altar Bread: This second absolutely necessary element of the Mass, usually in the West in the form of round wafers, is made of wheaten flour mixed with natural water and baked in an oven between two heated irons. It is generally made by nuns and must not be corrupted.

The Chalice: The gold-lined cup in which the wine is consecrated.

Altar Missal: It is the book at the altar from which the priest reads the various parts of the liturgy of the Mass.

Altar Rail: The altar, or Communion, rail separates the sanctuary from the body of the church. The faithful kneel here to receive Holy

Communion. The ritual orders that "a linen cloth be extended before those who receive Communion in order to catch the Sacred Particle, if by accident It should fall from the hands of the priest" (*The Ceremonies of the Mass*, p. 16). In many churches today the gilt paten, with handle attached, is substituted for the cloth.

Why Catholics Go to Mass

It is a grievous sin for a Roman Catholic to miss Mass on a Sunday or a Holyday of Obligation. This is the first commandment of the Roman Catholic Church—put in a positive, rather than a negative, setting.

It is enough for Roman Catholics to say that the faithful must attend Mass because the Church commands. Catholics are supposed to obey. Yet there are good and valid reasons back of this commandment. The first is that the Christian should *adore* God. The second is that there is a duty of *reparation*. In the third place, the faithful need to make *petitions* to God. And, lastly, the faithful owe a duty of *thanksgiving*. All these are present in the Mass, which puts those who participate, according to Roman Catholics, in direct communion with Him who died on Mount Calvary for the sins of the world.

"The priest we behold, the vestments, the candles, the elements, the prayers, are but the machinery through which this tremendous effect is accomplished. So that when you assist at Mass you are actually brought into immediate contact with Christ on Calvary, you have applied to your soul the merits of His Passion, and He discharges for you the necessary duties which you owe to God." (*The Ceremonies of the Mass*, p. 23)

The Roman Catholic Church commands its members to attend Mass for the good of their immortal souls.

Communion of Priest and People

After the priest in the Mass has consumed "the Body and Blood of our Lord," those who are to receive Communion approach the altar rail. (It must be borne in mind that in the Roman Catholic Church the priest partakes of both the elements, while the congregation partakes of the Eucharist under the appearance of bread alone. The Church believes it is unnecessary to serve both kinds, since Christ comes complete in either element.) The priest then removes from the tabernacle the *ciborium*, which contains the "Sacred Hosts," and after absolving the people of their sins he administers the sacrament to those at the altar, saying, *"May the Body of our Lord Christ preserve your soul to everlasting life. Amen."*

Why Latin Is Used

Latin is the universal language of the Roman Catholic Church. No matter where one may travel he will always find the same Latin and the same ceremonies used in the Mass. This makes the worshiper feel at home, and not a stranger. The Church began at a time when Latin was the best-known language throughout the world. It is still used, not only for the practical purpose of communication with Rome, but to express the unity and harmony of all Catholics in matters of religion. For the benefit of the worshipers, so that they may the better assist at the Mass, missals are printed in the vernacular.

Sacrifice on the Cross and of the Mass

In describing the difference between the original sacrifice of Christ on the Cross, and the sacrifice which takes place during the Mass, the *Baltimore Catechism* says: "The manner in which the sacrifice is offered is different: On the cross Christ physically shed His blood and was physically slain, while in the Mass there is no physical shedding of blood nor physical death, because Christ can die no more; on the cross Christ gained merit and satisfied for us, while in the Mass He applies to us the merits and satisfaction of His death on the cross."

What Mass Means to the Roman Catholic

In *Loss and Gain*, the real meaning of the Mass for Catholics is summarized by Cardinal Newman: "To me nothing is so consoling, so piercing, so thrilling, so overcoming, as the Mass, said as it is among us. I could attend Mass forever and not be tired— it is not a mere form of words, it is a great action, the greatest action that can be on earth. It is not the invocation merely, but, if I dare use the word, the evocation of the Eternal. He becomes present on the altar in Flesh and Blood, before whom Angels bow and devils tremble. This is the awful event which is the end, and is the interpretation of every part of the solemnity.

"So we, all around, each in his place, look out for the great Advent, waiting for the moving of the water. Each in his place, with his own heart, with his own intentions, with his own prayers, separate but concordant, watching what is going on, not painfully and hopefully following a hard form of prayer from beginning to end, but like a concert of musical instruments each different but concurring in a sweet harmony, we take our part with God's priest, supporting him yet guided by him.

"There are little children there, old men, simple laborers and students in seminaries, priests preparing for Mass, priests making their thanksgiving; there are innocent maidens and there are penitents, but out of these many minds rises one Eucharistic hymn and the great action is the measure and the scope of it."

THE PROTESTANT POINT OF VIEW
On the Sacrifice of Christ upon the Cross

Protestantism repudiates "the miracle of the Mass" because it believes that no miracle occurs and that one is not at all necessary.

Protestants cannot accept Roman Catholic belief concerning the sacrifice of the Mass. They believe that the whole principle of it is contrary to the teachings of the New Testament. They cannot find in the Bible anything to justify the Mass; they find many teachings which directly contradict it. They believe that Christ's death on the Cross, once and for all, is sufficient. There is no need for any repetition.[4] Moreover, most Protestants cannot accept the doctrine of the "real presence," that is, in bodily form. They believe that Christ comes to worshipers at Communion in various ways—along with the elements. Some believe in a physical presence. Most of them can see no advantage which might come through a miracle which does not already come to them by having Christ's real spirit present.

The Lord's Supper or Holy Communion, while being observed differently by various denominations, has a most significant place in the life of Protestant churches. Church members are richly blessed at the Communion Table in their spiritual fellowship with Christ. When all Protestants can agree to meet together at the Table, it will indicate that they have truly found their *living* Lord and are willing to share him spiritually with one another.

---

[4] At the Lund Conference it was declared that "In his [Christ] one perfect and sufficient sacrifice on Calvary he offered perfect obedience to the Father in atonement for the sin of the whole world. This was an act of expiation made once and for all and is unrepeatable."

Why Protestants Repudiate the Mass

Protestants have always taken a positive position in repudiating the Mass. They believe that Christ, once and for all, suffered and died on the cross for the salvation of sinners. They maintain, on the basis of Scripture (I Cor. 5:7; Heb. 10:26) that there remains no more reason for further sacrifice as far as Christ is concerned; that he is "our passover," having been sacrificed for us, and no further sacrifices prevail. The *Book of Common Prayer* speaks of Christ's "oblation of himself on the cross as a full, perfect and sufficient oblation and satisfaction for the sins of the whole world." The *Westminster Confession* puts it strongly, declaring that "sacrifice of the mass to be most abominously injurious to Christ's one only sacrifice, the alone propitiation for all the sins of the elect."

The Protestant position is well stated by Bishop Latimer: "According as the serpent was lifted up in the wilderness, so would Christ himself be exalted that thereby as many as trusted in him should have salvation. . . . They would have us saved by a daily oblation propitiatory, by a sacrifice expiatory or remissory. . . . Let us trust upon Christ's only death and look for none other sacrifice propitiatory than the same bloody sacrifice, the lively sacrifice, not the dry sacrifice but a bloody sacrifice. For Christ himself said, 'It is finished, I have wrought man's redemption and despatched the matter.' Christ, our passover, is offered, so that the thing is done and Christ hath done it once and for all and it was a bloody sacrifice."

Bishop Hooper, an early English reformer, called the Mass "an utter forsaking of the holy supper because it doth attribute and ascribe to itself that which appertaineth only to the blood of Christ on the cross, that is to say, satisfaction, purgation and remission of sins, with increase of grace." At the Third World Congress on Faith and Order it was declared: "Our Lord Jesus Christ in all his life on earth and chiefly in his death and resurrection has overcome the powers of darkness. In his one perfect and sufficient sacrifice on Calvary he offered perfect obedience to the Father in atonement for the sin of the whole world. This was an act of expiation made once and for all and is unrepeatable."

Not in the Bible

As far as Protestants can discover, the New Testament has nothing in it to justify the Mass, and has much in principle against it. Christ certainly did not indicate that he would die more than once on the Cross. His death was final and complete (John 16:1-28).

The Protestant opposition to the celebration of Mass rests on such Scriptural passages as these:

"Nevertheless I tell you the truth: 'It is expedient for you that I go away: for if I go not away, the Comforter will not come unto you; but if I depart, I will send him unto you'" (John 16:7).

"I go to my Father, and ye see me no more" (John 16:10).

". . . this same Jesus, which is taken up from you into heaven, shall so come in like manner as ye have seen him go unto heaven" (Acts 1:11).

"Now this I say, brethren, that flesh and blood cannot inherit the kingdom of God" (I Cor. 15:50).

"For the law of the Spirit of life in Christ Jesus hath made me free from the law of sin and death" (Rom. 8:2).

Paul never advocated the finding of the body of Christ in the Mass. But he did advocate "being in Christ" all the while, and becoming, as true Christians, living sacrifices (Rom. 12:1). He especially states, in Romans 6:8, 9, that Christ died only once. Therefore he could not die again, a bloodless sacrifice, in every Mass. "Now if we be dead with Christ, we believe that we shall also live with him. For in that he died unto sin once: but in that he liveth, he liveth with God." In Hebrews 9:27, 28, it is declared that "as it is appointed unto men once to die, but after this the judgment, so Christ was once offered to bear the sins of many."

PROTESTANT REFERENCE BOOKS: *The Divine-Human Encounter* by Emil Brunner, pp. 149-158; *The Jesus of History* by T. R. Glover, Chaps. VII and VIII; *Meditations on the Cross* by Toyohiko Kagawa; *The Life and Teachings of Jesus* by Charles Foster Kent, pp. 288-310; *Christ and His Cross* by W. Russell Maltby; *Our Fathers Faith and Ours* by David S. Schaff; *A Protestant Primer* by Clarence Seidenspinner, pp. 39 ff.; *Toward the Understanding of Jesus* by Vladimir G. Simkhovitch, Chaps. VIII and IX.

14

Heaven, Hell, Purgatory, and Indulgences

These four topics are linked together because in the Roman Catholic Church they all pertain to life after death. Moreover, in each case there is reality of the literal kind. Roman Catholics believe that there is a heaven, a hell, a place called purgatory, and that indulgences are directly related to the time a person has to remain in the torments of purgatory.

Roman Catholics are reminded often that for every person born into this world there will come a moment when he must leave it. That moment is all important. Unless a person is totally prepared to meet his Maker, with all his sins forgiven, death can mean an eternal tragedy. Therefore great emphasis is placed upon preparing to die in grace. This is why Roman Catholics make every possible effort to have a baby baptized, particularly if there is the possibility of its imminent death.

Whether Protestants will get to heaven all depends upon the attitude or intent, even though it be unexpressed, of the individual Protestant. The Roman Catholic position does allow for some Protestants to get to heaven, as well as to purgatory and hell.[1]

---

[1] The official Vatican letter, which rejected the interpretation of a Boston priest in 1947 regarding the article of Roman Catholic faith that there is no salvation outside the Roman Catholic Church, was republished on September 5, 1952. (Father Feeney will not acknowledge that a person may be saved through an implicit desire of the Roman Catholic Church.) The letter said in part: "It is clear that the doctrine presented as genuine Catholic teaching is far from being such, and can do nothing but grave harm to those who are in the Church and to those outside it." It declares that "good disposition of soul whereby a person wishes his will to be conformed to the will of God" is sufficient for salvation "when a person is involved in invincible ignorance" of the teaching of the Catholic Church. But it makes it very plain that "no one will be saved who, knowing the Church to have been divinely established by Christ, nevertheless refuses to

154

In this chapter there will be considered those life and death matters around which so much of the Roman Catholic faith and practice revolves day by day.

THE ROMAN CATHOLIC POSITION

The Meaning of Original Sin

Roman Catholics believe that on account of the sin of Adam, all his descendants "come into the world deprived of sanctifying grace and inherit his punishment." (*A Catechism of Christian Doctrine*, p. 45) This sin, which is in all people, except the Virgin Mary, is called original sin. It is called original because it comes down to people through their origin, or descent, from Adam. The chief punishments resulting from original sin are death, suffering, ignorance, and a strong inclination to sin. The penalties of original sin remain even after Baptism, although through Baptism, according to the Roman Catholic Church, original sin is taken away.

What Catholics Believe About Life Hereafter

It is the teaching of the Roman Catholic Church that death is a punishment for original sin; that the just who depart from this life free from all debt of temporal punishment are admitted at once to heaven, although there are various degrees of blessedness in heaven; that in heaven the faithful have a clear and direct knowledge of God and of the Three Divine Persons; that their happiness will last throughout eternity. It also teaches that persons who die in the state of mortal sin suffer eternal punishment in a place known as hell; that the souls of the just, who have not fully discharged their debt to God's justice, are cleansed by purgatorial pains after death and only then are admitted into heaven. It is the belief of the Catholic Church that the souls in purgatory can be relieved by such suffrages of the living as Masses, prayers, almsdeeds, and other good works; that on the Last Day all men will rise bodily from the dead, with the bodies which they had in this life; that they will at that time be brought

---

submit to the Church or withholds obedience from the Roman Pontiff." Father Leonard Feeney was officially excommunicated by the Roman Catholic Church on Feb. 13, 1953, the announcement being made by the Sacred Congregation of the Holy Office, the Vatican, on Feb. 16, 1953.

before the judgment seat of Christ and sentenced by him according to their individual deserts.

Heaven

Heaven, to Roman Catholics, is a place and state of eternal happiness. The chief factor of this is the ability to see God face to face, an experience known as the Beatific Vision. Other joys will be the companionship with Christ, the angels, and the saints, the fellowship with the faithful, and an understanding of the wonders of creation. In heaven the body (although it will be a transformed body) will share the joys of the soul. While all will enjoy the bliss of heaven, it will not be equal in degree, since it will differ according to the merits of each soul. Here man's will is fixed upon ultimate ends and will no longer fail, and the joys of heaven will never end.

Hell

Hell is also a place and a state, according to the Roman Catholic Church. It is the place and state of eternal punishment which consists (1) of the separation from God (pain of loss) and (2) real punishment for sins (pain of sense). The torment is a physical reality, although it may not be caused by an element exactly like earthly fire. In hell the punishment is not equal for all, but corresponds to the sinner's aversion from God. It should be noted that only those are punished in hell who depart this life with personal, grave, deliberate, and unrepented sin.

"Besides depriving the sinner of sanctifying grace, mortal sin makes the soul an enemy of God, takes away the merit of all its good actions, deprives it of the right to everlasting happiness in heaven, and makes it deserving of everlasting punishment in hell." (*A Catechism of Christian Doctrine,* pp. 48 and 49)

Saving Souls from Hell

Roman Catholics make every effort, through the sacraments of the Church particularly, to keep souls from going to hell. They also go to the very limit to keep babies from missing the eternal joys of heaven, for it is the teaching of the Roman Catholic Church that an unbaptized child is excluded from heaven. While it has not defined doctrines in regard to the specific fate of unbaptized children, the general teaching of Roman Catholic theologians is that they enjoy a state of natural happiness in limbo where they know and love God through their natural powers. Nevertheless, they will never reach heaven and enjoy the Beatific Vision.

In the *Manual for Nurses,* by Daniel E. Ostler, O.F.M., published by the St. Anthony Guild Press with the Imprimatur of the late Patrick Cardinal Hayes of New York, this admonition is given:

> *"The person who neglects to baptize a child in danger of death is guilty of mortal sin and will have to render an account before the judgment-seat of Jesus Christ.* If a child dies without Baptism, its soul is sent into eternity with the stain of original sin upon it. In such a state it can never see the Face of that God who created it, nor can it ever enter the Kingdom of Heaven for which it was destined." (p. 14)

Nurses are instructed to baptize the child when no priest can be reached in time. This will be a valid baptism so long as water is used along with the words, "I baptize thee—in the name of the Father and of the Son and of the Holy Ghost."

Canon 746 of the Roman Catholic Church gives these directions in unusual cases of infant baptism:

"1. An infant should not be baptized while still enclosed in its mother's womb, provided there is probable hope that, being rightly born, it may be baptized.

"2. If the infant's head should emerge and there is imminent danger of death, it should be baptized on the head; and if it is afterward born alive, it must not again be baptized, even conditionally.

"3. If some other member emerge, it should be baptized on the member if danger of death is imminent; but then if, being born, it should survive, it must be baptized again conditionally.

"4. If a pregnant mother should die, the fetus, having been extracted by those upon whom this duty devolves, should be baptized absolutely if it is certainly alive; if doubtfully alive it should be baptized conditionally.

"5. If a fetus was baptized in its mother's womb, it shall when born be baptized conditionally."

Nurses are told to baptize, at least conditionally, "monstrous and unusual forms of the fetus." (*Canon 748*) They are also told to summon a priest to administer the Last Sacraments (Penance in the form of confession, Holy Communion, and Extreme Unction) to a dying patient, or even when the patient is apparently dead. "Absolution and Extreme Unction can always be given,

at least conditionally, even if the patient be unconscious." (p. 26)
Canon 941 states: "When one doubts whether the sick person
has attained the use of reason; whether he is really in danger
of death; or whether he is dead—Extreme Unction shall be given
conditionally."

Purgatory

According to *A Catechism of Christian Doctrine,* "Those are
punished for a time in purgatory who die in the state of grace
but are guilty of venial sin, or have not fully satisfied for the
temporal punishment due to their sins. There will be no purgatory after the general judgment. Since we do not know how long
individual souls are detained in purgatory, there is need for
persevering prayer for the repose of the souls of all who die after
reaching the use of reason, except those who are canonized or
beatified by the Church. The souls in purgatory are certain of
entering heaven as soon as God's justice has been fully satisfied."
(p. 143)

The "poor souls in purgatory" will certainly suffer the loss of
the sight of God, and it is commonly taught, although it is not a
doctrine of the Church, that they also suffer physical pain by
some agency similar to the fire of hell.

The official pronouncement of the Roman Catholic Church is
sufficient proof for Catholics that there is a purgatory. But additional proof is offered from the Books of Maccabees, from tradition, and arguments from reason. The reasoning is as follows:
In the Bible it is stated that "there shall not enter (into heaven)
anything defiled" (Apoc. 21:27), and that "every idle word that
men shall speak, they shall render an account of it in the day of
judgment" (Matt. 12:36). On the basis of what we know about
human nature, it is reasonable to say that many who die in grace
are still burdened with venial sins. Such cannot possibly enter
heaven and, since they are not enemies of God, they will not be
sent to hell. Therefore there must exist a middle state in which
the just can be purified and then proceed to heaven.

Indulgences

If purgatory is misunderstood by Protestants, the doctrine of
indulgences is even more so. In fact, many Protestants believe
that this permits Catholics to "indulge in sin," and that this
privilege of sinning, without punishment, can be bought with a

price. This is not true. Roman Catholics repudiate absolutely any such thing.[2]

An indulgence, according to the official teaching of the Catholic Church, is not a pardon of sin, still less is it a permission to commit sin. It is rather a release from temporal punishment which is granted by the Church, outside of the Sacrament of Penance, to those whose sins have already been forgiven. While grace has been restored, usually there remain certain unpaid debts of temporal punishment. Some of these are cared for through penance following confession. The others must be paid for in purgatory by pain.

It is the teaching of the Roman Catholic Church that the time required in purgatory, to pay for venial sins, is shortened by the devotions of the faithful. "The faithful on earth, through the communion of saints, can relieve the sufferings of the souls in purgatory by prayer, fasting, and other good works, by indulgences, and by having Masses offered for them." (*A Catechism of Christian Doctrine*, p. 134)

There are two kinds of indulgences, *plenary*, which is the remission of all the temporal punishment due to sins, and *partial*, which is only remission of part of the punishment.

Plenary indulgences are granted, for example, to those who recite a third of the Rosary in the presence of the Blessed Sacrament (*The Raccolta*, No. 360, c.); to those who perform pious exercises of the Stations of the Cross (*The Raccolta*, No. 164); to those who recite devoutly the prayer, "Behold, O good and sweetest Jesus," before an image of Christ after Holy Communion (*The Raccolta*, No. 171).

Partial indulgences, of so many days or years, are granted for certain prescribed ejaculations (short sentence prayers), prayers, and good works. A long list of these are found in the official *Collection of Indulgenced Prayers and Works* issued from the Vatican. The partial indulgences range, each prayer, from a few days to several years (days and years here meaning relative, shorter or longer, periods).[3]

---

[2] "The Council of Trent . . . abolished all grants of Indulgence which were conditioned upon a pecuniary contribution towards a specified object." —*The Catholic Encyclopedia*.

[3] Many of the prayers are given, along with the days or years (indulgence), in the booklet *Keys to the Treasury of the Church*. Similar indulgences may be found in the official booklet used at Tuesday devotions in honor of St. Anthony, National Shrine of St. Anthony, New York City,

These indulgences, from the Spiritual Treasury of the Church, have been stored up through the centuries by means of "the infinite satisfaction of Jesus Christ and of the superabundant satisfaction of the Blessed Virgin Mary and of the Saints . . . which they gained during their lifetime but did not need." (*A Catechism of Christian Doctrine*, pp. 337-338) These can be expended by the Church to those who meet the specified conditions.

This power to distribute such indulgences is based upon Christ's words: "I will give unto thee the keys of the kingdom of heaven; and whatsoever thou shall bind on earth shall be bound in heaven; and whatsoever thou shalt loose on earth shall be loosed in heaven" (Matt. 16:19). Commenting upon this verse, Cardinal Gibbons says in his book, *The Faith of Our Fathers,* "By these words our Savior empowered His Church to deliver her children (if properly disposed) from every obstacle that might retard them from the Kingdom of Heaven. Now there are two impediments that withhold a man from the heavenly kingdom—sin and the temporal punishment incurred by it. And the Church having power to remit the greater obstacle, which is sin, has power also to remove the smaller obstacle, which is the temporal punishment due on account of it." (p. 308)

Roman Catholics are very sensitive on the matter of "selling" indulgences. They admit that there have been abuses, as in the case of John Tetzel, but they have taken official measures to stop such abuses and to forbid absolutely the taking of money for indulgences. A free-will offering, given in thankfulness, is not considered a fee and is permitted.[4]

Apostolic indulgences are those, either plenary or partial, attached to crucifixes, rosaries, medals, and other images blessed by the pope personally or by his delegates. These indulgences

---

or in the front of *A Catechism of Christian Doctrine,* Revised Edition, No. 3.

[4] Memberships are sold today in such organizations as the Paulist League. For $5.00 an individual Requiem Mass card can be secured. Family membership is $25.00.

According to an announcement in the Paulist Calendar (April, 1952), "*Aim:* offers perpetual remembrance for your deceased relatives and friends under the patronage of St. Catherine of Genoa in Our Mother Church, New York City.

"*Privileges:* Holy Mass is offered daily for those enrolled. They share in special Masses offered regularly at the Society's altar of St. Catherine. They participate in Masses, prayers and good works of Paulists throughout the world."

can be gained only by the first person who receives them and depend upon the saying of certain prayers, the doing of certain works of charity, or other good deeds. Indulgences can be gained for oneself. It must be remembered that no one knows, not even the pope, how long a soul has to remain in purgatory. It is also true that the actual results of the various indulgences are known by God alone. It is God, and God alone, who applies the indulgences. Roman Catholics believe that God is both loving and just.

Salvation Outside the Roman Catholic Church

This very important matter of finding salvation is treated officially by the Roman Catholic Church [5] in the following manner:

"When we say, 'Outside the Church there is no salvation,' we mean that those who through their own grave fault do not know that the Catholic Church is the true Church or, knowing it, refuse to join it, cannot be saved. 'Outside the Church there is no salvation' does not mean that everyone who is not a Catholic will be condemned. It does mean that no one can be saved unless be belongs in some manner to the Catholic Church, either actually or in desire, for the means of grace are not given without some relation to the divine institution established by Christ.

"They who remain outside the Catholic Church through no grave fault of their own and do not know it is the true Church, can be saved by making use of the graces which God gives them. Those who are outside the Church through no fault of their own are not culpable in the sight of God because of their invincible ignorance. Persons who make use of the graces God gives them, even though they are not members of the true Church, actually have the desire to become members inasmuch as they wish to use all the means ordained by God for their salvation."

Catholics are encouraged to persuade others to investigate the teachings of the Roman Catholic Church and to do everything possible to help non-Catholics, of their own free will, to become members of it.

The Communion of Saints

The official teaching of the Roman Catholic Church is, as found in *A Catechism of Christian Doctrine:* "By 'the communion

---

[5] *A Catechism of Christian Doctrine,* pp. 130-131.

of saints' is meant the union of the faithful on earth, the blessed
in heaven, and the souls in purgatory, with Christ as their Head.
The blessed in heaven comprise the Church triumphant; the
souls in purgatory, the Church suffering; and the faithful on
earth, the Church militant."

"Through the communion of saints, the blessed in heaven can
help the souls in purgatory and the faithful on earth by praying
for them. The prayers of the blessed in heaven are always
efficacious because they are always in accord with God's will."
(pp. 132-133)

Redemption Through Christ

Redemption, according to the teaching of the Roman Catholic
Catechism, is "that Jesus Christ, as the Redeemer of the whole
race, offered His sufferings and death to God as a fitting sacrifice in satisfaction for the sins of men, and regained for them
the right to be children of God and heirs of heaven." It is
pointed out that no creature could, of himself, make adequate
satisfaction for sin, which offends God. Every creature is *finite*
and therefore is unable to make *infinite* satisfaction. Although
God wished all to be saved, and although Christ died for all,
it is the teaching of the Roman Catholic Church that "only
those to whom the merits of His Passion are applied will
benefit by His death. The death of Christ was a sacrifice of
infinite merit and satisfaction, by which man was redeemed."

In the Roman Catholic Church the Stations of the Cross and
the Sorrowful Mysteries of the Rosary call to mind the chief
sufferings of Christ. Christ suffered and died on Good Friday,
revealing God's love for man and the evil, as well as the cost,
of sin; but He rose from the dead on Easter, glorious and immortal. He rose from the dead "to show that He is true God
and to teach us that we, too, shall rise from the dead." While
the Roman Catholic Church teaches that all men will rise from
the dead, only those who have been faithful to Christ will share
in His glory. On the Day of Judgment, Christ will come to
pronounce a sentence of eternal reward or of eternal punishment on everyone who has ever lived in this world.

THE PROTESTANT POINT OF VIEW
On the Meaning of Heaven and Hell

Protestantism rejects purgatory and indulgences because they are absolutely unscriptural and may result in serious moral and spiritual abuses.

The Protestant and Roman Catholic conceptions of heaven and hell agree in general. They differ radically, however, in regard to *who* will go to each place and *how* they will get there. Good works play a large part in the Roman Catholic system, while most Protestants believe in justification by faith as the way to heaven. We refer here to the majority orthodox view, and not the more liberal view stressing a combination of faith and good works. Purgatory and indulgences are alien to the Protestant conception of salvation as constructed from New Testament teachings.

Protestants can find nothing about purgatory or indulgences in the Bible. They consider them contrary to the spiritual concepts found in the teachings of Christ. Therefore all that Roman Catholics do and say about purgatory and indulgences cause Protestants great perplexity of mind and spirit. Here again is another area where Protestants and Roman Catholics are far apart. In this case they can come together not through understanding nor through appreciation, but only by the grace of God.

Protestants and Life Eternal

Jesus declared in Matthew 25:46 that "these shall go away into eternal punishment but the righteous into everlasting life." Protestants, basing their faith on this and other Scripture, think of eternal life as two separate states—heaven for the righteous, and hell for sinners (John 5:24)—although there are many interpretations of what these states mean. With one accord the Reformers refused to accept the doctrine of purgatory. According to the *Thirty-nine Articles*, purgatory was "vainly invented and grounded upon no warranty of Scripture, but rather repugnant to the Word of God." The Gallican Confession called it "an illusion, proceeding from the same shop from which have sprung monastic vows, pilgrimages, indul-

gences and all such things whereby men hope to merit forgiveness and salvation."

Heaven, for Protestants, is the final destination provided by
Christ's atonement. All who accept Christ as their Saviour,
and seek to follow him, will enter heaven. The test which
Christ himself formulated is found in Matthew 25. Hell, for
Protestants, is the place of eternal punishment for those who
deny Christ in thought and deed. John Wyclif spoke for all
Protestants when he declared: "Let .every man put his full
confidence and trust in God's mercy and in his own good life
and not in false pardons or vanities that men grant for love
and money. For such tricks avail not but deceive men that
trust in them."

According to David S. Schaff in *Our Fathers Faith and
Ours,* "Protestant thinkers at the present day may feel some
uncertainty in regard to the exact meaning of the Scriptures
concerning the resurrection from the dead and the time when
the future life begins but they agree in looking for the general
judgment in accepting Christ's assurance that 'he that believeth on the Son hath everlasting life,' and that no purgation
in an intermediate realm awaits Christian believers after the
present life." (p. 431)

Teaching of the New Testament

Protestants turn to the Bible for their belief in the future life.
Resurrection and immortality are among the cardinal teachings of the New Testament. Christ himself declared his going
unto his Father (John 16:28). Paul created particular doctrines regarding the future life. That Jesus believed in heaven
and hell is indicated in the Last Judgment scene (Matt. 25)
and the parable of the rich man and the beggar Lazarus
(Luke 16:19-31).

But nowhere in the Bible do Protestants find any references—
either directly or indirectly—to purgatory or to indulgences.
Because they are not in the Bible, and because they are opposed to a religion of the spirit, Protestants have from the beginning rejected such teaching.

Specific New Testament teaching regarding heaven and hell,
and the future life, is as follows: "And if thy right eye offend
thee, pluck it out, and cast it from thee; for it is profitable for
thee that one of thy members should perish, and not that thy
whole body should be cast into hell" (Matt. 5:29).

"Then shall he answer them saying, Verily I say unto you, Inasmuch as ye did it not to one of the least of these, ye did it not to me. And these shall go away into everlasting punishment: but the righteous into life eternal" (Matt. 25:45-46).

"And Jesus said unto him, Verily I say unto thee, Today shalt thou be with me in paradise" (Luke 23:43).

"In my Father's house are many mansions: if it were not so, I would have told you. I go to prepare a place for you" (John 4:2).

"And while they looked steadfastly toward heaven, as he went up, behold, two men stood by them in white apparel; which also said, Ye men of Galilee, why stand ye gazing up into heaven? This same Jesus, which is taken up from you into heaven, shall so come in like manner as ye have seen him go into heaven" (Acts 1:11).

"Now this I say, brethren, that flesh and blood cannot inherit the kingdom of God; neither doth corruption inherit incorruption. Behold, I shew you a mystery: We shall not all sleep, but we shall all be changed. In a moment, in the twinkling of an eye, at the last trump: for the trumpet shall sound, and the dead shall be raised incorruptible, and we shall be changed. For this corruptible must put on incorruption, and this mortal must put on immortality" (I Cor. 15:50-53).

"For we know that if our earthly house of this tabernacle were dissolved, we have a building of God, an house not made with hands, eternal in the heavens" (II Cor. 5:1).

"And I saw a new heaven and a new earth: for the first heaven and the first earth were passed away" (Rev. 21:1).

"He that overcometh shall inherit all things; and I will be his God, and he shall be my son. But the fearful, and unbelieving, and the abominable, and murderers, and whoremongers, and sorcerers, and idolators, and all liars, shall have their part in the lake which burneth with fire and brimstone: which is the second death" (Rev. 21:7-8).

PROTESTANT REFERENCE BOOKS: *American Freedom and Catholic Power* by Paul Blanshard, pp. 273 ff.; *The Idea of Perfection in Christian Theology* by R. Newton Flew, Chap. I; *A Protestant Manifesto* by Winfred E. Garrison, pp. 158-159, 183-184; *The Recovery of Ideals* by Georgia Harkness, pp. 191-197; the topics "heaven" and "hell" in Hastings' *Bible Dictionary; Creative Christianity* by Shailer Mathews; *An Interpretation of Christian Ethics* by Reinhold Niebuhr, Chap. III;

Our Fathers Faith and Ours by David S. Schaff, Chap. XXIII; *The Mysticism of Paul the Apostle* by Albert Schweitzer, Chaps. IV-VIII; *After Death* by Leslie D. Weatherhead; *Christian Doctrine* by J. S. Whale, Chap. VIII.

PART IV
Practices of Roman Catholics

15

Good Works of Charity

So much attention is usually given to Roman Catholic doctrines and rites that the humble daily works of mercy of the ordinary Catholic are overlooked. Besides faith and doctrine, and in addition to what happens within the sanctuary, Catholics are encouraged to act their faith and to follow the example of St. Francis and other saints.

Roman Catholics have the poor very much at heart. In their churches they have alms boxes prominently displayed. Charity with them is not only a part of good works, in which there is merit, but also a demonstration that the Roman Catholic Church itself is on the side of the poor. Pope Pius XI, in his encyclical letter *Divini Redemptoris,* calls for the practice of charity and help for the poor. "Sinful pleasures must be renounced and self must be forgotten for love of thy neighbor," the pope says. "There is a divine regenerating force in the New Commandment, as Christ calls charity. Its faithful observance will bring peace to the heart of the individual and to the world."

Protestants object to the Roman Catholic doctrine of salvation by good works (plus faith). Is their criticism fair and based on facts? In this chapter there will be a presentation of the "good works" side of Roman Catholicism.

THE ROMAN CATHOLIC POSITION

An Expression of Worship

It is the teaching of the Roman Catholic Church that "external worship is of no value unless it is joined with internal worship and is an outward manifestation of our internal convictions and sentiments." (*A Catechism of Christian Doctrine,* p. 165) In other words, the true Catholic is expected *to live* his religion daily.

The Chief Works of Mercy

Catholics are instructed that the chief works of mercy are: (1) to feed the hungry; (2) to give drink to the thirsty; (3) to clothe the naked; (4) to visit the imprisoned; (5) to shelter the homeless; (6) to visit the sick; (7) to bury the dead.

Eternal Rewards Through Good Works

The Roman Catholic Church believes in good works, along with faith, and as an expression of faith. Moreover, it believes that good works can help the Christian gain eternal rewards.

In *A Catechism of Christian Doctrine*, these declarations are propounded for the faithful:

"Our Lord taught explicitly that one can earn the eternal reward of heaven by performing the corporal works of mercy and that those who deliberately refuse to perform such works will be barred from heaven.

"One can feed the hungry, give drink to the thirsty, clothe the naked, and shelter the homeless not only by actually providing the necessities of life but also by working to correct economic abuses which cause unnecessary unemployment and poverty. Those who work to provide comfortable and sanitary housing for the poor perform a corporal work of mercy.

"One can visit the sick by paying a social call or by providing the necessary medical care as far as means and circumstances permit. Those who help support hospitals for the poor and home nursing organizations also perform this work of mercy. Doctors and nurses who attend the sick can gain the reward promised by Our Lord if they perform their duties for the love of God and not merely for money or for humanitarian reasons." (pp. 152, 153)

Includes Everyone

Everyone in the Roman Catholic Church is obliged to perform works of mercy. They vary according to the ability of the members and the needs of the neighbors. All of the ordinary deeds which are done day by day to relieve the need of others are works of mercy, if they are done in the name of Christ.[1]

---

[1] "When a person with the virtue of charity in his soul assists a needy neighbor on account of the words of Christ, 'as long as you did it to one of these my least brethren, you did it to me,' or simply because his Christian training tells him that the one in need is a child of God, the act is one of supernatural charity. It is likewise meritorious of eternal life."— *The Catholic Encyclopedia*.

Faith Plus Good Works

The Roman Catholic Church plainly teaches that "Without faith it is impossible to be saved." (*A Catechism of Christian Doctrine,* p. 91) Yet it says that good works must be added to faith, to prove that the faith is alive.

"Only if our consecration to God becomes visible to the world in charity, will the world believe. The responsibility to convert the world is on all Christians, since they are confirmed. Not all of them can teach and preach as priests and religious. But all can preach a greater sermon by their deeds." (*Our Parish: House of God and Gate of Heaven* by H. A. Reinhold, Paulist Press, p. 63)

Father Conway in his *Question Box* points out that Catholics accept the position that we are justified by faith. Yet he is quick to add "but not by faith 'alone.' " Then he goes on to say, "We are justified by a faith that worketh by charity." (pp. 223-224)

The Council of Trent declared, "In the act of justification, with the remission of his sins, man receives all at once, through Christ, on whom he is ingrafted, the infused gifts of faith, hope and charity. For faith without hope or charity, neither unites man perfectly with Christ, nor makes him a living member of His Body."

Two favorite Scripture passages with Catholics are: "Faith without works is dead" (Jas. 2:16), and "If I have all faith so as to move mountains and have not charity, it profiteth me nothing (I Cor. 13:2).

The Doctrine of Merit

The Roman Catholic Church teaches that there is merit in good works, not that reward rests in the works themselves but on the promise of Christ that He will reward faithful servants of His. If good deeds are done in His honor and service, aided always by divine grace, they are meritorious. St. Augustine is quoted as saying, "When God crowns our merits, He crowns His own gifts."

This doctrine of merit is defined by the Council of Trent as follows: "Eternal life is to be proposed to those who do good unto the end and hope in God, both *as a grace* mercifully promised to the children of God through Jesus Christ, and *as a reward* to be faithfully rendered to their good works and merits, in virtue of the promise of God Himself (II Tim. 4:7). . . . For since Christ Jesus Himself constantly communicated

His virtue to those who are justified, as the Head to the members
(Eph. 4:15), and as the vine to the branches (John 15:4), which
virtue always preceded, accompanied and followed their good
works, and without which they could be nowise agreeable to
God and meritorious; we must believe that nothing more is
wanting to the justified, nor is there any reason why they should
not be considered as having fully satisfied the divine law, as far
as the condition of this life admits, by such works as are done
in God, and truly merited the attainment of eternal life in due
time, if they die in the state of grace." (*Sess.* VI, Chap. XVI)

Catholic Charities

The Roman Catholic Church is noted for its many charities
in the form of hospitals (seven and a half pages of fine print are
needed, in the *National Catholic Almanac*, just to list the Catholic hospitals in the United States), relief agencies for the poor
and unfortunate, the deaf and blind, orphans, wayward girls,
institutions for handicapped children, foster homes, and homes
for the aged.

The Society of St. Vincent de Paul is the greatest Catholic lay
organization for charity purposes. There are 2,800 units of the
Society in the United States, with a total membership of 30,000
laymen. Each one is required to make a weekly visit to a poor
family. Its goals are: spiritual and material comforts for the
inmates of hospitals and institutions; care of poor and neglected
children, country vacations for the under-privileged, the pur-
chase of books for the poor attending parochial schools; providing Christian burial for the poor and friendless; furnishing food
and shelter for homeless transients; giving legal advice for those
who require it; and many other works of charity. In the past
twenty-five years it has distributed $50,000,000 to the poor.

In addition there are many charity organizations of Sisters,
much local parish charity work, special services for displaced
persons, charity projects of fraternal bodies like the Knights of
Columbus, and many specialized services conducted by the National Catholic Welfare Conference.

THE PROTESTANT POINT OF VIEW
On the Christian's Duty to His Neighbor

Protestantism does not accept the Roman Catholic doctrine of "good works" because the grace of God is a free gift and cannot be won or bought with a price.

Protestants should by all rights praise Roman Catholics for their good works of mercy—when they are not at the expense of public funds, and when they are divorced from the doctrine of merit. Good works, done in the name and spirit of Christ, are *good* no matter who does them. It is at this point of rendering Christian service, like helping refugees on an interdenominational and interfaith basis, that Roman Catholics and Protestants have learned to work together. While this does not mean that by so doing either has compromised their principles, it does demonstrate that, putting differences a little to one side, they can co-operate to a limited extent. At the present time such co-operation is rather tentative and semiofficial. While it means very little as far as real unity is concerned, it is something which many have greatly appreciated and believe should be encouraged.

On the Way to Salvation

Martin Luther in the Preface to his *Commentary on the Epistle to the Romans* explains how Christian faith saves a person completely, even to his daily living. He says, "Faith is a divine work in us which transforms us and begets us anew. It marks us in heart, temper, disposition and all our powers, entirely different men than we were before and brings with it the Holy Spirit. It is a living, busy, active, mighty thing. It is impossible that it should not be ceaselessly doing that which is good. As it is impossible to separate burning and glow from the flame, so it is impossible to separate good works from faith."

Good works, while not being a factor in obtaining eternal salvation, have always had a leading part in Protestant practice since the application of the Gospel message is found to be a fundamental teaching of Scripture. Luther, for example, in his *Freedom of a Christian Man* plainly declares: "Good works do not make a man good, but a good man doeth good works. True faith is a lively thing and can in no wise be idle. Therefore, teach we the people that God hath called us not to follow riot and wantonness but, as Paul said, 'He hath called us unto good works to walk in them.'"

Protestantism takes second place to no other religious faith in its ministry of love and mercy. This is demonstrated in its missionary programs, in its hospitals, and in its ever-widening area of social service and world relief. It is best illustrated in the lives of such men and women as Leo Tolstoy, Walter Rauschenbusch, Ida Scudder, E. Stanley Jones, Toyohiko Kagawa, Albert Schweitzer, and Jane Addams. According to the Oxford Conference official report, "The chief end of man is to glorify God, to honor and love him, in work and life as in worship. This love involves the obligation to love our neighbors as ourselves, a second commandment which Jesus declared to be like unto the first. . . . It must be emphasized that our obligation to the neighbor brings not so much from our recognition of man's native dignity as from the Christian revelation of God's purpose to restore that dignity through the redemption that is in Christ. The obligation is therefore a duty toward God and continues to be operative even when the neighbor does not obviously demand or deserve respect. We must love our fellow men because God loves them and wills to redeem them." (pp. 75-76)

Scriptural Basis for Protestant Beliefs

Protestants have never rejected Christian charity. It is a scriptural teaching (the Sermon on the Mount and I Cor. 13). What they have opposed is the attempt to make salvation rest upon the winning of merits and not upon the free will of a just and loving God. Once having been redeemed by the grace of God, and justified by faith, then there should be a constant flow of deeds of kindness and manifestation of love. The New Testament is full of such commandments as these:

"Therefore all things whatsoever ye would that men should do to you, do ye even so to them: for this is the law and the prophets" (Matt. 7:16).

"Wherefore by their fruits ye shall know them" (Matt. 7:20).

"Give ye them to eat" (Luke 9:13).

"Go, and do thou likewise" (Luke 10:37).

"And all that believed were together, and had all things common; and sold their possessions and goods, and parted them to all men, as every man had need" (Acts 2:44-45).

". . . we should remember the poor; the same which I also was forward to do" (Gal. 2:10).

"And let us consider one another, to provoke unto love and to good works" (Heb. 10:24).

"Seest thou how faith wrought with his works, and by works was faith made perfect? . . . For as the body without the spirit is dead, so faith without works is dead also" (Jas. 2:22, 26).

"And besides this, giving all diligences, add to your faith virtue; and to virtue knowledge; and to knowledge temperance; and to temperance patience; and to patience godliness; and to godliness brotherly kindness; and to brotherly kindness charity" (II Pet. 1:5-7).

"My little children, let us not love in word, neither in tongue; but in deed and in truth. . . . And this is his commandment, That we should believe on the name of his Son Jesus Christ, and love one another, as he gave us commandment" (I John 3:18, 23).

Following New Testament teaching, Protestants believe that no Christian, once being justified by faith, can be devoid of good works.

PROTESTANT REFERENCE BOOKS: *Social Salvation* by John C. Bennett; *The Social Triumph of the Ancient Church* by Shirley Jackson Case; *The March of Faith* by Winfred E. Garrison, Chap. X; *Applied Christianity* by Washington Gladden; *Christian Faith and Economic Change* by Halford E. Luccock; *Social Religion* by Douglas Clyde Macintosh; *Christianity and Social Progress* by Shailer Mathews; *The Social Gospel and the Christian Culture* by Charles Clayton Morrison; *The Contribution of Religion to Social Work* by Reinhold Niebuhr; *Jesus or Christianity* by Kirby Page; Walter Rauschenbusch's *A Theology for the Social Gospel, Christianity and the Social Crisis, Christianizing the Social Order.*

16

Why the Confessional
Is So Essential to Roman Catholics

One of the most common sayings of Roman Catholics, which Protestants often overhear, is, "I must go to confession." There is much more to this than meets the ear, for "going to confession" not only is frequently a compulsory matter but also involves one of the basic dogmas of the Roman Catholic Church, namely, penance.

What happens in the confessional box is wholly a personal matter. It is the place where the individual faces up to his personal sins, and asks for forgiveness. It is the place where sins are forgiven. And from the confessional Roman Catholics leave fit for heaven—unless or until they sin again.

There are many questions about the confessional which Protestants want answered. How can a priest actually forgive sins? What sins have to be confessed? How often does a Catholic have to go to confession? Does confession encourage people to go and sin again? These, and other important questions, will be answered in this chapter.

Christ said to the sinners of his day, "Thy sins are forgiven thee. Sin no more. Go in peace." He says the same words today, and he still forgives sins. But how can we find him, and how can we be sure that our sins are truly forgiven? Catholics claim to have the answer for both of these questions.

THE ROMAN CATHOLIC POSITION

Baptism Not Enough

According to the teaching of the Roman Catholic Church, the sacrament of Baptism is absolutely essential. It frees the soul of original sin. Even the newborn babe must be baptized and, if

176

there is imminent danger of death, the baby can be baptized in its mother's womb. Baptism provides spiritual regeneration and makes the person capable of receiving the other six sacraments. It imprints a "character" on the soul and admits the recipient to membership in the Church of Christ.

Even so, baptism may not be enough. Sins committed after baptism must also be forgiven. Another sacrament is provided for this purpose, the sacrament of Penance. Penance and the confessional go together, bringing to the Roman Catholic, in the confessional box, absolution.

The Sacrament of Penance

The teaching of the Roman Catholic Church regarding the sacrament of Penance, as based on its definition by the Council of Trent, is as follows:

1. The sacrament of Penance was instituted by Christ for the remission of sins committed after Baptism.

2. The words of Christ, "Receive the Holy Spirit; whose sins you shall forgive, they are forgiven them; and whose sins you shall retain, they are retained," [1] refer to the power of forgiving and retaining sin in the sacrament of the Penance.

3. It is only a priest or bishop who possesses this power; that he exercises it as a judge, with true authority to hear the self-accusation of the sinner, to give or withhold absolution, and to impose such penances as he thinks best.

4. Three acts are required of the penitent for the complete and perfect remission of sins: contrition, confession, and satisfaction.

5. Contrition conceived from such motives as the fear of hell, the loss of heaven, the filth of sin, and accompanied by a purpose of amendment, provided it excludes the affection for sin, is true sorrow, and prepares one to receive the grace of the sacrament.

6. The penitent must make a definite and specific confession of all grave sins, even those of thought, which he can call to mind; that private or auricular confession, as practiced in the Catholic Church from the beginning, is not a human invention or opposed to the ordinance of Christ.

7. A debt of temporal punishment sometimes remains after sin has been forgiven, but that it may be canceled by temporal afflictions willingly borne, by penitential works, and by the penance enjoined by the priest, for by such sufferings we are made

---

[1] John 20:22, 23.

like unto the suffering Christ, who alone can give our actions
the power to satisfy divine justice; that the debt of temporal
punishment may also be remitted by the Indulgences granted by
the Catholic Church.

8. For those who have fallen into grave sin after Baptism, the
sacrament of Penance is the only gate of salvation. Though it
sometimes happens that contrition is perfect through charity and
reconciles man with God before the sacrament of Penance is
actually received, nevertheless the reconciliation itself is not to
be ascribed to contrition alone but to contrition together with
the desire it includes of receiving the sacrament. It is also correct
and profitable to confess venial sins.

Power to Forgive Sins

Roman Catholics believe that the priest, properly ordained and
authorized, has the power to forgive sins, and that this power
comes directly from Christ. For Jesus said to his apostles, and to
their successors, "Receive the Holy Spirit; whose sins you shall
forgive, they are forgiven them; and whose sins you shall retain,
they are retained." According to the Catholic Church, "no man,
by his own power and authority, could possibly forgive sins. Only
God can do that because sin is an offense against Him. But the
priest, as God's representative, can forgive sins because God
has given him the power to do so." (*A Catechism of Christian
Doctrine*, p. 317)

Sins are forgiven when the priest says, "I absolve thee from
thy sins in the name of the Father, and of the Son, and of the
Holy Ghost. Amen."

Confessing Sins

The Catholic is required at times to go to confession and to
confess his sins to the priest that he may find forgiveness. The
question is, What sins must be confessed? The teaching of the
Roman Catholic Church at this point is: "It is necessary to confess every mortal sin which has not been confessed and forgiven; it is not necessary to confess our venial sins, but it is
better to do so." (*A Catechism of Christian Doctrine,* p. 317)

In order for a confession to be "entire" all mortal sins must
be told to the priest, giving their kind, the number of times each
sin has been committed, and any circumstances which may
change or add special significance to their nature.

By "kind" of sins is meant the class into which they fall, such as blasphemy, missing Mass, disobedience, theft, etc. Catholics are told that the best way to determine the different kinds of sin is to determine the virtue that has been violated or the commandment that has been broken. They have to confess whether the sin was in thought, word, or deed. In most prayer books there are lists of sins which help the Catholic to ascertain what sins he has committed.

The "circumstances" that change the nature of a sin are those which add some new element of wickedness to the act. For example, if a person kills another, he has committed a sin of murder. But if the person he has killed happens to be a priest, he has not only committed murder but has also committed the sin of sacrilege.

A person may forget to confess a mortal sin. But he must tell the sin the next time he goes to confession. To deliberately conceal a mortal sin in confession is a sacrilege, because by doing so a person abuses the sacrament of Penance, which is considered a sacred institution of Christ.

Making a Good Confession

In a leaflet published by St. Anthony's Guild, with the Imprimatur of Bishop Thomas A. Boland, entitled *Don't Be Afraid to Go to Confession,* and written by Giles Lawlor, O.F.M., these helpful hints are given to the faithful:

"All that is necessary for a good confession as regards the telling of your sins is the willingness to tell your mortal sins if they come to mind after an honest effort to remember them. This effort should be made with calmness, and you must not spend too long a time in the examination of your conscience.

"In the case of a person who has been away from confession for a year, if he has missed Mass, committed sins of impurity, practiced birth control, stolen or cheated, surely these things will come to his mind. If he makes a normal effort, five or ten minutes should be sufficient.

"If mortal sins have been forgotten, there remains the obligation to tell them the next time you go to confession. There is no reason for anxiety in the meantime, since the sin is already forgiven and since you are willing to tell the sin the next time you go to confession whether it be one or six months from now.

"It is not necessary to come to a decision as to whether the sin was mortal or venial in order to make a good confession. you accuse yourself, it is the priest's office to decide.

"If you need the proper information on any Commandment, you may always ask the priest; he is most willing to give it to you.

"The priest can absolve you from sin, but he cannot absolve you from a disease. The priest may help the doctor to convince you that it is your body or mind that is sick and not your soul.

"Sins you would not dare to tell your best friend you can safely tell to the priest. He is the only friend you may turn to when you have fallen to the lowest depths."

The Seal of the Confessional

The priest is bound—by natural, divine, and Church law—to keep absolutely secret whatever he hears in confession. "A priest who reveals the confession of the penitents shall be deposed with anathema," says the Second Synod of Dovin. *Canon Law 2369* declares, "The priest, who dares break the seal of Confession directly, remains under excommunication reserved in most special manner to the Holy See." Priests are forbidden to mention anywhere—in private or in public, in sermons or before courts of law—anything which they have heard in Confession.[2]

This law admits no exceptions. This means that a priest may not break the seal of confession, either to save his own life or that of another, to save his good name, or to further the aims of civil justice. That is, he cannot go to court and testify against anyone whose confession he has heard.

Penance After Confession

Roman Catholics are given a penance after confession in order that they may make some atonement to God for their sins, to receive help in avoiding them in the future, and to make some satisfaction for the temporal punishment due to them. It is therefore a sin to omit deliberately the penance imposed after confession—it is a mortal sin if the penance is grave and imposed for a grave sin; it is a venial sin if the penance is slight. If a person really intended to perform the penance at the time he received it, the sins he told in confession are forgiven; but he is guilty of a new sin afterward when he deliberately omits the penance.

The faithful are instructed to follow exactly the directions of the priest as to the manner and time of performing the penance.

---

[2] This matter is discussed in detail in Father Bertrand Kurtscheid's *A History of the Seal of Confession.*

They are also urged to fulfill the obligations of the penance immediately, or just as soon as it is possible.

The Price of Confession

No priest is allowed to take money for hearing a confession. It is absolutely forbidden by *Canon Law* 727. To administer a sacrament, such as Penance, for money, would be simony, and this is a grievous sin in the Roman Catholic Church.

Frequent Confession

Frequent confession is recommended for Roman Catholics for the good of their souls. This means weekly, biweekly, or possibly monthly confession. The goal of frequent confession is to assist the soul to attain a high degree of perfection, and to preserve and even to increase saving grace. Usually frequent confession concerns only venial or less important sins, sins that a Catholic does not have to confess unless he chooses to do so.

Points for the Examination of Conscience

In the back of a booklet published by the Benedictine Convent of Perpetual Adoration, Imprimatur of Carolius Hubertus Le Blond, called *Confession, Its Fruitful Practice* (pp. 50-61) is a rather long list of questions arranged under the Ten Commandments and the commandments of the Roman Catholic Church. There are far too many to list here, but a sample will indicate the nature of some of the questions which Roman Catholics put to themselves in Confession.

"Have I: Denied my religion? Doubted any article of Faith? Affiliated myself with a forbidden secret society? Taken part in non-Catholic church services? Read books, papers, etc., belittling morality, scoffing at virtue, and causing doubts in respect to the teachings of the Church? Complained or murmured against God's Providence? Neglected daily prayers or said them carelessly and with wilful distractions?"

"Have I: By act, participation, instigation, counsel, or consent, been guilty of anyone's death, or bodily injury? or of destroying the life of the unborn? Have I given way to anger and passion? Ill-treated others? Wilfully entertained thoughts of hatred, revenge, jealousy, aversion, resentment, or contempt for others?" etc.

"Have I: Committed impure acts? Alone, or with another? a relative? single or married? of my own or the opposite sex? Dwelt with pleasure on impure thoughts and imaginations? or consented to them in my heart? Wilfully desired to see or do anything impure? Used impure

language, allusions, words or double meanings? How many were listening? Have I listened with wilful pleasure to immodest language? Sung or listened to improper songs? Sinned by immodest touch or action, with myself, or with others? . . . Read immoral books? Lent or sold them to others? Written improper things? Voluntarily exposed myself to temptation by curiosity? by frequenting improper company? or places? sinful amusements? immodest dances? indecent plays? Have I been guilty of undue familiarities? Am I keeping sinful company now?" etc.

"*Have I* [as a physician]: Undertaken the care of persons seriously ill without sufficient science or experience? Rashly hazarded dangerous remedies? Made needless expense? Intentionally taken the life of a child unborn? Performed or advised forbidden operations? Failed to warn those in danger of death in time to receive the sacraments? Allowed infants to die without baptism through neglect?"

Making It Easy to Sin

The question has been raised as to whether confession does not encourage Catholics to sin again, knowing that they can be forgiven by the priest. The Roman Catholic answer to this is that confession is not made easy and that it strengthens, rather than weakens, character. It is pointed out that the confessional prevents sin, making Catholics realize the terrible nature of sin, its consequences here and hereafter.

Father Conway tells us (*Question Box,* p. 290) that "the confessor reminds the sinner that he cannot pardon sin, unless he atones for the past by restoring his neighbor's good name or property, unless he is sorry from a supernatural motive, and unless he promises to avoid in the future all the proximate occasions of sin. All priests know that hardened sinners find this difficult, for at times they will depart unabsolved rather than promise amendment."

Roman Catholics admit that some of the faithful go to confession in a mechanical, perfunctory manner. But they also insist that the vast majority of Catholics find in the confessional a new gateway to heaven, rendering the soul capable of again performing meritorious acts, which it could not do while in the state of mortal sin.

THE PROTESTANT POINT OF VIEW
On the Forgiveness of Sins

Protestantism rejects the Roman Catholic "Confessional" because it denies that the priest has the right to forgive sins and believes that every sinner should make his confession directly to God.

Protestants are being told by some today that they need the "confessional." But what is meant by this, and what Roman Catholics believe about Confession and Penance, are absolutely different things. One is moral, scientific, psychological; the other is theological, dogmatic, and supernatural. The former relates largely to personal problems, the other to personal sins. One is practiced by psychiatrists; the other can be performed only by those ordained as Catholic priests. Roman Catholics have, at the very heart of the Confessional, the sacrament of Penance. Here the priest is supposed to have special power from Christ to forgive sins.

From the Protestant point of view no one can forgive sins save Christ. God works through Christ to convert sinners. No extra intermediary is needed between God and man, except His Son. Protestants believe that God does forgive sins, and that Christ died on the Cross so that mankind might be saved. Confession, to the Protestant, is an outpouring of the heart to God, asking for forgiveness through Christ. This can happen at any time and at any place. God is good and he is more than ready to forgive those who seek him in humility and sincerity. Protestants are able to have contact with God and receive from him directly the forgiveness which a just and loving Heavenly Father feels they deserve.

Direct Access to Christ

Protestantism teaches that every believer has direct and immediate access to Christ, and to his throne of grace, and is assured of pardon quite apart from any priestly agency (Heb. 4:16). Forgiveness is a fundamental New Testament principle which asks that confession be made to God and to one another (Jas. 5:16). Jesus had a great deal to say about sin and the forgiveness of sins. In each case it was a matter of direct relationship with the Father (Matt. 23:4; Luke 11:46, 18:10-14; John 5:21; Mark 2:7; Rev. 1:18, 3:7).

Speaking of "the power of the keys" the *Augsburg Confession* says that it is "a power or commandment to preach the Gospel and to remit and retain sins, a power put into execution only by teaching or preaching the Word." The *Heidelberg Catechism* says that "the office of the keys is the preaching of the Holy Gospel and church discipline by which two things, the kingdom of heaven is open to believers and shut to unbelievers." The *Book of Common Prayer* puts it this way: "Almighty God, the Father of our Lord Jesus Christ, who desireth not the death of a sinner, but rather that he may turn from his wickedness and live, hath given power and commandment unto his ministers to declare and pronounce to his people, being penitent, the absolution and remission of their sins. He pardoneth and absolveth all those who truly repent and believe His Holy Gospel."

While Protestantism does not accept the confessional as an institution warranted by Scripture, it does recognize the function of the pastor as adviser and friend. But consultations on matters of religion and moral behavior, marriage and personal affairs, are with Protestants purely voluntary. Recognizing no mortal man as having the power to say, "I absolve thee," they seek to bring all people before a loving Father who is more ready to forgive than the sinner is to seek forgiveness. Moreover, knowing that it is scriptural to forgive wrongs committed against each other, Protestants are urged to cultivate the forgiving heart. Of late years many Protestant bodies have been very much in the mood of repentance. It was noted often at the first assembly of the World Council of Churches at Amsterdam. And it was part of the official message of the Lund Conference: "The word penitence has been often on our lips here at Lund. Penitence involves willingness to endure judgment—the judgment of the Lord to whom has been given the power to sift mankind and to gather into one the scattered children of God. We await His final triumph at the end of history. But, in God's mercy, tokens of judgment which are also calls to a new and active obedience come to us in our day also, here and now. Surely we cannot any longer remain blind to the signs of our times and deaf to His Word."

Scriptural Basis for Forgiveness

Protestants are opposed to the Roman Catholic Confessional. They have a scriptural basis for this opposition. In the first place, there is no New Testament teaching concerning anything pertaining to a Confessional and, in the second place, there are specific teachings that the sinner must seek forgiveness directly from God.

New Testament teachings regarding the confession of sins are found in these passages:

"If ye forgive men their trespasses, your heavenly Father will also forgive you. But if ye forgive not men their trespasses, neither will your Father forgive your trespasses" (Matt. 6:14-15).

"And when he saw their faith, he said unto him, Man, thy sins are forgiven thee" (Luke 5:20).

"Confess your faults one to another and pray one for another" (Jas. 5:16).

Forgiveness is one of the basic requirements of the Bible. We are taught that we must be as ready to forgive as to ask for forgiveness (Matt. 6:15). But nowhere does the Bible teach that sins against God can be forgiven by any man or priest.

PROTESTANT REFERENCE BOOKS: *American Freedom and Catholic Power* by Paul Blanshard, pp. 39, 134, 152; *Faith Is the Answer* by Smiley Blanton and Norman Vincent Peale, Chap. 87; *Pastoral Psychiatry* by John Sutherland Bonnell, Chap. VIII; *The Clinic of a Cleric* by W. A. Cameron, Chap. I; *The Art of Ministering to the Sick* by Richard C. Cabot and Russell L. Dicks, p. 202; *On Being a Real Person* by Harry Emerson Fosdick, Chap. VI; *Psychology and Religious Experience* by W. F. Halliday, pp. 240-244; *The Cure of Souls* by Charles T. Holman, pp. 241 ff.; *Health for Mind and Spirit* by W. L. Northridge, Chap. XII.

17

Devotional Life of Roman Catholics

In spite of their elaborate liturgies and ceremonies, Roman Catholics do not consider all of them absolutely essential to a life of devotion. They are spiritual aids, but there are more basic things than rites. The Roman Catholic Church, we are informed through Catholic teaching, does not insist on ritual, ceremonial, and exterior forms of worship to such an extent as to overshadow or destroy the vitalizing spirit which must animate the true worshiper's attitude toward God.

The Jesuit priest, Albert Muntsch, says in *Catholic Liturgy and Catholic Life*,[1] "The Church always teaches that the spirit alone vivifieth and is the essential requisite in worship of God. Hence she has no brief for mere external observance of the law at the expense of the spirit of faith, of devotion and charity, whose absence cannot be remedied by rigid Pharisaical attention to rites and ceremonies." (p. 14)

Because so much importance is placed upon personal devotion in the Roman Catholic Church, this chapter will be devoted primarily to those aspects of worship which each worshiper performs individually and alone, either in the sanctuary or at home.

THE ROMAN CATHOLIC POSITION

The Rosary

Since the Rosary has been considered in the chapter on Mary, all that is needed here is to point out that it is one of the chief items in the personal devotional life of the Roman Catholic. It should be kept in mind that the Rosary is not only a series of prayers, but also a string of reflections and meditations. For

---

[1] Published by Our Sunday Visitor Press, Imprimatur of Bishop John Francis Noll.

example, here is the first reflection and prayer in connection
with the Five Joyful Mysteries, "The Annunciation":

> " 'Let us contemplate, in this Mystery, how the Angel Ga-
> briel saluted our Blessed Lady with the title, Full of Grace,
> and declared unto her the Incarnation of our Lord and Savior
> Jesus Christ.'

> "Our Father, Hail Mary (ten times), Glory be to the Father,
> etc.

Let us pray.

> " 'O Holy Mary, Queen of Virgins, through the most high
> Mystery of the Incarnation of thy beloved Son, our Lord
> Jesus Christ wherein our salvation was begun, obtain for
> us, through thy most holy intercession light to understand
> the greatness of the benefit He hath bestowed upon us, in
> vouchsafing to become our Brother, and in giving Thee, His
> own beloved Mother, to be our Mother also. Amen.' "

The Sacramentals

The sacramentals of the Roman Catholic Church are quite
different from the sacraments, although they have, according to
Catholics, certain sacramental qualities. But unlike the sacraments they cannot, of themselves, produce spiritual benefits. In
The New Baltimore Catechism and Mass, No. 2, official Revised
Edition, the chief kinds of sacramentals are listed as three:
"(1) the *blessings* given by priests and bishops; (2) the driving
out from persons or things of *the evil spirits* that possess them;
(3) all *blessed objects*, such as: crucifixes, images, candles and
so forth." (p. 202)

The Roman Catholic Church calls these "holy actions" and
"things sacramental." They play an important part in the daily
devotional life of the faithful. It is the prayers, the faith, the
devotion which accompany the sacramentals, and the pious
thoughts which they inspire, that bring the real blessings. The
above Catechism points out very plainly that "to get any benefit
from the sacramentals we must use them with true faith and
piety; otherwise we shall be guilty of superstition."

Accepted on this basis the principal benefits obtained by the
use of sacramentals are: (1) actual graces; (2) the forgiveness
of venial sins; (3) the remission of temporal punishment; (4)
health of body and material blessings; and (5) protection from

evil spirits. The most commonly used blessed objects of devotion are holy water, candles, ashes, palms, crucifixes, images of Christ, of the Virgin Mary, and of the saints, medals, rosaries, and scapulars.

Holy Water: the water blessed by the priest according to the form in the "Rituale Romanum," and employed in just about every blessing of the Church. Upon entering a church, the holy water is taken up on the tips of the fingers, and the sign of the cross is made, this being symbolic of baptism and the banishment of original sin. It may also be used at bedtime or when rising in the morning, in moments of temptation and on numerous other occasions. According to the *National Catholic Almanac* (p. 233), holy water helps to promote spiritual and temporal health and "drive away the devil with his rebel angels. . . . The water thus blessed becomes a means of grace. By the reverent use of holy water, venial sin is blotted out."

Candles: After being blessed, candles are distributed to the faithful to be used in their homes on Candlemas day, the feast of the Purification of the Virgin Mary (February 2). According to *A Catholic Dictionary* (p. 69), "the blessed candles may be lit in times of trouble or temptation, during thunderstorms, childbirth, and at the hour of death." Votive candles, to be secured by a "little monetary offering," are lighted and dedicated to some special purpose. Resting before the Blessed Sacrament or a shrine, the votive candle serves as a projection of the worshiper's personality, remaining behind in the church to continue his prayer and petition.

Ashes: On Ash Wednesday ashes, which have been blessed, are placed on the foreheads of the faithful to remind them that they are but dust and ashes, and also that they should observe Lent with a humble and mortified spirit.

Palms: Blessed palms are distributed on Palm Sunday in commemoration of the triumphant entrance of Christ into Jerusalem.

Images: either a sculpture or a painting of Christ, the Virgin Mary, or some other saint. Images are regarded by Catholics as a complement to the liturgy or as an aid to private worship. They are venerated, but not worshiped. On this the Council of Trent says, "The images especially of Christ, of the Virgin Mother of God, and of the other saints, are to be had and kept in churches and due honour and reverence paid to them; not because it is believed that there is any divinity or power in them or that anything may be asked from them, or that any faith may be put in them as the heathen used . . . but because the honour shown to them is referred to the prototypes which they represent; so that, through these images which we kiss and before which we bow with bared heads, we worship Christ and honour the saints whose likeness they display."

Medals: A flat metal disk bearing a religious image of Christ, the Virgin Mary, or one of the saints, a shrine, etc. According to *A Catholic Dictionary* (p. 316), "they are mere signs of the prototypes to which due honour is accorded; in themselves they can have no efficacy, to look on them as mascots is superstition. The efficacy consists in the blessing of the Church calling down the goodness of God on the wearer, and sometimes in indulgences attached thereto."

Scapulars: two pieces of cloth, about 3 inches by 2 inches, joined by strings and worn back and front under the clothes. (A medal may be worn instead, having the Sacred Heart on one side and the Virgin Mary on the other.) There are seventeen recognized scapulars, each a badge of a religious institute, and with indulgences attached to wearing them.

Forty Hours' Devotion

This is a solemn exposition of the Blessed Sacrament for forty hours in commemoration of the forty hours during which the body of Christ was in the tomb. In the United States these hours are interrupted for the convenience of the faithful. "A plenary indulgence is granted to all contrite persons who have approached the Sacraments of Penance and the Eucharist, visited the church each day and recited five Our Fathers, Hail Marys and Glory Be to the Fathers, or one Our Father, Hail Mary and Glory Be to the Father for the intentions of the Holy Father." (*National Catholic Almanac*, p. 231)

Apostleship of Prayer (League of the Sacred Heart)

The "Apostleship of Prayer" is an association of millions of Catholics leagued together in prayer with "the Sacred Heart of Jesus"—the pious way of referring to the real, human heart of Christ which Catholics believe is present in every parish church in connection with Holy Eucharist. Membership is on a local basis with the sole obligation (not binding under sin) of offering daily prayers and good works, the daily recitation of a "decade" of the rosary, and sufferings for the intentions of Christ, the pope, and for the petitions of other members of the organization.

Each month the pope recommends to the members a special intention which is made known to members through little leaflets which are sent to every parish. "Promoters" are expected to attend to the distribution.

Holy Hour is a devotion held on the first Friday of each month so that members may meditate before the Blessed Sacrament, especially upon the Passion. Hymns, litanies, and other prayers are sometimes used as parts of the hour service, which is terminated with the benediction.

Stations of the Cross (Way of the Cross)

This popular devotion of Roman Catholics is in honor of the passion of Christ, noting the places where he stopped on his way to the Cross. It consists in moving from one to another of fourteen crosses and praying before each one. There are no set prayers, although special meditations have been prepared by approved sources.[2] This may be done alone, in the company of others, or in a group led by a priest. The custom originated in the fifteenth century with the Friars Minor.

All that is required for this simple devotion are fourteen crosses (or stations). They are now usually accompanied by images or tableaus, representing the events to be meditated upon. There is a tradition, verified by Saint Bridget's revelation, that Mary walked daily the *Via Dolorosa* and at each significant place on the way she knelt and prayed.

Pope Pius XI, in 1931, abolished all former indulgences previously granted for the Stations of the Cross and granted in their place the following:

"1. A plenary indulgence to those who make the Way of the Cross, each time they make it, even though it is repeated many times on the same day.

"2. A plenary indulgence

(a) to those who make the Way of the Cross on the day on which they receive Holy Communion; or

(b) to those who have made the Way of the Cross ten times and within a month receive Holy Communion.

"3. To one who begins the Stations of the Cross but does not complete the devotion, the Supreme Pontiff benignly grants an indulgence of ten years and ten quarantines for every station made."[3]

The fourteen stations are as follows:

I. Jesus Is Condemned to Death
II. Jesus Carries His Cross
III. Jesus Falls the First Time

---

[2] For example, *The Stations of the Cross,* published by St. Anthony's Guild, Paterson, N. J.

[3] Quoted from *The Stations of the Cross,* p. 15.

The Catholic Conception of Prayer

According to the Roman Catholic position, prayer is "the lifting up of our minds and hearts to God." (*Catechism*) Catholics, every time they pray, are asked to keep in mind these four intentions: (1) to *adore* God; (2) to *thank* Him for His favors; (3) to ask His *pardon* for sins and forgiveness of their punishments; (4) to beg of Him *graces* and *blessings* for one's self and for others.

In order to obtain God's help through prayer, the worshipers must pray with attention, with a conviction that they need God's help, with great desire for the graces they ask of God, with trust in God's goodness, and with perseverance. Distractions which are willful make prayers worthless. All prayers should begin and end with the sign of the cross, because the sign of the cross expresses two important mysteries: the Trinity and the Redemption.

Roman Catholics are instructed to pray especially for themselves, for their parents, relatives, friends, and enemies, for souls in purgatory, for the pope, bishops, and priests, and for the officials of their country.

Roman Catholics may use their own words in praying to God, and are encouraged to do so often. They are asked to learn the following prayers by heart: The Lord's Prayer, the Hail Mary, the Apostles' Creed, the Confiteor, the Glory be to the Father, and the acts of faith, hope, charity, and contrition.

Roman Catholics believe that God always hears prayers—although for various reasons He may not answer all of them—if they pray properly, because Christ has promised, "If you ask the Father anything in My name, He will give it to you."

Catholic Hymns

Protestants and Catholics share many of the great hymns of the Christian Church. However, much that is purely Roman Catholic in faith and practice is found exclusively in such Roman Catholic hymns [4] as the following:

Jesus, My Lord, My God

1. Jesus, my Lord, my God, my all!
   How can I love Thee as I ought?
   And how revere this wondrous gift,
   So far surpassing hope or thought?

Chorus:

Sweet Sacrament! we Thee adore,
Oh, make us love Thee more and more,
Oh, make us love Thee more and more.

2. Had I but Mary's sinless heart
   To love Thee with, my dearest King,
   Oh, with what bursts of fervent praise
   Thy goodness, Jesus, would I sing.

Daily, Daily Sing to Mary

1. Daily, daily sing to Mary
   Sing, my soul, her praises due;
   All her feasts, her actions worship,
   With the heart's devotion true.
   Lost in wond'ring contemplation,
   Be her majesty confess'd;
   Call her Mother, call her Virgin,
   Happy Mother, Virgin blest.

2. She is mighty to deliver;
   Call her, trust her lovingly;
   When the tempest rages round thee,
   She will calm the troubled sea.
   Gifts of heaven she has given,
   Noble Lady, to our race;
   She the Queen who decks her subject,
   With the light of God's own grace.

---

[4] The Roman Catholic hymns used here were taken from Father Mc-Guire's *The New Baltimore Catechism*, No. 1, Official Revised Edition.

Hymn to St. Joseph

1. With grateful hearts we breathe today
   The tender accents of our love.
   We carol forth a little lay
   To thee, great saint in heaven above.

Chorus:
   Oh Joseph dear, from thy bright throne,
   Incline thine ear unto our prayer.
   And o'er us all as o'er thine own,
   Extend thy fond paternal care,
   And o'er us all as o'er thine own,
   Extend thy fond paternal care,
   Extend thy fond paternal care.

2. More favored than earth's greatest king,
   Thou wert the guardian of that Child,
   Around whose crib full choirs did sing,
   With cadenced voices soft and mild.

Helps for Worship

Roman Catholics have a wealth of devotional material coming down from saints and mystics through the centuries. These are made available in attractive, but inexpensive form at Catholic bookstores. Leaflets and booklets on all phases of faith and practice are placed in convenient places for the faithful—and for prospective converts. Mass books, manuals of prayers, and other devotional helps are provided in very simple form so that they can be easily read, understood, and appreciated.

Sanctity of Life

Holiness of life is one of the chief ideals of the Roman Catholic Church. Freely admitting that its members are human beings, and are prone to all the sins and shortcomings of mortal men, nevertheless it does everything possible to lift the soul, and the daily life, of its members toward self-denial, sacrifice for others, and a true life of Christian devotion. This emphasis upon holiness of life is no better expressed, from the Roman Catholic point of view, than in the letters and encyclicals of Pope Pius XI, particularly those addressed to priests.

THE PROTESTANT POINT OF VIEW
On the Ways in Which to Worship God

Protestantism cannot accept the "sacramentals" of the Roman Catholic Church because they tend to make Christianity a mechanical affair and not something of the spirit.

Protestants come very close to Roman Catholics in their devotional life. Although they cannot accept the beads, images, and other objects particularly associated with the "sacramentals," they can appreciate the earnestness and sincerity of the vast majority of Catholic worshipers. They both find Christ, through different channels.

Protestants and Roman Catholics have much in common in regard to prayers, creeds, and the great hymns of the Church. A beautiful and sincere prayer, coming from the heart of a St. Francis of Assisi, can mean as much to a Protestant as it does to a Roman Catholic. So it is with church music and with architecture which has come down to us through the ages. How wonderful it is to find a bit of common ground upon which the faithful of the whole Christian Church can bow down and worship together. True, this must be done outside the regular rules, regulations, and doctrines of the Roman Catholic Church. But perhaps the time has come when, without violating any basic principle, we should step aside for a while and, as individual Christians, raise our hearts *together* in prayer.

Devotional Classics of Protestantism

The great devotional classics of Christendom, such as *The Imitation of Christ* and a hymn like Newman's "Lead Kindly Light," belong just as much to Protestants as they do to Roman Catholics. St. Francis' life, as well as his famous prayer, also belong to all true Christians who worship God "in spirit and in truth" (John 4:24).

Protestant worship is directed toward God and His Son Jesus Christ. Praise, prayer, the confession of sin and meditation, preaching and the reading of Scripture, all find their proper place in the Protestant service of worship. In many of the churches, litany and beautiful sacred music add to the worship

experience. Protestantism has produced such devotional material
as Bishop Andrews' *Prayers*, Jeremy Taylor's *Holy Living* and
Holy Dying, Bunyan's *Pilgrim's Progress*, and Law's *Serious Call*.
It has created hundreds of hymns and anthems. At the center of
Protestant worship is the experience of the sermon. Congrega-
tional singing adds to the sense of participation. The Communion
Table is present as a constant reminder of Christ's death on the
Cross for the salvation of mankind.

All Protestants are free to discover for themselves elements of
devotion in various Christian forms. They are not forced to worship at any special place or in any special manner. They may
worship at home as well as at the altar. Led by the Holy Spirit
they seek God's presence in private and in their churches, and
He speaks to them through prayer and through His Holy Word.
In their seeking they find Him.

Protestants have agreed that: [5] "We worship one God, Father,
Son and Holy Spirit, the Triune God, by whose Spirit all true
worship is inspired and unto whom all Christian worship is offered. . . .

"God Himself creates the faith by which we respond to Him
in worship, by encountering us and speaking to us (Gal. 2:20).
. . . God's encounter with us, and the response to Him in worship, involves the whole man (Matt. 22:37-40). It is made in
worship, in witness, and in Christian obedience and service. . . .
The response as expressed in worship involves adoration, confession, hearing the Word of God, intercession, invocation, oblation, praise, supplication and thanksgiving."

"Word and Sacrament are both the gifts of God. In the reading and preaching of the Word and the administration of the
Sacraments, God offers us His grace, imparts saving knowledge
of Himself and draws us into communion with Himself. All worship is by and within the family of God's people, alike in heaven
and on earth. Even in private prayer, the Christian is always
praying with the Church as a member of the communion of
saints. The worship of the congregation is both the basis of all
private prayer and devotion, and a powerful and essential Christian witness to the world."

New Testament Emphasis

The reason why Protestants stress a worship based upon spirit
and truth, free from mechanical and physical objects, is because

[5] Adopted by the Lund Conference.

this is the New Testament emphasis. Christ cleared the money-changers from the Temple (Matt. 21:12). He called for worship motivated by spirit and truth (John 4:23-24).

The Gospel of John has served Protestants for centuries as the ideal in devotional literature. The spiritual experience at Pentecost has set the tone for active worship (Acts 2:1-47). Paul at Mars Hill has given the philosophy of worship (Acts 17:22-34). And in his letters to the churches Paul instructs them to walk not after the flesh, but after the Spirit (Rom. 8:1).

Other passages giving the New Testament view of worship are: "If thou shalt confess with thy mouth the Lord Jesus, and shalt believe in thine heart that God hath raised him from the dead, thou shalt be saved. For with the heart man believeth unto righteousness; and with the mouth confession is made unto salvation" (Rom. 10:9-10).

"I beseech you therefore, brethren, by the mercies of God, that ye present your bodies a living sacrifice, holy, acceptable unto God, which is your reasonable service. And be not conformed to this world; but be ye transformed by the renewing of your mind, that ye may prove what is that good, and acceptable, and perfect, will of God" (Rom. 12:1-2).

"Know ye not that ye are the temple of God, and that the Spirit of God dwelleth in you? If any man defile the temple of God, him shall God destroy; for the temple of God is holy, which temple ye are" (I Cor. 3:16-17).

"In the church I had rather speak five words with my understanding, that by my voice I might teach others also, than ten thousand words in an unknown tongue" (I Cor. 14:19).

"God forbid that I should glory, save in the cross of our Lord Jesus Christ, by whom the world is crucified unto me, and I unto the world. For in Christ Jesus neither circumcision availeth any thing, nor uncircumcision, but a new creature" (Gal. 6:14-15).

"When ye pray, use not vain repetitions, as the heathen do; for they think that they shall be heard for their much speaking. Be ye not therefore like unto them: for your Father knoweth what things ye have need of before ye ask him" (Matt. 6:7, 8).

"Not everyone that saith unto me, Lord, Lord, shall enter into the kingdom of heaven; but he that doeth the will of my Father which is in heaven" (Matt. 7:21).

PROTESTANT REFERENCE BOOKS: *What I Owe to Christ* by C. F. Andrews; *Prayer* by Karl Barth; *Why I Believe in Religion* by Charles

Reynolds Brown; *So We Believe, So We Pray* by George A. Buttrick; *Today Is Mine* by Thomas Curtis Clark; Harry Emerson Fosdick's *The Meaning of Faith, The Meaning of Prayer, The Meaning of Service, A Great Time to be Alive* (Sermons); *Strengthening the Spiritual Life* by Nels F. S. Ferré; *Prayer and the Common Life* by Georgia Harkness; *Personal Religion and the Life of Devotion* by W. R. Inge; Rufus M. Jones's *How to Be a Transformed Person, Some Problems of Life, The Flowering of Mysticism, The Way to Power and Poise; A Testament of Devotion* by Thomas R. Kelly; Douglas V. Steere's *Doors Into Life, Introduction to the Devout Life, On Beginning from Within, Prayer and Worship;* Stanley I. Stuber's *The Christian Reader, Treasury of the Christian Faith; Pastoral Prayers* by Ernest Fremont Tittle.

18

World Missions and Social Justice

Believing that it has the only true religion, the Roman Catholic Church has, from the beginning, had an extensive world mission program in order to propagate the faith. In some cases it has won whole nations over to its belief. At other times it has become a powerful minority factor, always with the goal of increasing its membership until it wins all. But in every nation, at any time in history, it remains the same united Church, catholic, apostolic, and holy. In every country it aims to become, as soon as possible, a part of the national life, while still retaining all the characteristics of the Roman Catholic Church.

It was not until 1908 that the United States was officially taken from the list of the Church's mission territories. But by that time the Roman Catholic Church here had already begun its own home and foreign mission work. Today it has an extensive missionary program which, along with regular developments, has several new and most interesting features. For example, it is making creative use of all the facilities of mass communication.

THE ROMAN CATHOLIC POSITION

Missionary Territory

The whole world is the missionary territory of the Roman Catholic Church.[1] It does, however, have three phases of missionary development: (1) care of the faithful; (2) missions "to the heathen and Moslems";[2] and (3) territory not subject to the common law of the Western church but under the jurisdiction of the Congregation of Propaganda.

Foreign missions are under the direction of the Congregation of Propaganda and missionaries from among the secular clergy

---

[1] See *The Catholic Church in Action* by Michael Williams, The Macmillan Co., Chap. XIV.

[2] *A Catholic Dictionary*, p. 326.

are supplied by special colleges in various parts of the world. Most of the older religious orders do missionary work. This is particularly true of the Dominicans and Franciscans.[3] Jesuits are the largest missionary order.

According to *A Catholic Dictionary*, "the object of foreign missions is the conversion of the heathen to the faith of Christ and their incorporation in his Church, the appointed means of salvation. Medical missions, schools, material relief, etc., are the corporal works of mercy which necessarily accompany the Christian missionary; but his job requires of him no other intervention in native affairs, except it be for the express purpose of saving souls or imparting that minimum of education which should enable them to improve themselves from within and in their own way. The missionary is an emissary of Christ, not of a continent, a country, a culture or of commerce." (p. 326)

The last statistical survey shows that there are 489 missionary ecclesiastical divisions in 78 countries. These were served by 352 bishops and 137 other ordinaries [4] (24 of these being "natives"); 17,000 priests (4,800 natives); 6,180 brothers (2,150 natives); 47,000 nuns (16,700 natives); and 74,000 native catechists, representing 56 nationalities. There are also 720 hospitals, 37,000 schools with 2,250,000 pupils, 1,900 orphanages with 111,000 children, and 17,500 old people are cared for in 417 homes. The missionaries run 171 printing presses and publish 320 periodicals. There are 18,000,000 baptized Roman Catholics in these various missions, and 2,500,000 catechumens.

Catholic Negro Missions in the United States

Turning to Roman Catholic missionary work in the United States, there are several rather new developments including the Outdoor Apostolate, Negro Missions, and Indian Missions. Pope Pius XII, in his 1939 encyclical letter "To the Church in the United States" (*Sertum Laetitiae*), singled out Indian and Negro missions for his personal solicitude. In regard to the latter he said, "We confess that We feel a special paternal affection, which is certainly inspired of Heaven, for the Negro people dwelling among you; for in the field of religion and education We know

---

[3] "The Church, mindful of the order of the Saviour: 'Go, teach all nations' (Matt. 28:12), has always considered the preaching of the Gospel among the infidels and their conversion by her apostolic missionaries to be one of her principal duties."—*The Catholic Encyclopedia*.

[4] A cleric with ordinary jurisdiction over a specified territory.

that they need special care and comfort and are very deserving
of it. We therefore invoke an abundance of heavenly blessing
and We pray fruitful success for those whose generous zeal is
devoted to their welfare."

The Negro Roman Catholic population in the United States
is about 400,000 out of a total number of approximately 15,000,-
000. Churches for the special use of Negroes number 445, with
624 priests. There are 321 elementary schools with an enrollment
of 69,604 pupils. There is one ecclesiastical college and seminary
for Negroes, 12 boarding academies and vocational schools, and
some 30 complete high schools under Roman Catholic auspices.
In northern cities, efforts are made to incorporate Negroes into
white parishes.

In its work among Negroes the Roman Catholic Church, according to the *National Catholic Almanac,* has these two chief
objectives: "first, the religious welfare of the Catholics; secondly,
the propagation of the Faith among the non-Catholics. . . . Whilst
a majority of the adults are affiliated to the Negro branches of the
Protestant sects, millions of others have very meager religious
beliefs. These spiritually ignorant multitudes offer unquestion-
ably a vast field for missionary enterprise." (pp. 350-351)

Missionary work among the Negroes, Roman Catholic authorities admit, is not easy going. Much unfriendliness toward the
Roman Catholic faith is found, due "to ignorance of the Church
and to deep prejudices, bred by the hostile public opinion of
the communities in which they live. Besides this, most church
members are attached to and satisfied with their own churches."
(*National Catholic Almanac,* pp. 350-351)

In view of this open opposition, the Roman Catholic Church
is concentrating on aiding Negro children through schools and
social welfare. These friendly service projects, it feels, will in
time break down the major part of the resistance. Social service
centers are also being opened both to Catholics and to non-
Catholics among the Negroes, another indication that the Roman
Catholic Church is showing a real interest in Negroes. This interest is not strange to the Roman Catholic Church, for it "has
always demanded respect for basic human rights irrespective of
race or condition and has always manifested a deep sympathy
for the downtrodden." (*National Catholic Almanac,* pp. 350-351)

Catholic Indian Missions

Roman Catholics, beginning with the discovery of America, have had a special interest in behalf of the Indians. Pioneers, and still leaders in the Indian Missions, are the Franciscans, Jesuits, and Benedictines. The most effective work is being done through mission schools, many of them day schools.

In some cases, entire Indian tribes are now Roman Catholic. Here the work of the priests and Sisters is much the same as that done in poor rural communities. Most of the tribes, however, are "either partly pagan or Protestants. Here the work is predominantly missionary in character, to win these to the true Faith." (*National Catholic Almanac,* p. 352) About one-third of the Indians are now Roman Catholics.

The Outdoor Apostolate

The Outdoor Apostolate is a mission project with the purpose of extending the influence of the Roman Catholic Church particularly in rural areas of the United States. Most of this work, at present, is being conducted in the South. This mission is carried on out-of-doors and the chief aim is to attract non-Catholics. Trailer chapels are often used. At other times open meetings are held in parks, on lawns, or on street corners. Recordings, ranging from classical music to hymns, are used to attract the crowd.

The programs of the various mission groups—the "stand" to last from four days to two weeks—is usually about the same: a talk on a religious subject, religious movies with commentary by the priest in charge, a question box period, and a closing prayer. Efforts are made to cultivate personal friendships. And the people are always urged to help themselves to the many different kinds of leaflets which explain the Roman Catholic point of view on faith and morals.

Social and Economic Matters

If anyone is inclined to feel that the Roman Catholic Church is reactionary, he should examine its position in regard to social and economic matters. It has pioneered in labor relations, both in principle and in practice, for over half a century. The most famous of all pronouncements on Christianity's responsibility in the area of labor is the encyclical letter of Pope Leo XIII on "The Condition of Labor" (*Rerum Novarum*).

Other important official pronouncements giving the position of

the Roman Catholic Church on social and economic matters are
Quadragesimo Anno (Rebuilding Society's Social Order) by
Pope Pius XI in 1931; *Sertum Laetitiae* (To the Church in the
United States) by Pope Pius XII in 1939; and "The Church and
Social Order," by the archbishops and bishops of the Adminis-
trative Board of the National Catholic Welfare Conference in
1940. The latter is a reiteration of the teachings of the Roman
Catholic Church on ownership, property, labor, security, wages,
and the establishment of the social order.

Leo XIII and Labor

Pope Leo XIII wrote his history-making encyclical letter
Rerum Novarum in 1891. To say that he was ahead of his time,
in the position he took on working conditions and the rights of
labor, would be a grave understatement. The following quotations indicate some of Leo's chief concerns:

"It is surely undeniable that, when a man engages in remunerative
labor, the very reason and motive of his work is to obtain property,
and to hold it as his own private possession."

"There is nothing more powerful than Religion (of which the
Church is the interpreter and guardian) in drawing rich and poor
together, by reminding each class of its duties to the other, and especially of the duties of justice. Thus Religion teaches the laboring man
and the workman to carry out honestly and well all equitable agreements freely made, never to injure capital, nor to outrage the person
of an employer; never to employ violence in representing his own
cause, nor to engage in riot and disorder; and to have nothing to do
with men of evil principles, who work upon the people with artful
promises, and raise foolish hopes which usually end in disaster and in
repentance when too late."

"It cannot, however, be doubted that to attain the purpose of which
We treat, not only the Church, but all human means must conspire.
All who are concerned in the matter must be of one mind and must
act together. It is in this, as in the Providence which governs the
world; results do not happen save where all the causes cooperate."

"The first duty of the rulers of the State should be to make sure
that the laws and institutions, the general character and administration
of the commonwealth, shall be such as to produce of themselves
public well-being and private prosperity. . . . The more that is done
for the working population by the general laws of the country, the
less need will there be to seek for particular means to relieve them."

"The first concern of all is to save the poor workers from the cruelty
of grasping speculators, who use human beings as mere instruments
for making money. It is neither justice nor humanity so to grind men

down with excessive labor as to stupefy their minds and wear out their bodies. Man's powers, like his general nature, are limited, and beyond these limits he cannot go. . . . Daily labor, therefore, must be so regulated that it may not be protracted during longer hours than strength admits."

"Let it be granted, then, that, as a rule, workman and employer should make free agreements, and in particular should freely agree as to wages; nevertheless, there is a dictate of nature more imperious and more ancient than any bargain between man and man, that the remuneration must be enough to support the wage-earner in reasonable and frugal comfort. If through necessity or fear of a worse evil, the workman accepts harder conditions because an employer or contractor will give him no better, he is the victim of force and injustice."

"As far as regards the Church, its assistance will never be wanting, be the time or the occasion what it may; and it will intervene with great effect in proportion as its liberty of action is the more unfettered; let this be carefully noted by those whose office it is to provide for the public welfare."

Rebuilding the Social Order

After reviewing and reaffirming the teachings of *Rerum Novarum,* Pope Pius XI, in his encyclical letter "Rebuilding Society's Social Order" (1931), attacks Socialism at length, leaving for it no quarter. His conclusion is that "Even though Socialism contains some truth, it is built on a doctrine opposed to true Christianity. No one can be at the same time a sincere Catholic and a true Socialist." He admits that not a few Catholics are trying to be both. He is disturbed because so many workers have left the Church.

"To stem the tide of modern paganism and bring back Christ to His world," Pope Pius XI declares, "the apostle of the workingmen must be the workingman, the apostle of the employer, the employer. It is the duty of bishops and priests to select and train these lay apostles." And he strongly urges the Church to take practical measures to fulfill Leo's principles.

He closes by saying, "The world today needs such apostles if it is to be saved from ruin. It is Christ or chaos. The Church has nothing to fear for she knows that the gates of hell will never prevail. But modern ills and errors are ruining countless souls, and it is for all of us with the help of God's Grace to rescue these souls redeemed by the Blood of Christ."

Social Justice in America

Pope Pius XII, in his encyclical letter "To the Church in the United States" (*Sertum Laetitiae*), has a section dealing with social justice in which he emphasizes some of the principles laid down by Leo, and expresses satisfaction in knowing that these principles are being brought to bear in labor disputes. But he is troubled because of the lack of employment in the United States. At this point he says, "May it also be brought about that each and every able-bodied man may receive an equal opportunity for work in order to earn the daily bread for himself and his own. We deeply lament the lot of those—and their number in the United States is large indeed—who though robust, capable and willing, cannot have the work for which they are anxiously searching." This was written in 1939.

A Right Social Order

The archbishops and bishops of the Administrative Board of the National Catholic Welfare Conference make a splendid contribution in "The Church and the Social Order" by bringing within the scope of a booklet the essential teachings of the Roman Catholic Church in regard to ownership, property, labor, security, wages, and the establishment of social order. They mostly list the pronouncements of Pope Leo XIII and Pope Pius XI under these various topics, covering just about the same ground which we have already covered in this chapter.

Because this document was prepared in 1940, insurance against insecurity is stressed. The bishops question mildly the kind of economic system which permits widespread unemployment. "We do not wish to imply that individual employers as a class are willfully responsible for this present state of insecurity," they say, "but we do claim that a system which tolerates such insecurity is both economically unsound and also inconsistent with the demands of social justice and social charity."

The bishops rejoice in the fact that new legislation is being enacted for the benefit of the working class, which, though small, may be the beginning of a national policy. Although the ideal would be, from the bishops' point of view, to have a large measure of stability between prices and wages, they nevertheless advocate increases in wages "whenever and wherever the wages are inadequate to provide a decent living." They ask for patience in trying to reform an economic system "which has been predicated upon false principles" and point out that the remedy is not so simple as some may think. "The solution is to be found in clear thinking and in a right conscience. Relying upon God's Providence we dare not be pessimistic but at the same time we frankly recognize that a full restoration to a Christian social order is a matter of steady growth and not a sudden transition."

The Roman Catholic bishops, at the close of their presentation, strike a new note in emphasizing the fact that rugged individualism is not truly Christian. This is what they say: "Our economic life then must be reorganized not on the disintegrating principles of individualism but on the constructive principle of social and moral unity among the members of human society. In conformity with Christian principles, economic power must be subordinated to human welfare, both individual and social; social incoherence and class conflict must be replaced by corporate unity and organic function; ruthless competition must give way to just and reasonable State regulations; sordid selfishness must be superseded by social justice and charity. Then only can there be a true and rational social order; then only can we eliminate the twin evils of insufficiency and insecurity, and establish the divine plan of a brotherhood of man under the fatherhood of God."

THE PROTESTANT POINT OF VIEW
On World Missions and Social Justice

Protestantism objects to the world mission program of the Roman Catholic Church not because it is un-Christian, but because it is exclusively Roman Catholic.

Protestants, like Roman Catholics, have a missionary program which reaches around the world. Both seek to bring the saving gospel of Christ to the "lost." They supplement their work of evangelism with that of social service and education. In many respects this work of winning the world for Christ runs in parallel lines.

It is true that Protestants, particularly in South America, attempt to convert Roman Catholics. The difference between the two types of proselyting is that the conversion from Roman Catholicism to Protestantism constitutes a transfer of allegiance within the recognized fellowship of the Christian Church. This takes place not because Roman Catholics as individuals are considered "lost" souls, but because in certain areas, even under the very aegis of the Roman Catholic Church, they are badly neglected socially and economically—and many Protestants would add, morally and spiritually. Moreover, Protestants accept the principle of religious liberty for all and in accordance with this basic principle, related to human rights and fundamental freedoms, they believe that a person has the right to change his religious faith, of his own free will and as his conscience directs, and that within every free state every religious body must have the right to teach, preach, publish literature, and win converts. Protestants in America repudiate the claim that a single religious faith, either on the basis of dogma or inheritance, has the right to exclude other faiths from a free state, or that citizens of any nation are automatically born into a particular Church.

Protestants believe that they are called to carry Christ's work to the corners of the earth, to every nation, and to the end of time. As stated at Willingen, they believe that "the Church is sent to every inhabited area of the world. No place is too far or too near. Every group of Christians is sent as God's ambassadors to the people in its immediate neighborhood. But its responsibility is not limited to the neighborhood. Because Christ is King of Kings and Saviour of the world, each group of Christians is also responsible for the proclamation of His Kingship to the uttermost parts of the earth. . . . The Church is sent to every social, political and religious community of mankind, both to those near at hand and to those far off. It is sent to those who deny or rebel against the reign of Christ; and no weakness, persecution or opposition may be allowed to limit this mission. Such are the conditions which the Church must expect for its welfare. Faithfulness to Christ will require the Church to come to grips with the social, political, economic and cultural life of the people to whom it is sent."

Missions and the Bible

The Great Commission of our Lord (Matt. 28:18-20) has always been, and will always be, the supreme motivation of the Protestant missionary cause. Close second to this is the example set by the apostle Paul in his numerous missionary journeys. The world relief work of Barnabas (Acts 11:28-30), and the medical service of Dr. Luke (Col. 4:14), give ample scriptural support for the great Protestant missionary enterprise of today with its evangelistic, educational, relief, agricultural, and medical aspects.

Christian missions have additional scriptural support in such passages as these:

"Ye shall receive power, after that the Holy Ghost is come upon you; and ye shall be witnesses unto me, both in Jerusalem, and in all Judea, and in Samaria, and unto the uttermost part of the earth" (Acts 1:8).

"And he [Peter] said unto them, ye know how that it is an unlawful thing for a man that is a Jew to keep company, or come unto one of another nation: but God hath shewed me that I should not call any man common or unclean: . . . of a truth I perceive that God is no respecter of persons: but in every nation he that feareth him, and worketh righteousness, is accepted with him" (Acts 10:28, 34-35).

"Now there was in the church that was at Antioch certain prophets and teachers; as Barnabas, and Simeon that was called Niger, and Lucius of Cyrene, and Manaen, which had been brought up with Herod the tetrarch, and Saul. As they ministered to the Lord, and fasted, the Holy Ghost said, Separate me Barnabas and Saul for the work whereunto I have called them. And when they fasted and prayed, and laid their hands on them, they sent them away" (Acts 13:1-3).

Great Moral Principles

John Wyclif, the great Protestant reformer, laid down the moral principle that "It is not possible to imagine a case or think of a fiction in which it is allowable to tell a lie." It should be emphasized that the Protestant Reformation was far more than a protest against the theological abuses; it was a reaffirmation of basic moral and religious principles. To Protestants, religion is much more than abiding by the laws of an institution; it is possessing and living in everyday life the spirit and teachings of Christ. Protestants add to the Ten Commandments the principles of the Sermon on the Mount and the teachings of Paul.

Protestants have a conscience, and this conscience has been worked overtime as the Christian teachings have come face to face with the overwhelming social and economic problems of our day. At Delaware in March, 1942, leading churchmen faced the problems of war and peace, under the guidance of John Foster Dulles, and formulated a statement of propositions popularly known as the Six Pillars of Peace. At the biennial meeting of the Federal Council of Churches of Christ in America, held in Cincinnati, Ohio, December, 1948, a statement on "The Churches and Human Rights" was adopted. It began by saying: "The flagrant violation of human rights in our generation has denied basic Christian principles. It has outraged Christian feeling and has impeded the achievement of world order. Even in those lands which profess adherence to the Christian democratic tradition there are discriminatory restrictions and exploitations. The dignity of man and the obligation of Christian brotherhood are so clearly expressed in the Gospels that our failure to live up to their precepts is a reproach against us among non-Christian peoples. The churches cannot view this situation with unconcern."

At Detroit, in 1950, the Department of the Church and Economic Life, Federal Council of Churches, held a conference on the theme, "The Responsibility of Christians in an Interdependent Economic World." It adopted a statement which declared: "The Gospel is concerned with all the activities of man, individual and social. Therefore, as the custodian of 'the sacred and imperishable message of eternal salvation,' [the Church] is charged with a fourfold duty. . . . It must be the teacher of the principles of conduct; a voice of judgment; a guardian of moral and spiritual values already won; and the herald of a better day."

The Law of Christ

Protestants have been motivated by the great prophets of the Old Testament—Amos, Hosea, Isaiah, and Jeremiah—in their work of economic justice and social righteousness.

In the New Testament the parables of Jesus are filled with what we call today human rights and fundamental freedoms. So is the Sermon on the Mount. Christ had no patience with those who exploited human beings for their own private gain (Matt. 5–7). Paul, as well as James, spelled out in great detail how Christians should behave toward each other and in the community (Gal. 5:16-26; Jas. 2:12-18). That the early Christians took these teachings seriously is indicated by Acts 2:42-47.

Besides the parable of the Good Samaritan and the Last Judgment scene (Matt. 25), in which Jesus declared that those who will enter the Kingdom of Heaven are those who clothe the naked, feed the hungry, and visit the sick, this passage from Galatians sums up the Christian attitude of helpfulness: "Bear

ye one another's burdens, and so fulfil the law of Christ. . . .
Be not deceived: God is not mocked: for whatsoever a man
soweth, that shall he also reap. For he that soweth to his flesh,
shall of the flesh reap corruption; but he that soweth to the
Spirit, shall of the Spirit reap life everlasting. And let us not
be weary in well doing; for in due season we shall reap, if we
faint not. As we have therefore opportunity, let us do good unto
all men" (Gal. 6:2, 7-10).

PROTESTANT REFERENCE BOOKS: Kenneth Scott Latourette's series on
the expansion of Christianity is highly recommended: *Missions Tomorrow, Anno Domini, The Unquenchable Light, The First Five Centuries, The Thousand Years of Uncertainty, The Centuries of Advance,
The Great Century; Ecumenical Foundations* by William R. Hogg;
The Mission and Expansion of Christianity in the First Three Centuries
by Adolf Harnack (translated by James Moffatt); *The Christian Life
and Message,* Vol. I of the Report of the Jerusalem Conference; *The
Authority of the Faith,* Vol. I of the Madras Conference series; *Five
Decades and a Forward View* by John R. Mott; *Re-Thinking Missions,
A Layman's Inquiry After One Hundred Years; The Philosophy of the
Christian World Mission* by Edmund Davison Soper.

   Social Salvation by John C. Bennett; *The Recovery of Ideals* by
Georgia Harkness; *From Victory to Peace* by Paul Hutchinson (note
particularly Appendix); *Christian Ethics and Modern Problems* by
W. R. Inge; *Christianity and the Cultural Crisis* by Charles D. Kean;
The Principles of Christian Ethics by Albert C. Knudson; *Social Re-
ligion* by Douglas Clyde Macintosh; *An Interpretation of Christian
Ethics* by Reinhold Niebuhr; *Personalities in Social Reform* by
G. Bromley Oxnam; *The Social Principles of Jesus* by Walter Raus-
chenbusch.

PART V
Areas of Conflict

19

Education and the Public School

Controversy centers around the promotion of Roman Catholic education not only in the United States, but in other nations like France, Italy, and even Spain. In the United States the controversy arises especially in the matter of using federal funds for private or parochial schools. While this chapter will deal with this matter, its chief intent will be to outline the Christian position in regard to education in general, and Catholic education in particular.

Roman Catholics spend millions of dollars each year in maintaining separate schools for their children. They do this as a matter of principle. They believe that public schools, as they now exist in this country, are not good for Catholic children.

Back of the entire Roman Catholic school system, which consists of parochial or elementary schools, secondary and normal schools, seminaries and universities, is a basic philosophy of Christian education.[1] Whether we agree with it or not, it should be understood by Protestants. The purpose of this chapter will be to explain what Roman Catholics believe to be the ideal form of education, and how they attempt to apply their fundamental educational principles in a practical way on the local and national levels.

THE ROMAN CATHOLIC POSITION

The Official Catholic Position

The official position of the Roman Catholic Church regarding education is found in the *Code of Canon Law,* issued in 1918. In Section XXII, these regulations are found:

[1] The Roman Catholic position on religion in education is contained in a statement, "On Secularism and Schools," presented by the Roman Catholic Bishops of the United States on November 15, 1952, and printed in full in *The New York Times.*

213

"Parents are bound by a most grave obligation to provide to the best of their ability for the religious and moral as well as for the physical and civil education of their children, and for their temporal well-being." (*Canon 1113*)

"From childhood all the faithful must be so educated that not only are they taught nothing contrary to faith and morals, but that religious and moral training takes the chief place." (*Canon 1372*)

"In every elementary school religious instruction, adapted to age of the children, must be given." (*Canon 1373*)

"Catholic children must not attend non-Catholic, neutral or mixed schools. . . . It is for the bishop of the place alone to decide, according to the instructions of the Apostolic See, in what circumstances and with what precautions attendance at such schools may be tolerated without danger of perversion to the pupils." (*Canon 1374*)

"The Church has the right to establish schools of every grade, not only elementary schools, but also high schools and colleges." (*Canon 1375*)

The Church's Stand on Education

The stand of the Roman Catholic Church on education is presented in the following eight-point statement published in the *National Catholic Almanac* (p. 361):

1. Parents are responsible for the training of their children.
2. Parents may be assisted by the Church, the State, private societies or individuals in fulfilling this duty.
3. Teachers have their authority to teach by delegation from the parents.
4. The Church has the right to demand of the parents that their children be trained in religion and morality.
5. Since such training is not given in non-Catholic schools, parents who send their children to such schools are bound under pain of mortal sin to supply such training fully and adequately.
6. Since most parents are unable to supply full and adequate religious training to their children, it becomes in most cases their obligation to send the children to Catholic schools.
7. Parents may send their children to non-Catholic schools only when such practice is tolerated by the bishop of the diocese.
8. The State has the right to demand that the child be prepared for his duties as a citizen. Such training is given in parochial schools as well as public schools.

Basic Principles of Roman Catholic Education

Probably the best exposition of the Roman Catholic position in regard to education is found in the encyclical letter of Pope Pius XI on "Christian Education of Youth." It was written in 1929 to the Patriarchs, Primates, Archbishops, Bishops, and other Ordinaries in peace and communion with the Apostolic See, and to all the faithful of the Catholic world. Because of its great importance, and its authentic nature, it is quoted here quite liberally:

"Since education consists essentially in preparing man for what he must be and for what he must do here below, in order to attain the sublime end for which he was created, it is clear that there can be no true education which is not wholly directed to man's last end, and that in the present order of Providence, since God has revealed Himself to us in the Person of His Only Begotten Son, Who alone is 'the way, the truth and the life,' there can be no ideally perfect education which is not Christian education."

"From this we see the supreme importance of Christian education, not merely for each individual, but for families and for the whole of human society, whose perfection comes from the perfection of the elements that compose it."

EDUCATION BELONGS TO THE CHURCH

"Education is essentially a social and not a mere individual activity. Now there are three necessary societies distinct from one another and yet harmoniously combined by God, into which man is born; two, namely the family and civil society, belong to the natural order; the third, the Church, to the supernatural order."

"First of all education belongs pre-eminently to the Church, by reason of a double title in the supernatural order, conferred exclusively upon her by God Himself; absolutely superior therefore to any other title in the natural order."

EXCLUSIVE RIGHTS

"It is worthy of note how a layman,[2] an excellent writer and at the same time a profound and conscientious thinker, has been able to understand and express exactly this fundamental Catholic doctrine! The Church does not say that morality belongs purely, in the sense of exclusively, to her; but that it belongs wholly to her."

"Therefore with full right the Church promotes letters, science, art, in so far as necessary or helpful to Christian education, in addition to her work for the salvation of souls; founding and maintaining

[2] A. Manzoni in *Asservazioni sulla Morale Cattolica.*

schools and institutions adapted to every branch of learning and degree of culture."

"Nor does it interfere in the least with the regulations of the State, because the Church in her motherly prudence is not unwilling that her schools and institutions for the education of the laity be in keeping with the legitimate dispositions of civil authority; she is in every way ready to cooperate with this authority and to make provision for a mutual understanding, should difficulties arise."

BOTH PRIVATE AND PUBLIC

"Again it is the inalienable right as well as the indispensable duty of the Church, to watch over the entire education of her children, in all institutions, public or private, not merely in regard to the religious instruction there given, but in regard to every other branch of learning and every regulation in so far as religion and morality are concerned."

"It pertains to the State, in view of the common good, to promote in various ways the education and instruction of youth. It should begin by encouraging and assisting, of its own accord, the initiative and activity of the Church and the family, whose successes in this field have been clearly demonstrated by history and experience. It should moreover supplement their work whenever this falls short of what is necessary, even by means of its own schools and institutions."

JURISDICTION OF THE CHURCH

" 'Everything,' says Leo XIII, 'in human affairs that is in any way sacred, or has reference to the salvation of souls and the worship of God, whether by its nature or by its end, is subject to the jurisdiction and discipline of the Church. Whatever else is comprised in the civil and political order, rightly comes under the authority of the State.' "

"Whoever refuses to admit these principles, and hence to apply them to education, must necessarily deny that Christ has founded His Church for the eternal salvation of mankind, and maintain instead that civil society and the State are not subject to God and to His law, natural and divine. Such a doctrine is manifestly impious; contrary to right reason, and, especially in this matter of education, extremely harmful to the proper training of youth, and disastrous as well for civil society as for the well-being of all mankind."

LAY SCHOOLS BECOME IRRELIGIOUS

"From this it follows that the so-called 'neutral' or 'lay' school, from which religion is excluded, is contrary to the fundamental principles of education. Such a school moreover cannot exist in practice; it is bound to become irreligious.

"We renew and confirm their [Pius IX and Leo XIII] declarations, as well as the Sacred Canons in which the frequenting of non-Catholic schools, whether neutral or mixed, those namely which are open to Catholics and non-Catholics alike, is forbidden for Catholic children, and can be at most tolerated, on the approval of the Ordinary alone, under determined circumstances of place and time, and with special precautions. Neither can Catholics admit that other type of mixed school (least of all the so-called 'ecole unique,' obligatory on all) in which the students are provided with separate religious instruction, but receive other lessons in common with non-Catholic pupils from non-Catholic teachers."

NOT FIT FOR CATHOLIC STUDENTS

"The mere fact that a school gives some religious instruction (often extremely stinted) does not bring it into accord with the rights of the Church and of the Christian family, or make it a fit place for Catholic students. To be this, it is necessary that all the teaching and the whole organization of the school, and its teachers, syllabus and textbooks in every branch, be regulated by the Christian spirit, under the direction and material supervision of the Church."

STATE FINANCIAL AID FOR CATHOLIC SCHOOLS

"Let no one say that in a nation where there are different religious beliefs, it is impossible to provide for public instruction otherwise than by neutral or mixed schools. In such a case it becomes the duty of the State, indeed it is the easier and more reasonable method of procedure, to leave free scope to the initiative of the Church and family, while giving them such assistance as justice demands. That this can be done to the full satisfaction of families, and to the advantage of education and of public peace and tranquillity, is clear from the actual experience of some countries comprising different religious denominations. There the school legislation respects the rights of the family, and Catholics are free to follow their own system of teaching in schools that are entirely Catholic. Nor is distributive justice lost sight of, as is evidenced by the financial aid granted by the State to the several schools demanded by the families."

CRUSADE FOR ROMAN CATHOLIC EDUCATION

"In other countries of mixed creeds, things are otherwise, and a heavy burden weighs upon Catholics . . . to make adequate provision for what they openly profess as their motto: *'Catholic education in Catholic schools for all the Catholic youth.'* If such education is not aided from public funds, as distributive justice requires, certainly it may not be opposed by any civil authority ready to recognize the rights of the family, and the irreducible claims of legitimate liberty.

"Whatever Catholics do in promoting and defending the Catholic school for their children, is a genuinely religious work and therefore an important task of 'Catholic Action.'

"Let it be loudly proclaimed and well understood and recognized

by all, that Catholics, no matter what their nationality, in agitating
for Catholic schools for their children, are not mixing in party politics,
but are engaged in a religious enterprise demanded by conscience.
They do not intend to separate their children either from the body of
the nation or its spirit, but to educate them in a perfect manner, most
conducive to the prosperity of the nation."

Public Aid to Roman Catholic Schools in the U.S.A.

Catholic authorities in the United States, backed by the basic
principles of the Roman Catholic Church, maintain that laws—
local, state, and national—which now prohibit the use of public
funds for the support of "auxiliary services" for private or parochial schools are "unjust and discriminatory." This is because,
from the Catholic position, these prohibitory laws arbitrarily
deny tax aid to Catholic schools which, like public schools, prepare children for the responsibilities of American citizenship.[3]

Roman Catholic leaders see no reason why the inclusion of
religious instruction in a school system or curriculum should de-
prive it of tax support, just so long as it meets all the requirements of the compulsory educational laws. Catholics have ob-
jected to federal legislation which requires some states to use
all federal funds for public schools exclusively. They maintain
that a fair and equitable federal aid law must be based upon
the principle that money appropriated for all children should
benefit *all* children.

Because "auxiliary school services" has been ruled legal by the
Supreme Court, Catholics, according to a statement in the *National Catholic Almanac,* "have centered their attention on the
use of federal funds to furnish auxiliary school services, e.g., non-
religious textbooks, bus rides and health services for non-public
school children in every state receiving federal aid. They recom-
mend that a small part of each state's allotment of federal funds
be spent for these services even though no state or local funds
are so expended." They express objection to the plan whereby
each state is left free to decide for itself whether any federal
funds should be spent on non-public school children. At the

---

[3] "The State, therefore, has the duty to help parents fulfill their task of
religious instruction and training. When the State fails in this help, when
it makes the task more difficult, and even penalizes parents who try to
fulfill this duty according to conscience, by depriving their children of their
right under our Federal Constitution to auxiliary services, this can only be
regarded as an utterly unfair and short-sighted policy."—The Roman Catholic
Bishops' statement on "Secularism and Schools," November 15, 1952.

same time Catholics are working on the state level "to obtain for non-public school children those auxiliary school services that may be legally furnished to them."

Roman Catholic authorities do not believe that the First Amendment erects a high wall separating Church from State. They believe that the State should aid religion. The Bishops' statement on "Secularism and Schools" emphasizes this point. The principle is *equality of public support,* not absolute withholding of financial aid. Therefore Roman Catholics maintain that the Constitution will not be violated, either in spirit or in fact, if the federal government supports all religious faiths, on an equality basis, from the public treasury.[4]

Catholic Educational Institutions in the U.S.A.

A national summary [5] of the Catholic educational institutions in the United States is as follows:

	No. of Schools	Instructors			Students			
		Religious	Lay	Total	Men	Women	Unclassified	Total
Seminaries								
Major Seminaries	104	1,169	24	1,193	8,444	----	---	8,444
Minor Seminaries	139	1,539	62	1,601	15,521	----	---	15,521
Universities and Colleges								
For Men	79	3,352	8,340	11,692	184,359	43,209	---	227,568
For Women	129	3,648	1,703	5,351	2,701	62,982	---	65,683
Diocesan Teachers' Colleges and Normal Schools	31	655	71	726	424	6,132	---	6,556
Secondary Schools	2,150	22,643	4,189	26,832	209,624	264,605	8,443	482,672
Elementary Schools	8,289	58,946	3,233	62,179	1,103,421	1,097,258	102,286	2,304,965
Total	10,921	91,952	17,622	109,574	1,524,494	1,474,186	112,729	3,111,409

---

[4] See article, "Federal Aid and State Aid to Education," in the *National Catholic Almanac,* p. 365.

[5] Compiled in 1949 by the Department of Education, National Catholic Welfare Conference. The latest summary available at time of publication.

THE PROTESTANT POINT OF VIEW
On the Value of Christian Education

Protestantism is emphatically opposed to the Roman Catholic teaching and practice regarding public and parochial schools because it believes in the public school system and that secular education can and must be religious in principle without church support or control.

Probably the sharpest point of conflict between Protestants and Roman Catholics in the United States comes in the area of public support for private schools. Many individual Roman Catholics (if not the official hierarchy) advocate that public funds should not merely be used for auxiliary aid, such as books, health benefits, use of buses, and lunches, but also for the actual support of the program and maintenance of both Protestant and Roman Catholic schools. Most Protestants are intensely opposed to this, since it violates, according to their way of thinking, the principle of Church and State relationship as found in the First Amendment of the U.S. Constitution. But, even more basically, they are convinced that the public schools are the chief agency for developing the democratic spirit which is found so uniquely in this country.

Protestants are willing that Roman Catholics have their own schools. They support them in this right. They reserve the same right to have their own private schools. But they do not believe that either Protestant or Roman Catholic schools should have in full, or in part, financial aid from the public treasury. Protestants support as a policy one system of public schools which are provided, out of tax funds, for all the children of the nation. This does not mean that Protestants want a purely secular school system with no trace of morality or religion. Protestants desire a public school system which is morally sound and which imparts knowledge regarding the general background of religion. They look to the Church School and weekday religious education to provide specific religious and sectarian instruction, and to win and develop personal loyalty.

Roman Catholics are determined to give their children *Roman Catholic* education. Protestants appreciate this desire, but they are determined that it shall not be at government expense.

Even if Protestant schools were included in some legislation for financial aid to parochial schools, it would be opposed because, they believe, by the very acceptance of tax funds they would be doing a disservice to democracy and violating an American principle. This is the principle which protects religious liberty and keeps our churches free. When they speak of separation, Protestants intend that neither Church nor State will be the master of the other.

Protestantism's Contribution to Education

Protestantism, because of its dedication to truth wherever it may be found and its spirit of free inquiry, has been the source of popular education and the founder of schools, colleges, and great universities. This is true of Continental Europe, England, Scotland, and in missionary lands; it is especially true of America.

The Oxford Conference,[6] 1937, expressed the basic principles regarding Protestant education: "The church's largest contribution to education, like her supreme ministry to human life, is her gospel, with its interpretation of existence and its inspiration to live worthily. Where life is without meaning, education becomes futile. Where it is ignobly conceived, education is debased. Where it is viewed in the light of God's purpose in Christ, it assumes divine significance.[7] It is not the methods by which her gospel is taught to the educational system preferred by various nations and by various communions in the church. It is all-important that her gospel should supply the presuppositions of all education, by whatever agency it is given, and create the spiritual atmosphere which pervades any institution of true learning. 'In thy Light shall we see light.'"

The basic educational policies of Protestantism are listed as follows by the Oxford Conference:

1. "The church is concerned that every child and adult shall receive the fullest education consistent with his capacities and that no discrimination in educational opportunity be made on the basis of race or social status."

2. "For any education worthy of the name truth is supreme, and there must be freedom to seek and to teach it."

3. "It is the church's aim to educate free persons under law

---

[6] *The Oxford Conference Official Report*, Willet, Clark & Co., pp. 147, 148.

[7] This would, of course, be outside the public schools.

to Christ. . . . It is her conviction that personality attains this freedom and completeness only in obedience to God."

4. "The church is opposed to any education which stimulates unbridled individualism and must affirm the basis for social solidarity which God has given in the relationships of the family and the community."

5. "If the church is to discharge her teaching duty, she must bring her communions into a common front on educational issues and unite her forces in fulfilling this urgent task."

Protestants in America are emphatic in their insistence that, based upon the principle of separation of Church and State, public funds shall not be used for religious or parochial schools. This does not mean that Protestants are opposed to having a strong religious emphasis in the public school system.[8] The U.S. Supreme Court on April 28, 1952, in upholding the courts of New York in the matter of granting "released time" at the parent's request for weekday religious instruction outside public school property, declared, "We cannot expand it [the McCollum case decision] [9] to cover the present released time program unless separation of Church and State means that public institutions can make no adjustments of their schedules to accommodate the religious needs of the people. We cannot read into the Bill of Rights such a philosophy of hostility to religion." Protestants support this ruling.

In a previous decision (*Everson v. Bd. of Ed. of Township of Ewing*) the U.S. Supreme Court ruled on February 10, 1947, that the state of New Jersey could, on a general welfare basis, charge the cost of bus transportation of Roman Catholic parochial schools to the taxpayers. But in the same decision it was stated that "the First Amendment has erected a wall between

---

[8] In a formal message "To the Christian people of America," the National Council of the Churches of Christ in the U.S.A., with a membership of 30 denominations with 35,000,000 members, declared (Denver, Dec. 12, 1952): "A way must be found to make the pupils of American schools aware of the heritage of faith upon which this nation was established, and which has been the most transforming influence in western culture. This we believe can be done in complete loyalty to the basic principle involved in the separation of church and state."

[9] In this famous case, *People of Illinois ex rel Vashti McCollum v. Bd. of Ed. of School District No. 71, Champaign, Ill.*, the U.S. Supreme Court ruled in March, 1948, that local school boards cannot use public classrooms for weekday religious instruction. This decision still stands.

Church and State. That wall must be kept high and impregnable. We could not approve the slightest breach."

Scripture Texts

Jesus' whole approach to life, as noted in the Sermon on the Mount and in the parables, as well as in his daily deeds, is best indicated in the phrase "ye shall know the truth, and the truth shall make you free" (John 8:32). A free and inquiring mind, a seeking spirit, a desire to learn new truth, make Protestant education particularly suited to the way of life known under the term *democracy*.

Jesus' own training in the synagogues and in his home, and Paul's remarkable educational training (Acts 22:3), point up the Christian education program of Protestants. The fact that Luke was a highly educated physician (Col. 4:14) shows that while early Christianity made its appeal to the common people, it did not neglect the development of the mind as well as the spirit.

It is of course impossible to justify today's vast Christian educational program by specific Scripture texts. Yet the fact that our educational system grew very largely out of Protestantism in this country gives us good reason to believe that freedom of inquiry and the desire for knowledge first of all found their support in such scriptural passages as these:

"These things have I spoken unto you, being yet present with you. But the Comforter, which is the Holy Ghost, whom the Father will send in my name, he shall teach you all things, and bring all things to your remembrance, whatsoever I have said unto you" (John 14:25, 26).

"I beseech you therefore, brethren, by the mercies of God, that ye present your bodies a living sacrifice, holy, acceptable unto God, which is your reasonable service. And be not conformed to this world: but be ye transformed by the renewing of your mind, that ye may prove what is that good, and acceptable, and perfect will of God" (Rom. 12:1, 2).

One of the most basic texts in the field of Christian education is the one which shows the growth in the life of Christ: "And Jesus increased in wisdom and stature, and in favour with God and man" (Luke 2:52).

PROTESTANT REFERENCE BOOKS: *The Modern Rival of Christian Faith* by Georgia Harkness; *American Education and Religion*, edited by F. Ernest Johnson; *Crisis in Education* by Bernard Iddings Bell;

American Freedom and Catholic Power by Paul Blanshard, Chap. V; *God and the Day's Work* by Robert L. Calhoun; *Christian Higher Education*, Council of Church Boards of Education, 1940; *America's Way in Church, State and Society* by Joseph M. Dawson; *The Teaching of Religion in American Higher Education*, edited by Christian Gauss; *Education for Life* by John O. Gross; *Orientation in Religious Education* by Philip Henry Lotz; *The Church and Organized Movements*, edited by Randolph C. Miller (Chap. VII on "Christianity and Organized Education"); *The Clue to Christian Education* by Randolph C. Miller; *The University and the Modern World* by Arnold S. Nash. *Education and Liberty* by James Bryant Conant.

For the Roman Catholic viewpoint see *American Education and Religion*, and *Catholicism and American Freedom*, both by James M. O'Neill.

20

Roman Catholics and Democracy

What is the relation of the Roman Catholic Church in America to the Vatican in Rome? This is no academic question. It goes to the very heart of our democratic system. Are the members of the Roman Catholic Church under the absolute control of the pope only in moral and spiritual matters? Or, are they also under the control of the Roman hierarchy in matters of politics and civil obedience?

The relationship of the United States to the Vatican, particularly the exchange of official representatives, is involved here. Also involved is the often raised question of whether a Roman Catholic President of the United States would owe his first allegiance to the U.S. Constitution or to Rome.

In this chapter such questions will be answered. An honest attempt will be made to state the case for the Roman Catholic Church in regard to democracy, separation of Church and State, and religious freedom.

THE ROMAN CATHOLIC POSITION

Attitude Toward Democracy

The Roman Catholic Church is neutral as far as various forms of governments are concerned, except when they threaten the moral and spiritual life of the faithful, as in the case of Communism. It is above politics, at least in principle. The Church is the Church, and not a political organization.

This is brought out most forcefully in the encyclical letter of Pope Leo XIII, "Christian Democracy" (*Graves de Communi*) in which he warns Christian action groups against becoming political parties and then goes on to say, "The laws of nature and of the Gospel, which by right are superior to all human contingencies, are necessarily independent of all modifications of civil government, while at the same time they are in concord with

225

everything that is not repugnant to morality and justice. They are, therefore, and they must remain absolutely free from political parties, and have nothing to do with the various changes of administration which may occur in a nation; so that Catholics may and ought to be citizens according to the constitution of any State, guided as they are by those laws which command them to love God above all things, and their neighbors as themselves. This has always been the discipline of the Church. The Roman Pontiffs acted upon this principle, whenever they dealt with different countries, no matter what might be the character of their governments."

Pope Leo XIII asks all Roman Catholics to submit to the just commands of the rulers of the State.

In another encyclical letter, "On Civil Government" (*Diuturnum*), he leaves the form of government with the choice of the people, saying, "A society can neither exist nor be conceived in which there is no one to govern the will of individuals, in such a way as to make, as it were, one will out of many, and to impel them rightly and orderly to the common good; therefore God has willed that in a civil society there should be some to rule the multitude." But, he adds, when there is a conflict between Church and State, in regard to the matter of unjust laws, the Catholic must obey God rather than Caesar.

Good Citizenship

The Roman Catholic Church advocates good citizenship. It encourages its members to take an active part in the affairs of state. It teaches that "we are obliged to take an active part in the works of good citizenship because right reason requires citizens to work together for the public welfare of the country." (*A Catechism of Christian Doctrine*, p. 201)

According to an article in the *National Catholic Almanac,* "The Catholic citizen is in conscience bound to respect and obey the duly constituted authority provided faith and morals are thereby not endangered. Under no circumstances may the Church be subjugated by the State. Whatever their form may be, states are not conceded the right to force the observance of immoral or irreligious laws upon a people." (p. 110)

As Pope Pius XI puts it,[1] "The State must allow the Church freedom to fulfill her mission."

---

[1] Encyclical letter, "God and Liberty Against Satan and Slavery" (*Divini Redemptoris*).

Concordats

A concordat is a treaty between the Holy See and a sovereign nation concerning the interests of religion. Here the spiritual welfare of Roman Catholics is the first concern. The concordat does not necessarily mean that the Vatican approves the government or political system involved.

The Treaty of the Lateran, made between the Vatican and Italy in 1929, and incorporated into the constitution of the new Italian republic after World War II, not only created Vatican City as a sovereign state, but also made the Catholic faith the religion of Italy, along with the guarantees of its free exercise. Among other matters Italy recognizes that marriage is a sacrament and indissoluble, that instruction in Christian doctrine will be provided for in all public schools, and the person of the pope is inviolable and sacred.

The Italian constitution, although it recognizes Catholicism as the state religion, grants freedom to other faiths.

Vatican City State

The Lateran Treaty in 1929 brought into being the independent and sovereign Vatican City State. It is governed by the pope, who has full legislative, executive, and judiciary powers. It is also perpetually neutral and extra-national and enjoys all the rights and privileges of a sovereign nation, including diplomatic immunity.

The State of Vatican City comprises 108.7 acres. This territory includes principally the Vatican palace, its gardens and annexes, the basilica and piazza of St. Peter and the contiguous buildings. It has a population of less than a thousand, most of whom are clerics. It has its own post office, newspaper, radio station, etc. The pope delegates the actual management of Vatican City to a governor, who is a layman, and there is besides a consultative council, all named by the pope.

Pope Pius XI, when he took over the territory, declared, "It will, we hope, be clear that the Sovereign Pontiff has no more material territory than is indispensable for him if he is to exercise the spiritual power entrusted to him for the good of mankind . . . we are pleased that the material domain is reduced to so small an extent."

According to *A Catechism of Christian Doctrine*, "The present position of the Pope, as head of the Vatican City, shows to the world that he and his household are not the subjects of other temporal powers. When we speak of the temporal power of the Pope, we do not mean thereby merely to classify him with earthly rulers. The Pope's temporal power is a means to an end, guaranteeing that freedom of word and action which he must rightfully enjoy as the supreme spiritual ruler of the Church." (p. 125)

Since the pope is head of a temporal state, does it follow that Roman Catholicism is in part a Church and in part a State? In reply to this question, Fathers Rumble and Carty answer in *Radio Replies,* "In no way whatever can the Catholic Church be called partly a political State. . . . The Pope is the spiritual head of the Catholic Church, and I acknowledge spiritual allegiance to him as to my supreme Bishop. He happens also to be temporal ruler of the territory known as Vatican City, in order to be independent of Italian civil authority. But I am not a citizen dwelling in that territory, and have no political affiliations with it." (Vol. III, p. 91)

Father Rumble, who lives in Sydney, Australia, carries the point still farther when he says, "If the political interests of Vatican City ever really menaced the political interests of our Commonwealth, Catholics would be obliged in conscience to defend our country against Papal aggression. If the Pope sent two Cardinals and an altar boy in a rowing boat to annex Australia as a further temporal possession of the Holy See, it would be the duty of Catholics in Australia to enlist at once in the Army, Navy, and Air-force, and to concentrate on the task of repelling the invader even at the cost of their own lives."

The late Cardinal Gibbons, in *A Retrospect of Fifty Years,* also maintains that Catholics are not bound to obey the Pope if he should ever command them to be disloyal to their lawfully constituted civil authorities. "The Pope will take no such action . . . even though it is part of the Catholic Faith that he is infallible in the exercise of his teaching authority; but were he to do so, he would stand self-condemned, a transgressor of the law he himself promulgates." (p. 227)

Cardinal Newman in his famous letter of 1874, under the title *A Letter to the Duke of Norfolk,* makes it very clear that the Pope does not have *absolute* control of the Catholic citizen. He declares:

"When, then, Mr. Gladstone asks Catholics how they can obey the Queen and yet obey the Pope, since it may happen that the commands of the two authorities may clash, I answer, that is my *rule*, both to obey the one and to obey the other, but that there is no rule in this world without exceptions, and if either the Pope or the Queen demanded of me an 'Absolute Obedience,' he or she would be transgressing the laws of human society. I give an absolute obedience to neither."

Freedom of Worship

Although the matter of the Roman Catholic attitude toward religious liberty was dwelt upon briefly in Chapter 3, it should be noted here that what Protestants mean by freedom of worship, and what Roman Catholics mean by it, are two quite different things. Roman Catholics begin with the premise that the Roman Catholic faith, and it alone, is the true faith. All other religions are in error, at most to be tolerated. This means that although Protestants may be given, under certain conditions, freedom to worship, the ideal situation is to have the State support Roman Catholicism as the official authorized religion in a completely Roman Catholic country.

This position is made clear in *A Catholic Dictionary* when it declares that freedom of worship is "the inalienable right of all men to worship God according to the teaching of the Catholic Church. No state can justifiably prevent the exercise of this right; and indeed it has a duty to foster this true worship. . . . But to avoid greater evil or to achieve a higher good, public authority can tolerate false religions, so long as they do not teach open immorality." (pp. 201-202)

When Mexico, on the basis of a new constitution, withdrew support from Roman Catholicism as the official religion of the State, and placed the Church under certain civil laws, the Vatican expressed a most solemn protest. This was followed up by the encyclical letter of Pope Pius XI, "The Church and Mexico," in which he commended the clergy for standing up for the "rights of the Hierarchy" even in the face of persecution, and declared that the Holy See "had to condemn" a secular paper because of its attacks on the Catholic Church, and said, "Add to this that not only is religious instruction forbidden in the primary schools, but not infrequently attempts are made to induce those, whose duty it is to educate the future generations, to become purveyors of irreligious and immoral teachings, thus obliging the parents to make heavy sacrifices in order to safeguard the innocence of their children."

Although the government of Mexico, in 1929, publicly declared that the new constitution had no intention of destroying the "Identity of the Church," or of ignoring the hierarchy, yet Pope Pius XI maintained that the specific measures adopted, such as granting licenses for the priestly ministry, the limiting of the number of the clergy, and the failure to recognize the hierarchy officially, did mean that the State was attacking "the liberty of the Church, which liberty the Church can never renounce." He advised the clergy of Mexico to continue with its ministry, but under protest.

Freedom of religion, from the Roman Catholic point of view, means full liberty for the "one true religion."

"The Catholic Church, even if our country became entirely Catholic, would not wish to assume purely civil government. Free and easy divorce laws would be repealed; the sale of birth-control requirements would be prohibited; and various other un-Christian liberties would be withdrawn. But where legislation did not conflict with God's laws, it would be unaffected by the predominance of the Catholic religion." (Fathers Rumble and Carty in *Radio Replies,* Vol. I, p. 296)

"A Catholic would not be inconsistent with any principle of his faith if he held that in the circumstances that prevail at the present time, it would be the most feasible plan to have complete religious toleration throughout the whole world. But it must be remembered that a Catholic cannot advocate such a plan on the basis that all religions have a genuine, God-given right to exist. Such a right belongs only to the one religion founded by Jesus Christ for all men. Catholics can uphold only the policy of equality of *civil* rights for all denominations. . . . In a country like the United States, where the religious affiliations of the citizens are so numerous and so diverse, and where no single denomination is predominant, complete equality for all religions is undoubtedly the most commendable policy. . . . The Catholics of America are just as anxious as their Protestant and Jewish neighbors to maintain and to promote civil equality for all religions throughout our land. If the word 'rights' is taken in the sense of *civil rights* in the United States or in countries where there are similar religious conditions, Catholics have no hesitation in stating that all religions should have equal rights." (Francis J. Connell in *Freedom of Worship,* published by the Paulist Press, Imprimatur of Francis Cardinal Spellman, pp. 13, 15)

Separation of Church and State

The relation of Church and State in the United States rests on the first amendment of the Bill of Rights of the U.S. Constitution, namely, "Congress shall make no law respecting an establishment of religion, or prohibiting the free exercise thereof."

Much discussion has taken place over the correct interpretation of this amendment. Many prominent Roman Catholics contend that it does not mean that there should be a wall of separation between Church and State, but that they should be mutually helpful. They do not agree with the opinion of the Supreme Court, in the McCollum case, and some Catholics even call it "the greatest threat to our civil liberties in recent times." [2]

Roman Catholics believe that the government, through the use of public funds, should co-operate with education that includes religion. They do not ask that Congress establish any religion, or give preference to any, but that it give equal co-operation to all faiths. They cite as an example the following: "If aid is given Catholic hospitals and refused those operated under Methodist auspices, it is clearly a case of favoritism. But if all sectarian hospitals are aided, the sects which do not operate hospitals validly cannot accuse the government of discrimination against them." (Jeffrey Keefe, O.F.M., in *American Separation of Church and State*, published by the Paulist Press, p. 23)

The summary of the whole matter is found in these words of George E. Reed of the Legal Department of the National Catholic Welfare Conference, "Specifically, the Virginia Senate stated that although the amendment 'goes to restrain Congress from passing laws establishing any national religion, they might, notwithstanding, levy taxes to any amount for the support of religion.' . . . Unfortunately the Supreme Court of the United States has rejected this view. The departure from the historical concept of the First Amendment lies in the mandate against 'aid to all religion.' The majority of the constitutional experts have indicated that the First Amendment was never intended to bar non-preferential aid to religion but that on the contrary such co-operation between Church and State has played a significant role in the development of this country." [3] Catholic

---

[2] James H. O'Neill in *Religion and Education Under the Constitution.*
[3] Article in *National Catholic Almanac*, pp. 647-649.

authorities (along with some Protestants) are waging a campaign to have this McCollum decision of the U.S. Supreme Court reversed.

THE PROTESTANT POINT OF VIEW
On the Basis of Religious Liberty

Protestantism is strongly opposed to the Roman Catholic position regarding Church and State because it firmly believes that there must be a free church in a free state, without preferential treatment of any kind whatsoever to any church, sect, or religion.

Protestants developed very largely in the environment of democracy. Roman Catholicism, on the other hand, has lived through the centuries in a variety of political governments and, because of its hierarchy, does not adjust easily to democratic principles and practices. It lives, in theory at least, above politics and encourages the faithful to express loyalty to their own form of government. In the ideal, and sometimes in actual practice, Roman Catholics demand that the State become the servant of the Church. Other religious faiths are then "tolerated," but they are never allowed true freedom in the full sense—both religious and civil.[4]

Religious freedom, to the Protestant, is freedom to preach, worship, and to evangelize openly. It is the right to practice one's faith without government or Church interference, so long as such practice does not injure others or endanger the State. Most Protestants believe that sending an official U.S. representative to the Vatican is a violation of the principle of religious freedom and separation of Church and State. Sending a special envoy to the Vatican would be to single out a particular faith for official recognition. Protestants vigorously protest against this,

---

[4] The Spanish Constitution, Article 6, while recognizing the Roman Catholic Church as the state religion, states that "no one will be molested for his religious beliefs nor in the private exercise of his cult." But Protestants are not allowed the privileges of *public* worship. Pedro Cardinal Segura y Saenz, Archbishop of Seville, has recently attempted to force the government to deny Protestants even the limited toleration provided for in the Constitution.

In Italy, recently, certain Protestant "cults," as denominations are called there, have been denied the right of public worship.

as they do against the official recognition of any or all religious faiths by the State. Again, this does not mean that Protestants oppose the Roman Catholic religion as such; but it does mean that although looking with favor upon close relationships between governments and churches, there must be a mark of separation between the two. Otherwise the State might try to dominate the Church, or in some cases, the Church might actually control the State. From the Protestant point of view, true liberty cannot exist, either for the State or the Church, under such conditions.

The U.S. Constitution

"Congress shall make no law respecting an establishment of religion or prohibiting the free exercise thereof or abridging the freedom of speech and the press." This is from the Constitution of the United States of America. The Supreme Court in several decisions has ruled that this "has erected a wall between church and state." (Mr. Justice Black, *Everson vs. Township of Ewing,* Majority Opinion, February 10, 1947)

These rights were written into the Constitution because Protestants brought to this nation, and championed, the cause of religious freedom. This was particularly true of Roger Williams who established Rhode Island upon the foundation of religious and civil liberty. Here he put into practice the principle of separation of Church and State which became a part of the legislation supported by the Founding Fathers. In Pennsylvania, as the result of the labors of William Penn, the principle was established that true religion can consort only with liberty of opinion and conscience, never with the spirit of persecution. Penn also maintained that neither a good Christian nor a good citizen can be made by force. He therefore advocated toleration as the unifying factor of the New World. Virginia, largely due to Baptist influence, a few days before the Declaration of Independence was signed, abolished the state church and declared that all men are equally entitled "to the free exercise of their religion according to the dictates of their conscience."

One of the most complete definitions of religious liberty, from the Protestant viewpoint, was made in 1942 by Dr. Luther A. Weigle in his presidential address before the biennial meeting of the Federal Council of the Churches of Christ in America (now a part of the National Council of the Churches of Christ in the

U.S.A.) at Cleveland.[5] In this three-point declaration, dealing with the rights of the individual, the church, and the citizen, Dean Weigle indicated the following rights for the individual:

"1. To believe as reason and conscience dictate.
2. To worship God in the ways which reason and conscience dictate.
3. To live and act in accordance with such belief and worship.
4. To express religious belief in speech.
5. To express religious belief for the purpose of persuasion, to convince and convert others.
6. To educate his children in his religious faith.
7. To join with others in the organized life and work of a church, congregation, or other religious fellowship.
8. To withdraw from such affiliation with a religious organization or community . . . to change belief.
9. To disbelieve in God, to deny religion, and to act, speak, persuade, educate, and affiliate with others in ways appropriate to this disbelief or atheism."

Both the Oxford Conference on Church, Community and State (1937) and the Madras Conference under the sponsorship of the International Missionary Council went on record favoring freedom in private and public worship; freedom of the church to preach and teach, in public as well as in private; freedom to carry on Christian service and missionary activity; freedom to determine conditions of membership and the reception of members; and freedom of the church to have such rights and facilities as are open to citizens and associations in general, so that the recognized ends of the church may be achieved. (For an exposition of these points please see *The Oxford Conference Official Report*, pages 72-73, and *The World Mission of the Churches*, Findings and Recommendations of the International Missionary Conference, Madras, page 124.)

In a "Statement on Religious Liberty," in 1944, the Federal Council of Churches and the Foreign Missions Conference of North America adopted the following pronouncement on the meaning of religious liberty:

"The right of individuals everywhere to religious liberty shall be recognized and, subject only to the maintenance of public order and security, shall be guaranteed against legal provisions

---

[5] *Religious Freedom*, Biennial Report, 1942, Federal Council of Churches, pp. 32-34; also in *Religious Liberty: An Inquiry* by M. Searle Bates, pp. 303-305.

and administrative acts which would impose political, economic, or social disabilities on grounds of religion.

"Religious liberty shall be interpreted to include freedom to worship according to conscience and to bring up children in the faith of their parents; freedom for the individual to change his religion; freedom to preach, educate, publish, and carry on missionary activities; and freedom to organize with others, and to acquire and hold property, for these purposes."

In 1949, the Third Study Conference on the Churches and World Order, meeting at Cleveland, reaffirmed a strong resolution on religious liberty, which was originally adopted by the World Council of Churches in 1948.

Although, according to Winfred E. Garrison in *A Protestant Manifesto* (p. 196), "even in the middle of the twentieth century more Protestants are members of state-connected churches than of free churches," the position of the Protestant churches in America is strongly for absolute separation of Church and State. Typical of statements adopted by other Protestant bodies is the following adopted by the American Baptist Convention at Boston in 1950: "Whereas, we as American Baptists have seen anew the significance and necessity of the principles of religious freedom and the separation of Church and State which our forefathers first proclaimed and practiced in this land . . . reaffirm at this mid-century our support of . . . the absolute separation of Church and State." (*Year Book of the American Baptist Convention,* 1950, p. 192)

Human Rights in Scripture

It is not without reason that the cause of democracy is the strongest in countries where Protestants are in the majority. Protestants accept the teaching of Scripture concerning human rights (Luke 10:30-37), the sanctity of the individual soul (Luke 17:2), and the proper relationships between church and state (Matt. 22:21). When Jesus declared that we should render unto Caesar what belongs to Caesar, and render unto God what belongs to God, he laid the foundation for a democratic state. Add to this Peter's teaching that "We ought to obey God rather than men" (Acts 5:29), and we have a strong basis for democratic action. Freedom, liberty, soul liberty, freedom of conscience, separation of church and state, are the great words and principles of Protestantism. They did not originate in men's minds. They were first of all created in the inspired writings of the Bible.

To be specific we refer to the following passages:

"Be kindly affectioned one to another with brotherly love; in honour preferring one another; not slothful in business; fervent in spirit; serving the Lord; rejoicing in hope; patient in tribulation; continuing constant in prayer; distributing to the necessity of saints; given to hospitality. . . . Be of the same mind one toward another. Mind not high things, but condescend to men of low estate. Be not wise in your own conceits" (Romans 12: 10-13, 16).

"There is neither Jew nor Greek, there is neither bond nor free, there is neither male nor female: for ye are all one in Christ Jesus" (Gal. 3:28).

"Stand fast therefore in the liberty wherewith Christ hath made us free, and be not entangled again with the yoke of bondage" (Gal. 5:1).

"Masters, give unto your servants that which is just and equal; knowing that ye also have a Master in heaven" (Col. 4:1).

"For perhaps he [Onesimus] therefore departed for a season, that thou shouldest receive him for ever; not now as a servant, but above a servant, a brother beloved" (Philem. 1:15-16).

PROTESTANT REFERENCE BOOKS: *Religious Liberty*, M. S. Bates; *Separate Church and State Now* by Joseph M. Dawson; *A Protestant Manifesto* by Winfred E. Garrison; *Protestant Panorama* by Clarence W. Hall and Desider Holisher; *Man and the State* by William Ernest Hocking; *Tradition, Freedom and the Spirit* by David Jenkins; *Separation of Church and State in the United States* by Alvin W. Johnson and Frank H. Yost; *The Catholic-Protestant Mind* by Conrad Henry Moehlman; *Democracy and the Churches* by James Hastings Nichols; *Reference Manual on U.S. Diplomatic Representation at the Vatican*, published by the National Council of Churches; *Religious Liberty* by Cecil Northcott; *Church and State in the United States* by Anson Phelps Stokes; *Religion in Colonial America* by William W. Sweet.

21

The Vatican and Its World Power

It will be helpful, if we are to understand the Vatican and its world power, to have at the very beginning a few definitions of terms associated with the Vatican. *Holy See* means specifically the episcopal territory (or throne) of Rome, but in general has come to mean the pope as supreme pontiff, together with those who are associated with him in government at the Church's headquarters. *Papacy* means the office of the pope, or the system of ecclesiastical government in which supreme authority is vested in the pope. *Vatican* means the official residence of the pope at Rome, but figuratively it signifies the papal power and influence. *Hierarchy* (ecclesiastical) means the organization of the ranks and orders of the Roman Catholic clergy in successive grades: (1) one part ("Order") which has the power over worship and the administration of the sacraments; (2) the other part (Jurisdiction) has power over the members of the Roman Catholic Church. Put these key words together and they spell tremendous spiritual and moral power—and, many would add, political power.

THE ROMAN CATHOLIC POSITION

The Composition of the Catholic Hierarchy

At the head of the governing body of the Roman Catholic Church [1] is the pope who carries the titles Bishop of Rome, Vicar of Jesus Christ, Successor of St. Peter, the Prince of the Apostles, and Supreme Pontiff. He not only has primacy of honor, but also has supreme and full power over the Universal Church, Patriarch of the West, Primate of Italy, Archbishop and Metropolitan of the Roman Province, and Sovereign of the State of Vatican City.

---

[1] The official title is "The Holy Catholic Apostolic Roman Church."

237

The College of Cardinals serves as the Senate of the pope. It assists him in the government of the Church, the cardinals being his chief advisers and helpers.

Four patriarchs serve in Constantinople, Alexandria, Antioch, and Jerusalem, and the pope acts as the patriarch for all the Western Church.

An archbishop serves as the bishop of a diocese (archdiocese) and has authority, which is limited and defined by canon law, over the bishops of the dioceses of a defined territory (province).

Bishops are the supreme ecclesiastical rulers of their respective dioceses.

Consistories are assemblies of cardinals presided over by the pope.

A Council is an assembly of the Catholic Church, called together by its lawful head, to decide questions concerning faith, morals, or ecclesiastical discipline. (For a full treatment of this subject, the reader is referred to *The Catholic Encyclopedia*.)

Although the pope has full and absolute jurisdiction in the governmental affairs of the Church, it is practically impossible for him to administer personally the affairs of the universal Church. Therefore, popes have established various groups of churchmen who are given particular areas of responsibility. These bodies fall under these categories:

I. Congregations [2]

Supreme Sacred Congregation of the Holy Office

"Guards the Catholic doctrine in faith and morals; judges heresy and those suspected of heresy; protects the dogmatic doctrine of the sacraments; decides in matters concerning the Eucharistic fast of priests celebrating Mass; in matters concerning the Pauline privilege, the marriage impediments of disparity of cult and mixed religion, and is able to grant dispensations from these two impediments; examines and condemns books and publications dangerous to faith and morals, and gives dispensations for reading them; judges all questions pertaining to the dogmatic doctrine of indulgences, new prayers, and devotions." [3]

---

[2] For a fuller treatment of the functions of the various Congregations at the Vatican see *The Catholic Church in Action* by Michael Williams, The Macmillan Co., Imprimatur of Patrick Cardinal Hayes.

[3] All quotations in this section are taken from the *National Catholic Almanac*.

Sacred Consistorial Congregation

"Prepares matter to be discussed at consistories; constitutes new dioceses, provinces, and cathedral and collegiate chapters for all territories not subject to the Propagation of the Faith; divides dioceses; proposes bishops, apostolic administrators, coadjutors, and auxiliary bishops," etc.

Sacred Congregation for the Oriental Church

"All matters of whatever kind which pertain to the discipline, the persons, or the rites of the Eastern Church, as also mixed questions either of persons or things which arise owing to the relation to the Latin Church, constitute the object of this Congregation's care."

Sacred Congregation of the Sacraments

"Regulates the discipline of the seven sacraments; . . . probes reasons for dispensations; has exclusive competence in legitimation of birth; receives and answers questions regarding the obligations of Holy Orders and the validity of Orders of Matrimony."

Sacred Congregation of the Council

"Has authority over discipline of secular clergy and laymen. Oversees pious legacies, work, Mass stipends, benefices, and offices, ecclesiastical goods, both movable and immovable, diocesan taxes, taxes of the Episcopal Curia, etc.; has power to dispense from the conditions for obtaining a benefice; to permit laymen to acquire ecclesiastical goods usurped by the civil power."

Sacred Congregation of Religious

"Has jurisdiction over the government, discipline, studies, property, and privileges of all religious, including lay members of Third Orders; gives dispensations to religious from the common law."

Sacred Congregation for the Propagation of the Faith

"Entrusted with the care of all mission territory—those places where no hierarchy is established. . . . Societies and Seminaries founded to train missionaries are under the supervision of this Congregation."

Sacred Congregation of Rites

"Supervises and determines all things which pertain to ceremonies and rites in the Latin Church; grants dispensations in such matters; gives insignia and privileges of honor; treats of all business concerning the beatification and canonization of the Servants of God or concerning the relics of these same."

Sacred Congregation of Ceremonies

"Regulates ceremonies in the papal chapel and court and the sacred functions which the cardinals perform outside the papal chapel; decides questions of the precedence of cardinals and legates whom the various nations send to the Holy See."

Sacred Congregation of Extraordinary Ecclesiastical Affairs

"Constitutes and divides dioceses, promotes suitable men for vacant sees, whenever these affairs must be settled in conjunction with civil powers; handles matters referred to it by the Holy Father through the Cardinal Secretary of State, especially concordats and those matters which have a relation to the civil laws. Under the Congregation is the Pontifical Commission for Russia."

Sacred Congregation of Seminaries and Universities

"Superintends all those matters which pertain to the government, discipline, temporal administration, and studies of seminaries; to it also is committed the direction of the government and studies in universities depending upon the authority of the Church, even those directed by the religious; examines and approves new institutions; confers academic degrees and grants the faculty and establishes norms for the conferring of these."

Sacred Congregation of the Basilica of St. Peter

Its duty is the care of the building and upkeep of St. Peter's.

II. TRIBUNALS

Sacred Apostolic Penitentiary

"Jurisdiction to judge all cases of conscience, non-sacramental as well as sacramental; also decides questions concerning the use and concession of indulgences, without however encroaching on the rights of the Holy Office as to the dogmatic doctrine involved in these or in new prayers or devotions."

Supreme Tribunal Apostolic Signature

"The supreme tribunal of the Roman Curia; handles all cases of appeal; settles controversies as to the jurisdiction of the inferior tribunals."

Sacred Roman Rota

"Handles cases demanding judicial procedure, without prejudice to the rights of the Holy Office or the Congregation of Sacred Rites."

III. Offices

Apostolic Chancery

"Sends out Apostolic Letters and Bulls concerning the provision of consistorial offices and benefices, the establishment of new dioceses, provinces and chapters, and other affairs of major importance."

Apostolic Datary

"Should have knowledge of the suitability of candidates to be promoted to non-consistorial benefices; sends letters of appointment to such candidates; sends dispensations from conditions required for these benefices; exacts the tax imposed by the Holy Father in conferring these benefices."

Apostolic Camera

"Has the care and administration of the temporal goods and rights of the Holy See, especially when it is vacant."

Secretariate of State

"Prepares matters to be brought up before the Congregation of Extraordinary Ecclesiastical Affairs. Handles ordinary affairs. Sends out Apostolic Briefs."

Secretariate of Briefs to Princes and of Latin Letters

"To translate in Latin the acts of the Supreme Pontiff, which have been committed to it by him."

Papal Legates and Other Representatives

There are four classes of papal legates, the first being *Legates a latere*, who are cardinals appointed by the pope to represent him at specific functions, usually those of national importance. *Nuncios* are representatives of the pope at a foreign government whose duty it is to handle the affairs between the Apostolic See and the state. In all Roman Catholic nations the Nuncio is dean of the diplomatic corps. *Inter nuncios* are legates of lower rank whose duty it is to foster relations between the Vatican and the state. They are sent to governments of lesser importance. *Apostolic Delegates* are nondiplomatic legates sent to foreign countries to watch over the conditions of the Church and state.

Vatican representatives, of one kind or another, are found in most of the countries of the world, although the apostolic nunciaturs have been closed in the Communist nations of Albania, Bulgaria, China, Czechoslovakia, Estonia, Hungary, Latvia, Lithuania, and Rumania. The posts in Greece and Syria, as of

1951, were not filled. The following countries now have Vatican representatives: Argentina, Australia (New Zealand and Oceania), Austria, Belgian Congo (and Ruanda Urundi), Belgium, Bolivia, Brazil, British East and West Africa, Canada, Chile, Colombia, Costa Rica, Cuba, Dominican Republic, Ecuador, Egypt, El Salvador, Ethiopia, France, French West Africa, Germany, Great Britain, Guatemala, Haiti, Honduras, India, Indo-China, Indonesia, Iran, Iraq, Ireland, Italy, Japan, Jerusalem (Palestine, Jordan, and Cypress), Korea, Lebanon, Liberia, Luxembourg, Mexico, Netherlands, Nicaragua, Pakistan (East and West), Panama, Paraguay, Peru, Philippines, Poland, Portugal, South Africa, Spain, Switzerland, and Turkey.

Diplomatic Representatives to the Vatican

Most of the nations of the world sent representatives to the Vatican. At the present time, the following countries are represented:

Nation	Rank
Argentina	Ambassador Extraordinary and Plenipotentiary
Austria	Envoy Extraordinary and Minister Plenipotentiary
Belgium	A. E. and P.
Bolivia	A. E. and P.
Brazil	A. E. and P.
Chile	A. E. and P.
China	Charge d'Affaires, *ad interim*
Colombia	A. E. and P.
Costa Rica	E. E. and M. P.
Cuba	A. E. and P.
Dominican Republic	A. E. and P.
Ecuador	A. E. and P.
Egypt	E. E. and M. P.
El Salvador	E. E. and M. P.
Finland	E. E. and M. P.
France	A. E. and P.
Great Britain	E. E. and M. P.
Haiti	A. E. and P.
India	E. E. and M. P.
Indonesia	E. E. and M. P.
Ireland	A. E. and P.
Italy	A. E. and P.
Lebanon	E. E. and M. P.

Nation	Rank
Liberia	E. E. and M. P.
Lithuania	E. E. and M. P.
Monaco	E. E. and M. P.
Netherlands	E. E. and M. P.
Nicaragua	E. E. and M. P.
Order of Malta	E. E. and M. P.
Pakistan	Ch. d'A., *ad interim*
Panama	E. E. and M. P.
Peru	Ch. d'A., *ad interim*
Philippines	A. E. and P.
Poland	A. E. and P.
Portugal	A. E. and P.
San Marino	E. E. and M. P.
Spain	A. E. and P.
Syria	Ch. d'A.
Uruguay	E. E. and M. P.
Venezuela	A. E. and P.
Yugoslavia	Ch. d'A., *ad interim*

Summary of World Strength of the Catholic Church

There are about 400,000,000 Catholics in the world. They are located in the following countries: [4] Aden (see Saudi Arabia); Alaska, 19,782; Albania, 877,477; Andorra (French), 5,000; Angola, 681,157; Argentina, 14,955,245; Australia, 1,387,833; Austria, 5,841,863; Azores, 278,000; Bahamas (British West Indies), 11,378; Balearic Islands, 417,719; Basutoland (British), 197,215; Bechuanaland and Southern Rhodesia (British), 85,850; Belgium, 8,345,319; Bermuda (British), 2,000 est.; Bolivia, 3,851,022; Brazil, 53,200,000; Bulgaria, 57,000; Burma, 130,832; Cameroons (British), 52,240; Cameroons (UN Trust Territory under French administration), 499,320; Canada, 4,986,552; Canary Islands (Spanish), 774,723; Cape Verde Islands (Portuguese), 168,109; Ceylon, 507,418; Chile, 5,500,000; China, 3,251,347; Colombia, 10,450,000; Congo (Belgian), 3,511,025; Costa Rica, 807,260; Cuba, 4,000,000 est.; Cyprus (British), 4,800; Czechoslovakia, 8,500,000; Dahomey (French), 111,787; Denmark, 22,000; Dominican Republic, 2,211,834; Ecuador, 3,123,000; Egypt, 200,000; El Salvador, 1,675,000; England and Wales, 2,837,000; Eritrea (under British control), 75,000; Estonia, 2,327; Ethiopia, 39,000; Falkland Islands (British), 354; Finland, 1,112; Formosa, 12,746;

---

[4] From *Annuario Pontificio*, 1951.

France, 33,714,635; French Equatorial Africa, 343,581; French India, 193,700; French West Africa, 416,995; Gambia (British), 3,555; Germany, 23,550,000 (all zones); Gibralter, 21,250; Gold Coast and Togoland (British), 293,000; Greece, 29,139; Guadeloupe, 305,000; Guam, 32,209; Guatemala, 3,011,550; Guiana, British, 52,500; Guiana, French, 15,000; Guinea, French, 22,877; Guinea, Portuguese, 8,139; Guinea, Spanish, 112,959; Haiti, 2,500,000; Hawaiian Islands, 145,000; Honduras, 1,502,000; Honduras, British, 35,263; Hungary, 6,122,583; Iceland, 500; India, 3,654,939; Indonesia, 911,072 est.; Iran, 17,873; Iraq, 200,000; Ireland, 2,710,000; Ireland, Northern, 500,000; Israel, 23,000; Italy, 45,631,713; Ivory Coast (French), 123,810; Jamaica, British West Indies, 83,513; Japan, 157,241; Jordan, 49,138; Kenya and Zanzibar (British), 324,143; Korea, 181,776; Latvia, 506,500; Lebanon, 455,552; Liberia, 9,271; Libya, 53,700; Lithuania, 2,100,-000; Luxembourg, 289,500; Macao (Portuguese), 33,047; Madagascar (French), 698,975; Madeira (Portuguese), 249,747; Malaya, 92,929; Malta, 308,000; Manchuria, 203,680; Martinique, French West Indies, 259,000; Mauritius, Island (British), 155,000; Mexico, 24,268,008; Monaco, 20,000; Morocco (French), 360,000; Morocco, 113,164; Mozambique, 183,563; Nepal, 500; Netherlands, 3,703,672; New Guinea (British), 24,933; New Guinea (Netherlands), 56,758; New Guinea (UN Trusteeship), 115,707; New Zealand, 204,287; Nicaragua, 1,142,622; Nigeria, 657,917; Norway, 4,905; Nyasaland, 281,259; Oceania, 219,476; Pakistan, 224,995; Panama, 610,000; Paraguay, 1,611,000; Peru, 8,070,039; Philippines, 16,000,000 est.; Poland, 22,000,000 est.; Portugal, 7,782,800; Puerto Rico, 2,030,000; Portuguese India, 418,564; Reunion (French), 229,488; Rhodesia, Northern, 342,387; Rumania, 3,100,000; San Marino, 11,000; Saudi Arabia, 5,840; Scotland, 1,000,000; Senegal (French), 62,969; Seychelles Islands (British), 31,437; Sierra Leone (British), 11,079; Somalia, 8,500; Soudan (French), 17,822; Southwest Africa, 25,964; Spain, 28,324,025; Sudan, 85,103; Surinam (Dutch Guiana), 33,825; Swasiland (British), 12,001; Sweden, 16,000; Switzerland, 1,750,000 est.; Syria, 114,597; Tanganyika (British), 742,224; Thailand, 52,557; Togoland, 111,613; Tunisia (French), 280,000; Turkey, 55,084; Uganda (British), 1,050,277; Union of South Africa, 666,525; Union of Soviet Socialist Republics, 8,000,000 est.; United States, 28,634,878; Uruguay, 1,885,000; Vatican City, 970; Venezuela, 5,225,000; Viet Nam, 1,519,622; West Indies (British), 367,983;

West Indies (Dutch), 112,440; West Indies (U.S.), 4,775; Yugoslavia, 5,670,600.

The Index of Forbidden Books

No better illustration of the control which the Roman Catholic Church has over her members around the world is afforded than the official *Index of Forbidden Books*.[5] These books banned by the Vatican are forbidden everywhere and in whatever language they may be translated. Roman Catholics who publish, sell, loan, or keep them, without special permission, are subject to excommunication (1. excommunication reserved in a special way to the Holy See; 2. nonreserved excommunication). (*The Code of Canon Law*)

For the protection of the faith and morals of Catholics the Holy See issues, from time to time, a list of books which the faithful are forbidden to read. (Another prohibition, but on a national basis and different level, is the list of forbidden motion pictures issued by the League of Decency, of the Committee on Motion Pictures, a special Bishops' committee.) The *Index*, however, does not contain all the books which Roman Catholics are forbidden to read, but only those which have been placed before the Holy See for official action.[6] Special permission may be received, for valid reasons, to read books listed on the *Index*.

Closely connected with the *Index* is the *Imprimatur*. Canon Law demands that some books, such as those dealing with Holy Scripture, devotional and prayer books, writings on matters of faith and morals, must have ecclesiastical censorship prior to publication. After such books have been examined by the diocesan censor and approved for Catholic readers, the term *Nihil obstat* ("there is nothing objectionable") is granted. In granting this permission to have the book published, the Ordinary does not *per se* approve the contents. It does, however, indicate that the writing has already passed ecclesiastical censorship and therefore may be read by the faithful "without detriment to faith or morals."

Books which are forbidden reading according to the *Index*, as prescribed by Canon Law, are editions of the Bible by non-

---

[5] For a full treatment of *The Index of Forbidden Books*, with lists, see *What Is the Index?* by Redmond A. Burke, Bruce Publishing Co.

[6] *The Index Expurgatorius* is a list of passages deleted from certain books, after which they may be read and circulated. This is different and separate from the *Index*.

Catholics; books which defend heresy and schism, books which attack religion or good morals; books by non-Catholics on religion, unless they do not contain anything contrary to the Catholic faith; commentaries, notes, and translations of the Bible published without Catholic approval; books which deride any Catholic dogma; books which, when dealing with the Masonic, or similar secret orders, contend that these are useful and not opposed to the Roman Catholic Church; books which deal with obscene or impure topics; etc. Catholics are forbidden to read such books whether they are on the *Index* or not.

THE PROTESTANT POINT OF VIEW
On the Matter of Gaining World Power

Protestantism is firmly against the apparent attempt of the Vatican at world domination because it fears the control of moral and spiritual affairs by a pope at Rome and opposes governmental representation at the Vatican State both on political and religious grounds.

Protestants may envy the power and authority of the Roman Catholic Church, but they cannot justly condemn a Church *as a Church* no matter how powerful it becomes. They can criticize and attempt to correct those aspects of the Church's operation in worldly and civic affairs which have proven injurious to other faiths and to the State itself. Protestants may not like the system of the Roman hierarchy. That is a matter for Roman Catholics to accept or reject, not Protestants. Protestants do have a concern when the Roman Catholic hierarchy begins to take over functions, responsibilities, revenue, and sometimes property, outside its own sphere. Public property and common tax funds must not be used for any Church.[7]

This power of domination does not apply only to things. It also applies to ideas, to ideals, and to services and forms of entertainment for all the people. The Roman Catholic Church may have a perfect right, if it desires, to forbid its own members to read certain books, see particular plays, or view some motion pictures. But it has no right to prevent the rest of the community from doing so. That is, the Roman Catholic Church has no right to

---

[7] For a discussion of the Catholic Church in politics see *Faith Is a Weapon* by Thomas B. Morgan, G. P. Putnam's Sons.

set itself up in every community as a general censor. No one objects to its emphasis upon purity and good morals, but all those who still value the privilege of individual choice and action cannot permit an outside organization, no matter what its motives may be, to rule arbitrarily on what nonmembers of the Roman Catholic Church may see, read, hear, or do. This is as true of medicine and birth control as anything else. The Christian Church must grow strong *as a whole*. The world needs a strong Church. But to make the Roman Catholic Church strong at the expense of Protestantism is to rob living Christianity of its freedom. And to have Roman Catholics in positions of power who must obey the *ex cathedra* voice of the pope, in all matters of faith and morals, can create disunity within the nation and lead to moral confusion in regard to the established laws and customs of the country.[8]

Moreover, the whole question of chief allegiance enters the picture at this point. Roman Catholics claim that they must obey the pope only in matters which pertain to faith and morals, and not in regard to secular or political matters. But what happens here in America when a civic issue is created by Roman Catholics on moral grounds? Such a case developed, involving the Welfare and Health Council of New York City. Early in 1953 the Roman Catholic Charities of New York and Brooklyn threatened to withdraw if the Planned Parenthood Committee of Mothers' Health Centers was allowed membership. Here was a situation where Roman Catholics, on the basis of Roman Catholic morality, attempted to dictate to the entire community. If this issue should ever be taken to the U.S. Supreme Court on the one hand, and to the pope at Rome on the other, the first loyalty of American citizens who are Roman Catholics would be severely tested. Even a President of the United States, if he happens to be a Roman Catholic, must obey the pope when he speaks *ex cathedra* in the realm of faith and morals. In a world where faith and morals are so closely linked with government and civic affairs, the ecclesiastical gap separating the differences in supreme loyalty is not too realistic.

---

[8] The "moral and faith" influence of the Vatican can hardly be separated from medical practice, politics, education, books, movies and television, and policies relating to Rome and to Roman Catholic nations.

Not a Super-Church

Without any implications that the World Council of Churches is a super-church, a hierarchy, or even has power over its constituent members, it is being set here as the closest counterpart which Protestantism has to the Vatican. Yet it is so different, in organization, program, and spirit, that it should be emphasized again—it is not a Church, nor does it have any central ecclesiastical authority; it is exactly what its name indicates, a *council of churches*. This is brought out very plainly in Chapter III of *The Quest for Christian Unity* by Robert S. Bilheimer, the American program secretary of the World Council of Churches.

Organized at Amsterdam, Holland, in 1948, it was in a real sense the logical outgrowth of the great world missionary conferences of Jerusalem in 1928 and Madras in 1938, as well as the faith, life and work conferences of Stockholm (1925), Lausanne (1927), Oxford (1937), and Edinburgh (1937). After a delay of years because of the outbreak of World War II, and working during this period with a Provisional Committee, official representatives of 148 churches (denominations or communions) met to organize the World Council of Churches. The basis of membership was that any church body might become a member which "accepts Jesus Christ as God and Saviour."

Some of the chief positions taken at the first Assembly of the World Council of Churches are as follows: "War as a method of settling disputes is incompatible with the teaching and example of our Lord Jesus Christ. The part which war plays in our present international life is a sin against God and a degradation of man."

"The Churches must also attack the causes of war by promoting peaceful change and the pursuit of justice. They must stand for the maintenance of good faith and the honouring of the pledged word; resist the pretensions of imperialistic power; promote the multilateral reduction of armaments; and combat indifference and despair in the face of the futility of war; they must point Christians to that spiritual resistance which grows from settled convictions widely held, themselves a powerful deterrent to war."

"We denounce all forms of tyranny, economic or religious, which deny liberty to men."

"We oppose aggressive imperialism—political, economic or cultural—whereby a nation seeks to use other nations or peoples for its own ends."

"The United Nations was designed to assist in the settlement of difficulties and to promote friendly relations among the nations. Its purposes in these respects deserve the support of Christians."

"The Church has always demanded freedom to obey God rather than men. We affirm that all men are equal in the sight of God and that the rights of men derive directly from their status as the children of God. It is presumptuous for the state to assume that it can grant or deny fundamental rights. It is for the state to embody these rights in its own legal system and to ensure their observance in practice."

This program of practical Christian co-operation, as represented in the World Council of Churches, is significant:

1. Relief action on behalf of the war-stricken churches.
2. Upholding the Christian standard of conduct toward friend and foe.
3. Organizing interchurch aid looking toward rehabilitation of church life.
4. Co-ordinating services for refugees and displaced persons.
5. Enlisting youth in the Christian world community.
6. Building a world fellowship in Christ of men of good will.
7. Giving Protestant Christendom a united voice and a center of united action.

Chief Positions

It is impossible to reconcile the power and hierarchy of the Roman Catholic Church with the teaching of Scripture. The New Testament teaches very clearly that domination, authority, power, are not attributes of the Christian Church. Christ himself severely rebuked the scribes and the Pharisees for assuming to be spiritual rulers (Matt. 23; 24:1-2). He also rebuked his own disciples for desiring the chief positions in the Kingdom (Luke 9:46-48). Christ's teaching was, "Blessed are the poor in spirit: for theirs is the kingdom of heaven. . . . Blessed are the meek: for they shall inherit the earth" (Matt. 5:3, 5).

Paul declared that "we look not at the things which are seen, but at the things which are not seen; for the things which are seen are temporal; but the things which are not seen are eternal" (II Cor. 4:18), and in Hebrews 9:24 it is indicated that "Christ is not entered into the holy places made with hands, which are the figures of the true; but into heaven itself, now to appear in the presence of God for us." Protestantism, being Bible centered, could see the dangers to true Christianity in power, pomp, and glory. As long as it keeps its eyes on the New Testament it will continue to hold this position.

In the New Testament the church was a Christian fellowship which met, not in a great cathedral, but in a private home. This is indicated in passages such as: "Greet Priscilla and Aquila, my helpers in Christ Jesus: who have for my life laid down their own necks: . . . likewise greet the church that is in her house" (Rom. 16:3-5). In regard to the qualifications of a bishop, Paul writes in I Timothy 3:2-5: "A bishop then must be blameless, the husband of one wife, vigilant, sober, of good behaviour, given to hospitality, apt to teach; Not given to wine, no striker, not greedy of filthy lucre; but patient, not a brawler, not covetous; One that ruleth well his own house, having his children in subjection with all gravity; (For if a man know not how to rule his own house, how shall he take care of the church of God?)"

PROTESTANT REFERENCE BOOKS: *The Quest for Christian Unity* by Robert S. Bilheimer; *Our Protestant Faith* by William R. Cannon, Jr., Chap. X; *Ecumenical World Foundations* by William Richey Hogg; *Toward a Reborn Church* by Walter Marshall Horton; *The Christian Outlook* by Kenneth Scott Latourette; *On This Rock* by G. Bromley Oxnam; *A Protestant Primer* by Clarence Seidenspinner, pp. 54-59; the official report of the First Assembly of the World Council of Churches, Amsterdam, the Netherlands, 1948.

22

Church Union—From the
Roman Catholic Point of View

Protestants and Roman Catholics have many things in common. They both have Christ as Lord and Saviour; they are both of the Christian tradition; they both have at least two sacraments,[1] Baptism and the Lord's Supper (the Catholic Church recognizes "Protestant" baptism under certain conditions); they share many hymns together; and much of their devotional literature, including the Bible, is the spiritual heritage of both. These, and many works of mercy, such, for example, as working together for refugees and world relief, indicate that Protestants and Catholics are not as far apart as many would have us believe.

On the other hand, the Roman Catholic Church has established certain basic principles which do not make for Church unity. As we will see in this chapter, Catholics believe in church unity of a certain kind. Whether all Christians can ever unite on the basis proposed so often by the various popes is exceedingly doubtful—unless new definitions and new practices are worked out. But this much is certain, there are good Roman Catholics and there are good Protestants. On the basis of Christ's own test, these Christians, who have so much in common, should find ways and means, without compromising their fundamental convictions, of having fellowship together and working in common for the great principles of the Kingdom.

THE ROMAN CATHOLIC POSITION

It would be possible to compile, from various Roman Catholic sources, material on the position of the Roman Catholic Church in regard to church union. For lack of space, and the

---

[1] Many Protestants call these ordinances or memorials.

251

desire to present as true a picture as possible in the briefest compass, we use one source—the encyclical letter of Pope Leo XIII on "The Unity of the Church" (*Satis Cognitum*). Every Protestant move toward complete Christian unity will have to take serious recognition of the arguments of Pope Leo XIII. Although presented over fifty years ago,[2] they still represent the views of the Church concerning unity.

The Other Sheep Outside the Fold

Pope Leo XIII begins his encyclical letter by referring directly to the "sheep that have strayed."[3]

"It is sufficiently well known unto you that no small share of Our thoughts and of Our care is devoted to Our endeavor to bring back to the fold, placed under the guardianship of Jesus Christ, the chief Pastor of souls, sheep that have strayed. Bent upon this, We have thought it most conducive to this salutary end and purpose to describe the exemplar and, as it were, the lineaments of the Church. Amongst these the most worthy of Our chief consideration is *Unity*. This the divine Author impressed on it as a lasting sign of truth and of unconquerable strength. The essential beauty and comeliness of the Church ought greatly to influence the minds of those who consider it. Nor is it improbable that ignorance may be dispelled by the consideration; that false ideas and prejudices may be dissipated from the minds chiefly of those who find themselves in error without fault of theirs."

"If those about to come back to their most loving Mother (not yet fully known, or culpably abandoned) should perceive that their return involves not indeed the shedding of their blood (at which price nevertheless the Church was bought by Jesus Christ) but some lesser trouble and labor, let them clearly understand that this burden has been laid on them not by the will of man but by the will and command of God."

---

[2] Written in 1896, this encyclical letter, "The Unity of the Church," was issued in 1949 by the Paulist Press as the text for discussion clubs.

[3] "Those who have been baptized but do not belong to the Catholic Church, heretics and schismatics of divers confessions, are not called infidels but non-Catholics. The relation in which all these classes stand to the Catholic Church is not the same; in principle, those who have been baptized are subjects of the Church and her children even though they be rebellious children; they are under her laws or, at least, are exempt from them only so far as pleases the Church."—*The Catholic Encyclopedia.*

Only One True Church

Pope Leo XIII now begins, in his encyclical letter, to outline the Catholic basis for belief in only one true Church.

"The mission of the Church is to save *that which had perished:* That is to say, not some nations or peoples, but the whole human race, without distinction of time or place. . . . Wherefore, by the will of its Founder, it is necessary that this Church should be one in all lands and at all times. To justify the existence of more than one Church it would be necessary to go outside in the world, and to create a new and unheard-of race of men."

"Furthermore, the Son of God decreed that the Church should be His mystical body, with which He should be united as the head. . . . Scattered and separated members cannot possibly cohere with the head so as to make one body."

"So the Christian is a Catholic as long as he lives in the body; cut off from it he becomes a heretic—the life of the spirit follows not the amputated member." [4]

Agreement of Minds Necessary

"Agreement and union of minds is the necessary foundation of this perfect concord amongst men, from which concurrence of wills and similarity of action are the natural results. Wherefore, in His divine wisdom, He ordained in His Church *Unity of Faith;* a virtue which is the first of those bonds which unite men to God, and whence we receive the name of the *faithful—one Lord, one faith, one baptism.* That is, as there is one Lord and one baptism, so should all Christians, without exception, have but one faith."

The Nature of Faith

After pointing out in detail how Christ appointed the apostles as his ambassadors and how, in turn, they appointed successors, bishops to fulfill his world mission, Pope Leo XIII proceeds to describe the meaning of faith.

"Wherefore, as appears from what has been said, Christ instituted in the Church a *living, authoritative,* and *permanent Magisterium,* which by His own power He strengthened, by the

---

[4] "Anyone becomes a schismatic who, though desiring to remain a Christian, rebels against legitimate authority, without going as far as the rejection of Christianity as a whole, which constitutes the crime of apostasy."—*The Catholic Encyclopedia.*

Spirit of Truth He taught, and by miracles confirmed. He willed and ordered, under the gravest penalties, that its teachings should be received as if they were His own. As often, therefore, as it is declared on the authority of this teaching that this or that is contained in the deposit of divine revelations, it must be believed by every one as true."

"Faith, as the Church teaches, is 'that supernatural virtue by which, through the help of God and through the assistance of His grace, we believe what He has revealed to be true, not on account of the intrinsic truth perceived by the natural light of reason, but because of the authority of God himself, the Revealer, who can neither deceive nor be deceived.'" [5]

He who dissents even in one point from divinely revealed truth absolutely rejects all faith, since he thereby refuses to honor God as the supreme truth and the *formal motive of faith.*"

Only Way to Salvation

Pope Leo XIII proceeds to say that it is "undoubtedly the office of the Church to guard Christian doctrine and to propagate it in its integrity and purity."

"The Church alone offers to the human race that religion—that state of absolute perfection—which He wishes, as it were, to be *incorporated* in it. And it alone supplies those means of salvation which accord with the ordinary counsels of Providence."

"The power of performing and administering the divine mysteries, together with the authority of ruling and governing, was not bestowed by God on all Christians indiscriminately, but on certain chosen persons."

"The Church, therefore, is man's guide to whatever pertains to heaven."

Peter and the Keys of Heaven

"When Christ promised to give to Peter the keys of the kingdom of heaven, He promised to give him power and authority over the Church."

"Above all things the need of union between the bishops and the successors of Peter is clear and undeniable. This bond once broken, Christians would be separated and scattered, and would in no wise form one body and one flock. . . . It must be clearly understood that bishops are deprived of the right and power of

---

[5] Vatican Council.

ruling, if they deliberately secede from Peter and his successors; because, by this secession, they are separated from the foundation on which the whole edifice must rest."

"But the Episcopal order is rightly judged to be in communion with Peter, as Christ commanded, if it be subject to and obeys Peter; otherwise it necessarily becomes a lawless and disorderly crowd."

"The authority of the Roman Pontiff is supreme, universal, independent; that of bishops limited, and dependent. 'It is not congruous that two superiors with equal authority should be placed over the same flock; but that two, one of whom is higher than the other, should be placed over the same people is not incongruous. Thus the parish priest, the bishop, and the Pope, are placed immediately over the same people.' " [6]

Basis of Unity

At the close of his encyclical letter Pope Leo lays down, in dogmatic fashion, the one and only basis of unity as far as Christendom is concerned.

"What Christ has said of Himself We may truly repeat of Ourselves: *Other sheep I have that are not of this fold; them also I must bring and they shall hear My voice.* Let all those therefore, who detest the widespread irreligion of our times, and acknowledge and confess Jesus Christ to be the Son of God and the Savior of the human race, but who have wandered away from the Spouse, listen to Our voice. Let them not refuse to obey Our paternal charity. Those who acknowledge Christ must acknowledge Him wholly and entirely. 'The Head and the body are Christ wholly and entirely. The Head is the only-begotten Son of God, the body is His Church; the bridegroom and the bride, two in one flesh. All who dissent from the Scripture concerning Christ, although they may be found in all places in which the Church is found, are not in the Church; and again all those who agreed with the Scriptures concerning the Head, and do not communicate in the unity of the Church, are not in the Church.' " [7]

"Let such as these take counsel with themselves, and realize that they can in no wise be counted among the children of God,

---

[6] St. Thomas Aquinas.

[7] St. Augustine, *Contra Donatistas Epistola.*

unless they take Christ Jesus as their Brother, and at the same
time the Church as their Mother."

"We most earnestly commend to His loving kindness all those
of whom We have spoken."

THE PROTESTANT POINT OF VIEW
On the Reality of a United Christian Force

**Protestantism cannot accept the Roman Catholic con-
ception of church union because it is wholly outside
its own ideas of the Christian fellowship, Christian co-
operation, and the prayer of Christ that they all might
be one.**

Church unity (as distinguished from organic church union)
is something to be greatly desired and sought after. It is a dis-
grace to have constant strife among the various divisions of the
Christian Church. Great progress has been made in bringing
together denominations of similar belief and practice, and also
in interdenominational co-operation through the National Council of the Churches of Christ in the U.S.A., the International
Missionary Council, and the World Council of Churches. Yet,
as far as union between Protestants and Roman Catholics is concerned, little, if any, progress has been made. It is true that
during recent years popes have extended to Protestants invita-
tions to reunite with "the one true Church." What must be
clearly understood here is that such a union would have to take
place purely on Roman Catholic terms. In other words, it would
be a *return* and not a reunion. All Protestants would have to
become Roman Catholics. All the basic Roman Catholic principles and practices, as outlined in this primer, would have to be
accepted. There is no possibility of a compromise with the
Roman Catholic Church.

Under these circumstances the best plan for Protestantism is
to strengthen and to unite its own forces. It must never, because
of inner competition, become the victim of outside forces. It has
great principles which the world greatly needs. In being morally
and spiritually great it must treat its fellow Christians in the
Roman Catholic Church with understanding—but with firmness.
Blind prejudice will do it far more harm than good. There are
areas of co-operation open to all true Christians. May Protestants

never be guilty of failing to co-operate in practical ways with the Roman Catholic Church, and *vice versa,* when such co-operation means helping needy people and extending the Kingdom of God!

The Power of God

The evidence of many Protestant conferences is that Protestant churches are becoming stronger by moving toward co-operation and unity of purpose and program. Concrete examples of this have been mentioned. Two of the latest conferences to stress the need of unity were the International Missionary Council's world conference on "The Missionary Obligation of the Church," held at Willingen in July, 1952, and the Third World Conference on Faith and Order held at Lund, Sweden, in August of 1952. While dealing primarily with the missionary obligation of the Church, and the creative adjustments which must be made to face successfully the issues of a world in conflict, the Willingen Conference could not escape the connection between mission and unity. Unity thus became a part of the official program. In a "Statement on the Calling of the Church to Mission and Unity," this pronouncement was made:

"Division in the Church distorts its witness, frustrates its mission, and contradicts its own nature. If the Church is to demonstrate the Gospel in its life as well as in its preaching, it must manifest to the world the power of God to break down all barriers and to establish the Church's unity in Christ. *Christ is not divided.*

"We believe that through the ecumenical movement God is drawing His people together in order that He may enable us to discern yet more clearly the contradictions in our message and the barriers to unity which are also hindrances to effective witness in a divided world. We can no longer be content to accept our divisions as normal. We believe that in the ecumenical movement God has provided a way of co-operation in witness and service, and also a means for the removal of much that mars such witness and service."

At Lund, the challenge to strengthen through co-operation was no less pronounced. Although facing up squarely to the many unsolved problems and disagreements among Protestants, in regard to faith, order, and practice, it nevertheless adopted such positive pronouncements as the following:

"We have not resolved our differences nor brought forth before the world a simple method of achieving unity. Yet we have safeguards against complacency of a far more important kind. This Conference, by its very existence as well as by repeated emphases, has called the churches both to a deeper awareness of their common faith and to a more resolute effort to translate awareness of their common faith and to a more resolute effort to translate that faith into terms clearly visible in their common life. More perfect agreement waits upon a more adventurous courage and upon a more urgent effort of the will. . . .

"We have seen clearly that we can make no real advance towards unity if we only compare our several conceptions of the nature of the Church and the traditions in which they are embodied. But once again it has been proved true that as we seek to draw closer to Christ we come closer to one another. We need, therefore, to penetrate behind the divisions of the Church to a deeper and richer understanding of the mystery of the God-given union of Christ with His Church. We need increasingly to realize that the separate histories of our churches find their full meaning only if seen in the perspective of God's dealings with His *whole* people."

Stress upon Unity in the New Testament

"Neither pray I for these alone, but for them also which shall believe on me through their word; that they may be one; as thou, Father, art in me, and I am in thee, that they also may be one in us," prayed Jesus, as recorded in John 17:20, 21.

All that is necessary is to list, without comment, the following verses in order to show how much emphasis there really is in the New Testament on Christian unity:

"These all continued with one accord in prayer and supplication, with the women, and Mary the mother of Jesus, and with his brethren" (Acts 1:14).

"And they, continuing daily with one accord in the temple, and breaking bread from house to house, did eat their meat with gladness and singleness of heart" (Acts 2:46).

"Now the God of patience and consolation grant you to be likeminded one toward another, according to Christ Jesus: that ye may with one mind and one mouth glorify God" (Rom. 15: 5, 6).

"Now there are diversities of gifts, but the same Spirit. . . . For to one is given, by the Spirit, the word of wisdom; to another the word of knowledge, by the same Spirit; to another faith, by the same Spirit; to another the gifts of healing, by the same Spirit; to another the working of miracles; to another prophecy; to another discerning of spirits; to another divers kinds of tongues; to another the interpretation of tongues; but all these worketh that one and the selfsame Spirit, dividing to every man severally as he will. For as the body is one, and hath many members, and all members of that one body, being many, are one body, so also is Christ. For by one Spirit are we all baptized into one body, whether we be Jews or Gentiles, whether we be bond or free; and have been all made to drink into one Spirit" (I Cor. 12:4, 8-13).

"There is neither Jew nor Greek, there is neither bond nor free, there is neither male nor female: for ye are all one in Christ Jesus" (Gal. 3:28).

"There is one body, and one Spirit, even as ye are called in one hope of your calling; one Lord, one faith, one baptism, one God and Father of all, who is above all, and through all, and in you all" (Eph. 4:4-6).

PROTESTANT REFERENCE BOOKS: *Man's Disorder and God's Design*, the Amsterdam Assembly Series, 1949; *Faith and Order*, Proceedings of the World Conference, Lausanne, 1927, edited by H. N. Bates; *The Stockholm Conference*, 1925, The Official Report of the Universal Christian Conference on Life and Work, edited by G. K. A. Bell; *The Quest for Christian Unity* by Robert S. Bilheimer; *Toward a United Church* by William Adams Brown; *Ecumenical Foundations* by William R. Hogg; *Toward a Reborn Church*, Walter Marshall Horton; *The Jerusalem Meeting of the International Missionary Council*, 1928, eight volumes; *World Chaos or World Christianity* by Henry Smith Leiper; *The Madras Series*, 1938, seven volumes; *The Oxford Conference Official Report*, 1937; *The Church Looks Forward* by William Temple; *For the Healing of the Nations* by Henry Pitt Van Dusen; *World Christianity, Yesterday, Today, and Tomorrow*, by Henry Pitt Van Dusen.

23

Summary: How Protestants Differ from Roman Catholics

The Roman Catholic Archbishop of Utrecht and the four Roman Catholic bishops of the Netherlands prepared a pastoral letter which was read in all of their churches on a Sunday in August, 1948, explaining why the Roman Catholic Church was not participating in the First Assembly of the World Council of Churches which was opening at Amsterdam on this same Sunday. While admitting that the assembly would be followed with interest, and that the question of Christian unity concerned the "Mother Church," even more than it did the Protestants, the letter went on to plead with "non-Catholic Christians" to return to the one true Church, and asked the members of the "Holy Catholic Church" to observe on the following Sunday "a solemn, or at least a sung Holy Mass.. . . to obtain from God that all may share in the unity of the Holy Church."

The aloofness of the Roman Catholic Church in not participating in the Amsterdam assembly was not due to fear of losing prestige or from tactical considerations. "This attitude solely proceeds from the conviction of the Church that she must be unshakably true to the task with which Jesus Christ has entrusted her. For she is the one holy Catholic and apostolic Church which was founded by Jesus Christ in order that His work of salvation might be carried on through her unto the end of all times; she is the mystical Body of Christ; she is Christ's Bride."

The following statement made by the Roman Catholic Bishops indicates how difficult it is for Protestants and Roman Catholics to meet on equal grounds to discuss the possibility of the reunion of the Christian fold.

"That [the unique position of the Roman Catholic Church] is why the divisions between the Christians can only be put an end to in one way: by a return to Her; by a return within the unity which has always been preserved within Her. If, however, the Catholic Church were to participate in the endeavor towards a new religious unity and this on an equal footing with the others, then by doing so she would in fact admit that the unity, willed by Christ, does not continue within her and that, therefore, there really is no Church of Christ. But such a thing she never can admit."

For the Present at Least

At the very same time that this pastoral letter was being prepared, another encyclical letter was being drawn up by 329 archbishops and bishops of the "Holy Catholic Church," in this case meaning those churches in fellowship with the Anglican Communion. Presided over by the Archbishop of Canterbury, this 1948 Lambeth Conference also desired the unity of the Church. It asked God's blessing upon the World Council of Churches meeting at Amsterdam, and reaffirmed a previous Lambeth Conference statement that "there can be no fulfilment of the Divine purpose in any scheme of reunion which does not ultimately include the great Latin Church of the West, with which our history has been so closely associated in the past, and to which we are still bound by many ties of common faith and tradition."

But the encyclical letter (*Mortalium Animes*), issued by Pope Pius XI in 1928, was cited which made "it once again abundantly plain that the only method of reunion which Rome will accept is that of submission to the Papacy. There are no signs whatever of any abatement of this demand in the last twenty years. Nor is there any possibility of its acceptance by the Churches of the Anglican Communion." The Bishops of the Anglican Communion then went on to make this statement which all Protestants can support: "It should be remembered that in addition to the question of the position of the Papacy, there are still most serious divergences in faith and practice between ourselves and the Roman Catholic Church, which make the prospect of hopeful approaches toward intercommunion unpromising for the present."

Points of Agreement

Since Roman Catholicism and Protestantism are in the same course of Christian history up until the Reformation, there are many points at which they come together in agreement. Without taking account of the special refinements developed by the theologians on both sides, it can be said in general that there are points of agreement relating to: The Apostles' Creed; the Nicene Creed; redemption as indicated in the incarnation and Cross of Christ; the doctrine of the Trinity; the events in the earthly ministry of Christ; the manifestation of the Holy Spirit; the existence of sin; atonement through Christ's death upon the Cross; the reality of God; the forgiveness of God; the justice of God; the presence of grace; the need of salvation; the assurance of eternal life; the Bible as the Word of God; the frequent use of the Lord's Prayer; the existence of the Christian Church; the basic requirements of worship; the nature of prayer; the scriptural authorization of at least two sacraments; a Christian way of life; a missionary motivation and program.

All of these areas of general agreement have not been treated at great length in this primer largely because misunderstandings arise at points of special interpretation, and bitterness is most prevalent in the realm of particular practice. We have been working here in the framework of things which make for better understanding and appreciation. But in considering Roman Catholicism as a whole—and it must be taken as one single piece if it is to be fully comprehended—these points should be included in the Roman Catholic pattern.

Protestant Disagreements

While Protestantism has kept, as its very own, much of the Christian belief and practice which is the common inheritance of all Christendom, there are, as has already been noted in "The Protestant Point of View" sections in each chapter, certain pronounced disagreements. While attempting to be as factual as possible, we will list some of the chief differences which exist between Roman Catholicism and Protestantism.[1] (Although an attempt has been made in the following listing to be as specific as possible, the reader may want to place "some" before Protestants.)

1. Protestants believe that the Church belongs to all true Christians and is "a community of forgiven sinners"; Roman Catholics believe that the Church belongs only to those who are members

---

[1] All quotations relating to Protestantism are taken from *Faith and Order*, the official report of the Third World Conference at Lund, 1952.

of the Roman Catholic Church, either knowingly or unknowingly. (See pages 4-13 for a full explanation.) [2]

2. Protestants believe that only "Christ is head of the Church which is His Body"; Roman Catholics believe that the pope is head of the visible Church on earth as the Vicar of Christ. (See pages 5-11.)

3. Protestants believe in justification by faith—that salvation comes only by the grace of God; Roman Catholics believe that salvation is secured by faith *plus good works*—only as channeled through the Roman Catholic Church. (See pages 18-22; 170-173.)

4. Protestants believe that the Protestant Reformation was a return to the creative principles of the New Testament; Roman Catholics think of the Reformation as something forced upon a self-reforming Church and as alien to the true Christian faith. (See pages 17-22.)

5. Protestants believe that the democratic inheritance of America was created and nurtured almost exclusively by Protestantism; Roman Catholics claim a large share in the democratic nature of America. (See pages 24-33.)

6. Protestants believe that no human being is, or can be, infallible; the Roman Catholic Church teaches that when the pope speaks *ex cathedra* he is infallible. (See pages 39-49.)

7. Protestants believe that Peter was one of Christ's chief apostles; Roman Catholics believe that he is "the Rock" upon which the Church is founded. (See pages 40-48.)

8. Protestants believe that the Ten Commandments are the basis for individual and social morality; Roman Catholics add to the Ten Commandments the six Precepts of the church. (See pages 50-60.)

9. Protestants believe in voluntary church attendance; Roman Catholics demand Church attendance. (See pages 56-60.)

10. Protestants believe that the financial support of the church and the clergy should be on a purely voluntary basis; Roman Catholics stress the obligation of making financial contributions. (See pages 56-60.)

11. Protestants believe that "while there are indications of diversity in worship in the New Testament, nevertheless the

---

[2] Because these brief statements cannot be complete in themselves, the reader is referred to the sections of this primer where each point has special treatment. A warning is given against using any of these statements out of their fuller context, or as an attack on the doctrines of the Roman Catholic Church.

preaching of the Word and the administration of Baptism and the Lord's Supper were everywhere marks of the Church's unity," and therefore Protestants have only two sacraments or ordinances, namely, Baptism and the Lord's Supper; Roman Catholics have seven sacraments: Baptism, Confirmation, Holy Eucharist, Penance, Extreme Unction, Holy Orders, and Matrimony. (See pages 63-74.)

12. Protestants believe that Baptism is not absolutely essential to salvation; Roman Catholics hold that all who are not baptized will go to hell. (See pages 65-74.)

13. Protestants believe that both elements of the Lord's Supper, that is, bread and wine, should be received by the communicant; the Roman Catholic Church reserves the wine exclusively to the clergy. (See pages 67-74; 149.)

14. Protestants of various denominations believe that Christ is present at the Lord's Table in spirit, along with the elements; Roman Catholics believe that the bread and wine are actually changed by the miracle of transubstantiation into the *real* flesh and blood of Christ. (See pages 67-74.)

15. Protestants believe in the priesthood of all believers and that the clergy,[3] although specifically called and commissioned to special Christian service, is not of a different nature than the Christian laity; Roman Catholics make a sharp distinction between clergy and laity. (See pages 75-82.)

16. Protestants believe that no one has the right or power to forgive sins save God alone; the Roman Catholic Church teaches that the priest can and does forgive sins. (See pages 78-82.)

17. Protestants believe that clergymen have the right to marry; the Roman Catholic Church enforces clerical celibacy. (See pages 77-82.)

18. Protestants believe that the Christian life is a "vocation" in the highest sense of that term and that the laity should have a prominent and official part in the life of the Church; Roman Catholics stress the sanctity of the priesthood and place the entire management and control of the Church in the hands of the hierarchy. (See pages 83-93.)

19. Protestants believe, for the most part, that all people after death enter either the state of heaven or hell; Roman Catholics

---

[3] Churches having an episcopally ordained clergy place greater stress upon priestly orders.

also believe in heaven and hell, but add an intermediary stage to heaven known as purgatory. (See pages 99-108.)

20. Protestants claim the right to discipline both clergy and laity for infractions of doctrine and practice; the Roman Catholic Church exercises the power of anathema and excommunication. (See pages 102-108.)

21. Protestants have no single ecclesiastical body which can adopt doctrines or church practices that are binding on all Protestant churches throughout the world; the Roman Catholic Church either through the pope, or councils called by him, can define dogmas which are absolutely binding upon every Roman Catholic throughout the world. (See pages 103-108.)

22. Protestants believe that most of the Bible existed before the organized Church; Roman Catholics believe that the Church is the mother of the Bible. (See pages 109-117.)

23. Protestants believe that the Scriptures are all-sufficient for Christian life and practice; the Roman Catholic Church teaches that Tradition must be accepted along with the Scriptures as interpreted by the Church. (See pages 110-117.)

24. Protestants have a Bible of 66 books; Roman Catholics have a Bible of 72 books. (See pages 112-116.)

25. Protestants believe that they have a right to read any version or translation of the Bible; the Roman Catholic Church forbids its members to read any version or translation not specifically authorized by itself. (See pages 112-116.)

26. Protestants give the individual the right to interpret the Scripture; the Roman Catholic Church insists upon being the interpreter for the individual. (See pages 113-116.)

27. Protestants believe that Mary was the mother of Jesus; Roman Catholics believe that Mary is the "Mother of God." (See pages 119-130.)

28. Protestants believe that Jesus had brothers and sisters; the Roman Catholic Church teaches that Mary had no other children save Jesus. (See pages 121-130.)

29. Protestants teach in their creeds that Christ was born of the Virgin Mary; Roman Catholics believe not only in the Virgin Birth of Christ, but also in the immaculate conception of Mary. (See pages 121-131.)

30. Protestants believe that Mary's body was natural and must wait for the general resurrection of the dead in Christ; the Roman Catholic Church teaches that Mary's physical body has already ascended into heaven. (See pages 122-131.)

31. Protestants honor Mary as the mother of Jesus; Roman Catholics venerate Mary and direct their prayers to her. (See pages 123-129.)

32. Protestants credit Mary with no miracles; Roman Catholics believe that Mary has performed and does perform miracles. (See pages 124-129.)

33. Protestants believe that marriage is a holy institution and a sacred bond; Roman Catholics believe that the marriage of baptized persons constitutes a sacrament of the Church. (See pages 132-143.)

34. Protestants warn against the dangers of mixed marriages, but have no specific church laws forbidding the marriage of Protestants to Roman Catholics; the Roman Catholic Church forbids mixed marriages and they are allowed only by special dispensation. (See pages 135-141.)

35. Protestants, under certain circumstances, permit divorces; the Roman Catholic Church teaches that a couple united in the sacrament of Matrimony can never, by any human power, be divorced. (See pages 135-143.)

36. Protestants have no moral or spiritual laws forbidding the practice of birth control; the Roman Catholic Church forbids the use of any method of artificial birth control. (See pages 138-143.)

37. Protestants believe that Christ suffered "uniquely in His once-and-for-all death"; Roman Catholics believe that in the sacrifice of the Mass "Christ through the ministry of the priest, offers Himself to God in an unbloody manner under the appearance of bread and wine." (See pages 144-153.)

38. Protestants practice a form of worship which is largely fluid and individual and conduct their worship services in the vernacular; in the Roman Catholic Church worship is largely fixed and objective and Latin is used universally. (See pages 150-153.)

39. Protestants are free to worship where they please; Roman Catholics are forbidden to worship in Protestant churches. (See pages 51; 181.)

40. Protestants, in the main, believe that God will receive to Himself unbaptized babies who die in infancy; the Roman Catholic Church teaches that an infant, dying unbaptized, will never be able to enter heaven. (See pages 156-165.)

41. Protestants believe that full forgiveness of sins may be received from God and that it is not necessary for those who are forgiven to pay for sins after death; Roman Catholics believe

that some sins cannot be entirely atoned for upon earth and that the granting of indulgences helps to alleviate the unpaid debts of temporal punishment in purgatory. (See pages 158-166.)

42. Protestants believe that the Communion of Saints consists of "the fellowship of the whole company of believers on earth and in heaven"; Roman Catholics believe that it is "the union of the faithful on earth, the blessed in heaven, and the souls in purgatory." (See pages 161-166.)

43. Protestants believe that good works should result from the faith of the Christian, but that they are not an essential part of the process of salvation; the Roman Catholic Church teaches that "one can earn the eternal reward of heaven by performing the corporal works of mercy." (See pages 169-175.)

44. Protestants believe that it is proper to confess sins to God and to each other, but that only God through Christ has the power to forgive sins; the Roman Catholic Church teaches that in the Confessional the priest himself can absolve those who confess their sins. (See pages 176-185.)

45. Protestants believe that prayer should be from the heart, directed to God Himself, and thus encourage personal, impromptu prayers; the Roman Catholic Church believes that prayer can be directed through saints and has an elaborate system of formal prayers to be recited. (See pages 186-197.)

46. Protestants believe that true worship is of spirit and truth, and is devoid of physical objects having spiritual benefits; Roman Catholics have "sacramentals" such as blessed beads, crucifixes, images, candles, holy water, medals, and scapulars. (See pages 187-197.)

47. Protestants, because they believe that "the Church by its very nature is an evangelizing fellowship," have a missionary program which is directed to all those outside the Christian churches, but Roman Catholics are not specifically included; the Roman Catholic Church definitely includes Protestants in its missionary enterprise. (See pages 198-207.)

48. Protestants freely permit their children to attend secular public schools; the Roman Catholic Church forbids the attendance of Roman Catholic children at "non-Catholic, neutral or mixed schools," and they can do so only by special ecclesiastical permission. (See pages 214-224.)

49. Protestants take the stand, on the basis of the separation of Church and State, that public tax money should not be used to support religious or parochial schools; Roman Catholics encour-

age the use of public funds for parochial schools on the principle that it is the duty of the State to help support the cause of true religion. (See pages 218-224.)

50. Protestants have no legal and binding arrangements with governments; the Roman Catholic Church has an arrangement of treaties or "concordats" with specific governments. (See pages 227-236.)

51. Protestants have no independent and sovereign government of their own; Roman Catholics have the Vatican City State of which the pope is the absolute ruler and to which representatives of other governments are accredited. (See pages 227-236.)

52. Protestants believe in, and practice, religious freedom for all faiths and for those of no particular faith; the Roman Catholic Church allows "equality of *civil* rights for all denominations," but it only "tolerates" what it considers to be false religions. (See pages 229-236.)

53. Protestants believe the conscience of the individual Christian should be the guide in the reading of books and the viewing of plays, movies, and television; the Roman Catholic Church has a formal system of censorship for all its members. (See pages 245-250.)

54. Protestants have a world fellowship through various world alliances and through the World Council of Churches, but they have no central system of government or control; the Roman Catholic Church is organized as a hierarchy, with the pope as its supreme authority. (See pages 237-250.)

55. Protestants believe in Christian co-operation and are making progress toward various forms of church unity, although denominational bodies retain autonomy; the Roman Catholic Church believes itself to be "the one true Church," and will consider union only on the basis of a return to its own fold. (See pages 251-259.)

Brief Résumé of Protestant Beliefs

This excellent résumé of the beliefs commonly held by Protestants was formulated and adopted by 220 delegates at Lund:

"In His eternal love the Father has sent His Son to redeem creation from sin and death. In Jesus Christ, God's Son became Man. By word and deed He proclaimed on earth the arrival of God's Kingdom, bore away the sins of the world on the Cross, rose again from the dead, ascended into heaven, to the throne of His Kingdom, at the right hand of God. At Pentecost God poured out His Spirit upon the Church, giving all who believe in Jesus Christ the power to become God's children. Through the indwelling of His Spirit Jesus Christ dwells in the midst of His Church. As Lord and King He will come again to judge the quick and the dead and to consummate the eternal Kingdom of God in the whole creation."

The Church Triumphant

Protestantism stands for the Church Triumphant and nothing upon earth has the power to separate true Protestants from the daily as well as the final victory which comes from being an active member of Christ's eternal Kingdom. This triumphant spirit is well illustrated in the martyrdom of the fifteenth-century reformer Savonarola. As he was about to be burnt at the stake in Florence, the Bishop of Vasona in his embarrassment at condemning such a noble Christian to death bungled the usual formula and said instead, "I separate thee from the Church militant and triumphant." But the martyr corrected him, saying "From the Church militant, not triumphant; for this is not thine (*hoc enim tuum non est*)." The Bishop accepted the correction and said, "Amen. May God number you therein."

The Church belongs to the Spirit and it is of God. In the Church we become free and are caught up in the spirit of Truth. Members of the Church are children of hope and always look forward to the greater revelation in Christ. Salvation comes to the individual, to the Christian cause, and to the Church Triumphant not through any human merit, but through the saving power of the Cross. This is the Protestant faith. And this is where Protestants stand—ever pressing forward to greater spiritual, moral, and social triumphs through Christ.

We only who believe in Jesus Christ the power to bring us into filial relationship through the indwelling of the Spirit in Jesus Christ has in the midst of His Church. As Lord and King He will reign... place for the quick and the dead and to reverence. He raised kingdom of God in the whole creation.

The Church Triumphant

Protestantism stands for the Church Triumphant and no longer upon earth but the power to separate true Protestants from the faith, as well as the final victory which comes from humiliation... never reminded of Christ's eternal Kingdom, one permanent spirit as well illustrated in the martyrdom of the Mexican reformer Savonarola. As he was about to be burnt at the stake in Florence, the Bishop of Vienne, in his robes... ceremony of degradation, spoke such words. "Outlaw in deed," and did the words "from the triumphant and the militant," but the master remarked this. "From the Church militant and triumphant he this is not however to excommunicate me?" The Bishop accepted the correction and said "From the Church militant were then...

The Church, then, is the Spirit, and it is of God. It is through persons free and are caught up in the spirit of truth. Standards of the Church are followed to him, and also to him forced to the inner revelation of Christ. Salvation comes to the individual, to the human being, and not the Church triumphant and through acts human nent, but through the spirit power of the Cross. This is the Protestant faith. And this is why Protestants stand ever pressing forward to greater spiritual, moral, and social triumphs through Christ.

INDEX

Index

273